The psychology and education
of gifted children

The psychology and education of gifted children

PHILIP E. VERNON, GEORGINA ADAMSON
and   DOROTHY F. VERNON

WESTVIEW PRESS • BOULDER, COLORADO

First published in 1977
by Methuen & Co Ltd
11 New Fetter Lane, London EC4P 4EE
Published in 1977 in the United States of America by
Westview Press, Inc.
1898 Flatiron Court
Boulder, Colorado 80301
Frederick A. Praeger, Publisher and Editorial Director
© 1977 Philip E. Vernon, Georgina Adamson, Dorothy F. Vernon

Library of Congress Cataloging in Publication Data
Vernon, Philip Ewart.
The psychology and education of gifted children.

Bibliography: p.
1. Gifted children--Education. I. Adamson, Georgina,
joint author. II. Vernon, Dorothy F., joint author.
III. Title.
LC3993.V47   371.9'5   77–23220
ISBN 0–89158–728–4

Printed in Great Britain

Contents

Preface

Why *another* book on gifted children? There are so many already, and they are mostly inspired by the same philosophy; namely that highly intelligent or talented children are potentially the most valuable resource of modern society; that far too often this resource is being wasted through inadequacies in the education that most schools provide, and that there are many ways in which their conditions of upbringing and schooling can be improved. However, over the past fifteen years or so there have been numerous developments in psychology, and in educational procedures, which are particularly relevant to the understanding and stimulation of gifted children. More is known regarding the nature of intelligence and its development. We realize that it varies quite considerably during childhood growth, and is greatly dependent on environmental influences, though this does not mean that we can readily increase the IQ at will. At the same time there is a strong hereditary component both in general, and more specialized, abilities. These specialized types of ability or talents are considerably more diverse than was assumed by earlier writers on intelligence. There are also a number of rather technical, but important, points in the interpretation of test IQs which, so far as we know, have not found their way into any other book on the gifted.

Then there has been a spate of interest in creativity, and a good deal of confusion between the creative production of outstanding artists or scientists, and the rather trivial results of so called creativity, or divergent thinking, tests. As regards education, we have seen, in Britain, mounting criticisms and eventual decline of selective secondary education (the eleven-plus); also attacks on any kind of homogeneous grouping or streaming. In North America, to an even greater extent, testing for educational predictions has come under fire, and it is difficult to win support for special education for gifted children, owing to suspicions of 'elitism'. However, there are many arguments for and against different approaches to the education of children of superior mentality which we have tried to present judiciously. Other trends which need to be taken into account include computer managed instruction, curricular developments, particularly in mathematics and science, and the advocacy of what is called normalization in the education of exceptional children. However, these topics are treated only briefly, and we do not attempt to go into detailed exposition of educational procedures or materials for the gifted.

Thus it is the integration of educational considerations with a good deal of basic psychology and mental testing which we regard as the justification for this book. Since all three authors were brought up under the British educational system, but have worked in Canadian schools and universities for many years, it is an advantage to be able to compare the views and the practices in both countries and in the United States. This involves us in some mixture of terminologies, and we apologize to the British reader who is unfamiliar with, say, North American school grades, and to the Canadian and American who is unfamiliar with infant, primary, and with secondary modern or grammar schools, and with British spelling.

The main purpose of the book is to provide the kind of information which should be useful to teachers who are being trained for work with the gifted, at a fairly non-technical level. That is, we assume that the reader is acquainted with such terms as 'mean' scores and 'correlation coefficients', though not, say, with 'factor analysis' or 'multiple regression equation'. We hope also that it will be helpful to education and psychology students, and to teachers and educational administrators generally, who are interested in gifted children and their education; and to many parents whose children show promise of exceptional ability, and who wish to know more about their prospects and upbringing. Regretfully we have decided to exclude case studies, or anecdotes about particular gifted children. True, they might add considerably to the interest and readability of such a book, but they do take up more space than can be spared at a time when publishing costs are so high.

Grateful acknowledgements are made to Mrs Ruthe Lundy and to Dr F.A. MacKinnon and Mr D.L. Hicks, who provided us with much first-hand information regarding the operation of schemes for gifted children in Palo Alto, California, and

Saskatoon, Saskatchewan, respectively. Also to Mr G.A. McLennan for using some of his valuable spare time to read and comment on the manuscript

1 Introduction

It is surely ironic that the most able and talented children in western societies, such as Britain, the United States and Canada, by and large receive the worst education. There are many exceptions of course: that is, schools, or classes within schools, which try to cater for the particular needs of the gifted. But any special provision is apt to be costly, in so far as it involves small classes under highly qualified teachers, and expensive materials. Many private schools do serve the need, but they have to charge fees, and this restricts their clientele mainly to wealthy families. Public educational systems often make special provision for unfortunate children at the bottom of the scale — those who are physically handicapped or mentally retarded, sometimes for the culturally deprived or the emotionally maladjusted and young delinquents. This is equally costly, indeed more costly, in terms of personnel, buildings and equipment, and in addition usually involves a body of highly trained psychologists to diagnose handicaps and to assist in assigning the children who most require special help to appropriate schools or other forms of treatment. The various school authorities, and the tax payers, are usually willing to finance these humanitarian services (though many would say that they are too niggardly); but it is much more difficult to persuade them to make similar provisions for the gifted, despite the obvious point that the latter are likely to make far more valuable contributions to the good of the community in the future, when they become the scientists, artists, teachers and leaders of the next generation. The very fact that these children *are* able militates against them; they generally learn easily, and do well in and enjoy school and cause little trouble, and this means that they do not seem to constitute a pressing problem. They already have an advantage, so why give them more? However, we shall see later that many of them do have difficulties, and that conventional schooling may turn them into poor learners, and waste their talents.

Moreover, a rather large proportion tend to come from upper- or middle-class homes (partly because those from working-class homes are less likely to be recognized), and such homes can do a lot to make up for what the gifted miss at school. Hence the politicians and the public, and some educational administrators, have a further excuse for shirking the issue. Nevertheless, the situation is by no means hopeless: many educationists and parents are aware of the problem and have stirred up support for a variety of changes in school organization and curriculum, or instituted fruitful experiments, some of which we will describe below. Special provisions for the gifted have been running, in parts of the US and Canada, for over fifty years. There is no simple or universal answer to the question — how to allow for individual differences between pupils in a mass educational system, which of necessity must be run economically. But we can learn a lot from what has been tried, and how it has worked, as well as from psychological studies of the characteristics and development of gifted children.

Brief historical and comparative survey

Throughout history, different societies have held various views as to the appropriate education of the most able, and how it may best be accomplished. In Greece, over 2000 years ago, Plato distinguished the 'men of gold', with superior intellects, from those of 'silver' and 'iron or brass'. As children they should be instructed in such subjects as philosophy, metaphysics and science, which would be beyond the ability of those who were destined to become soldiers or artisans.

Until well into the nineteenth century there was very little problem, since so few children were educated anyway. Those that were mostly came from wealthy families. In England, the sons were sent to so-called 'public schools' such as Eton and Winchester. Classes were small and likely to be grouped according to ability level. For other sections of the population there were the old-established grammar schools, which were also fee-paying, but usually admitted a proportion of able working-class children who won scholarships. Thus they too catered mainly for pupils of above average ability. Similarly, Germany had its Gymnasium, France its Lycée. Gradually, elementary education for the whole population was introduced in European countries, but the system remained highly élitist. Until well into the twentieth century, only the upper- and middle-class children and a few of the most able working-class, could advance to higher secondary or university education. Moreover, streaming, or homogeneous grouping, was customary; hence, at least in a rough and ready way, the exceptionally talented were picked out and enabled to progress at approximately their own rate, instead of having to be taught along with pupils of only moderate or inferior ability. Naturally the systems of school organization varied greatly from one country to another; but they did allow the most able to rise to the top, even though they obviously provided few opportunities for 'mute inglorious Miltons' from the great mass of the peasant and working-class population.

In the United States, the earliest colleges (e.g. Harvard, 1636) were highly selective and a few independent, private schools were set up, mainly in New England. Nevertheless, the opposed philosophy of egalitarianism became predominant, holding that education should be available to all, regardless of wealth or privilege. In addition, particularly in the nineteenth and twentieth centuries, the common school was seen as a unifying force for Americanizing the children of immigrants from many lands, whose parents spoke many tongues. Initially, it did not work too badly, since the dull and disinterested could and did drop out of school at an early age, leaving mainly the more academically motivated, who were able to progress to the higher grades. But with the increasing spread of educational facilities and increasing realization among parents of the benefits of secondary and college education, the range of ability among those who stayed on widened, till now more than three-quarters of the population complete high school, and a majority in some States go on to some form of tertiary education. Since both homogeneous grouping, and acceleration to allow the brighter to proceed more rapidly, are frowned upon (though currently being employed with increasing frequency), the difficulties of educating the whole range of ability among pupils, grouped simply by age, have become more and more apparent. Some of the slower or more backward children repeat grades and thus become academic retardates, but only a small proportion who are seriously handicapped, physically or mentally or both, are specially catered for. In Canada, school organization is generally similar to the USA, with only a few high-prestige fee-paying schools on the British model.

In the 1930s, and particularly following World War II, more democratic ideals began to spread throughout most European countries. Thus in the UK sufficient 'grammar' (i.e. high) schools were built to take, on average, 20 per cent of the elementary school population at the age of eleven, on the basis of a selection examination — the notorious 'eleven-plus'; and more opportunity was offered to those who failed this hurdle to be upgraded later or to take advanced secondary courses. Comprehensive schools, which, like American high schools, are non-selective, were introduced in the fifties and sixties, and now cater for more 11-18 year old students than do the grammar and independent secondary schools. However, most of these continue to practise streaming; that is, the most able pupils in any year-group are in the top class, then the next slice, and so on down to the lowest class which will tend to consist of the very backward and virtual non-readers. The same sort of grouping by ability is typical also in the larger primary (elementary) schools, though an increasing number are now switching over to mixed-ability classes. Unlike North America, the pace of adoption or non-adoption of comprehensive and unstreamed schooling depends considerably on pressures exerted by the political party that happens to be in power at the moment. When the overall organization of schooling is so controversial an issue, little attention is paid to the special needs of the highly gifted.

Some implications of individual differences

As early as the 1920s psychologists such as Terman and Thorndike in the United States and Burt and Thomson in Britain had constructed objective group tests of intelligence, and of achievement in different school subjects, which made it possible to assess children's abilities on age scales. For example a bright child aged 9 years might show the intellectual capacity equivalent to that of the average 12 year old, and score at 11-year or sixth-grade level* on tests of reading and

*It would become tedious always to list the UK equivalents of North American grades, or vice versa, and as the American system is simpler, it will generally be adopted. British readers are merely asked to remember that subtracting 5 from a child's age in years will normally specify what grade he

arithmetic. Terman pointed out that in an average unselected class, covering the whole range of ability for that age, the variations are so enormous as to make it absurd to try to teach all children the same topic at the same rate. For example, at 10 years a few children may have the mental capacity or intelligence of 14 or 15 year olds, and others the capacity of 7 year olds, or even lower if the severely defective have not been weeded out. The range in mathematical and language abilities could be almost as great, though most teachers would frankly disbelieve that some of their fifth-grade pupils could cope with ninth-grade work, others only with second-grade. Naturally the brighter ones will probably not have been taught some of the concepts and skills usually studied at ninth grade, though if standardized tests are applied to fifth-graders it may well be found that they have picked them up on their own; and had they been allowed to progress at their own natural rate, they would readily have kept up with children much older than themselves. The range of variation in younger classes is not so marked: at 5 years it is likely to be only half as great as at 10, hence it is more feasible to give uniform instruction to all first-graders. On the other hand, the range is even greater in the secondary school, though sometimes alleviated since, as noted above, many of the dullest drop out, or else are working in a grade, or two grades, lower than usual for their age.

Terman and Burt advocated the organization of classes on a mental age rather than chronological age basis, though they realized that a compromise would be necessary. Otherwise, if, say, all children of mental age 10 were put together, it would

---

is in (e.g. 6 year olds will mostly be in Grade 1). If British terminology is used, the approximate age equivalents are:

5 year olds — Infants 1	8 year olds — Junior 2
6 2	9 3
7 ...... Junior 1 (or sometimes Infants 3)	10 4

All of these are 'primary' school — no longer called 'elementary'. In secondary schools:

11 year olds — Form 1	15 year olds — Form 5
12 2	16 .... 6 (first year)
13 3	17 .... 6 (second year)
14 4	18 .... 6 (third year)

mean including pupils whose chronological ages ranged from about 14 to 6. Such a policy also implied that intelligence tests accurately measured each child's basic or innate capacity for acquiring school learning, which — as we shall see later — is only partially true. Nevertheless, if acceleration or retardation in accordance with achievement were more fully adopted, and more attention paid to children's IQs in class allocation, it would be possible to arrange more homogeneous groups or streams, and thus to do more for the gifted as well as for the dull. It would mean that a very significant proportion of the most able students would be able to cover the conventional school and university curriculum in two years less than the average student takes, and thus become qualified for productive professional or other highgrade careers two years earlier, which would be of obvious benefit to society. There are, however, various difficulties and disadvantages both in acceleration and other methods of adjusting instruction to individual differences, and these will be discussed in chapters 9-11.

The gifted child in the classroom

The more highly developed an educational system, and the greater the efficiency with which it covers the entire child and adolescent population, the more likely it is to become institutionalized and rigidly standardized, and the less concerned with the needs of the individual child. Administrators and supervisors naturally prefer a neat arrangement where every child of a given age is being taught the same syllabus from the same textbook at the same time. Most parents likewise prefer a standard system with which they are familiar. Another drawback is that the larger the number of children to be educated, the greater the number of teachers needed. And although teachers have to possess good academic qualifications, the unfortunate fact is that they tend to be drawn from the second-grade rather than from top-notch students. The latter, who possess greater initiative and intelligence, tend to aim at professions or other jobs which give them more scope for self-direction than the rather restricted (and not too well-paid) job of teaching. It has been stated also that those teachers who conform most efficiently to the system are more likely to be rewarded by promotion than the individualists or pioneers; though we doubt whether this is justified. Obviously these are broad generalizations which are unfair to large numbers of dedicated and able teachers who keep mentally alive and continue throughout their careers to search for original ways of interesting and stimulating their pupils. Fortunately the professions of teaching and of educational administration do attract, and provide scope for, a wide range of different personalities and abilities, who make different contributions to educating the young. But the clash between good education and bureaucratization is inevitably greater than in the days when schools were less organized and more selective.

It would be unfair also to impute that even average teachers, let alone good ones, fail to take account of individual differences, or expect all members of a class to acquire the same knowledge and skill at the same rate. They normally repeat their instruction in different ways at different levels of complexity, and set exercises of different degrees of difficulty; and they recognize that each child is an unique person who requires different handling. However, there is a tendency to pitch the instruction at the level of the pupil about three quarters' way down the list in achievement (i.e. the twenty-fifth percentile), so that the least able or most poorly motivated don't get left too far behind; and then, in so far as time allows, the teacher will give individual help to the weaker pupils. Inevitably this means that the brightest quarter, and still more so the exceptionally gifted, are way ahead, and have nothing to do, except perhaps additional exercises of the same kind. And since they are usually more keen and able than the majority, they receive least attention: good marks and praise, perhaps, but these do not compensate for boredom. Leta Hollingworth, a psychologist who made major contributions to the education of very highly intelligent children, remarked that the pupil of IQ 140 wastes half his time in the ordinary classroom, and the one with an IQ of 180+, almost all of it (cf. Hildreth, 1952).*

Being inventive, such children usually find something to do, like talking to or helping their neighbours, trying out their own ideas, or reading. They may just daydream and look forward to the more interesting activities they can carry on at home.

*All references to books and articles are given in the final bibliography, and may be identified by author and date.

But they can also develop the bad habits of slapdash work, scarcely bothering to listen to the teacher's painstaking instruction, and thus achieve far less than they are capable of. They can easily become complacent and, when later they do get to work along with intellectual equals, lack the necessary drive and persistence. They may show off or become troublesome in other ways. Having acquired a lot of unusual information or skills, outside school, they ask questions, or suggest new and more effective methods, e.g. of solving mathematical problems, which differ from the teacher's routine approach, and are, therefore, unwelcome and treated sarcastically. Naturally it is disconcerting when they upset a teacher's carefully prepared lesson plan. Thus their attempts to make use of their brains are damped down and frustrated. By the age of 10 or so, some of them are as intelligent as, or more so than, the teacher himself or herself, though, of course, less mature, and therefore are apt to become a threat to good discipline and orderly instruction. So that although, as already mentioned, the majority are better motivated and much quicker to learn than average, it is by no means uncommon for them to be referred to the schools' psychologists as under-achievers or behaviour problems. Teachers tend to equate docility and conformity with ability, and are genuinely astonished when told that such a child is much above average and chiefly needs to be given more challenging work to do.

Always, though, we must remember the wide variety of competence and skills among teachers. Some are far more capable than others of individualizing instruction even in the ordinary classroom, of welcoming and encouraging and getting the best out of the brighter children without neglecting the dull or the average; whereas others are much more limited and inflexible. But just as it is generally recognized that most teachers cannot be expected to cope with the severely handicapped, so it is reasonable to allow that they will have difficulties in providing for those who are at least as much above average as the severely handicapped are below average.

Social attitudes

A further handicap to the gifted children is that society, particularly North American society, tends to be suspicious of the child who is 'different', and prefers the well-rounded socially and emotionally adjusted child, who shows the interests conventional to his or her sex and age, rather than the academically distinguished or artistically gifted. 'Gifted' is associated with geniuses or young prodigies, and genius is traditionally, though unjustifiably, associated with neurosis, or even insanity. The very bright child, according to traditional lore, is poorly developed physically, short-sighted, no good at athletics; also precocity is a flash-in-the-pan that doesn't last. Moreover, the real geniuses in adult life, such as Darwin, Einstein, or Winston Churchill, were far from brilliant at school. Cases can be cited to bolster all these beliefs, provided the much larger number who prove the exact opposite are ignored. We will outline some of the evidence later. Yet at the same time the public is avidly interested in the exploits of geniuses and prodigies such as those who appear on TV quizzes; and in these days where giftedness is beginning to become more fashionable, some parents do harm to their children's natural growth by exploiting and over-pressuring them.

Not only do most parents and teachers tend to mould children towards conventionality; the peer-group exerts an even more compelling influence towards uniformity in attitudes and values as well as in dress, manner and speech. In this it is backed up by the stereotypes so frequently exhibited on television. It may welcome some forms of exceptionality such as social leadership, particularly in antisocial gangs, and it approves of strongly masculine physique and athletic skills. A.J. Tannenbaum, in a study of American adolescents in 1962, found predominantly negative attitudes towards academic superiority and positive valuation of athletic achievement. Moreover, even the brighter pupils accepted these stereotypes and were apt to conceal their talents and intellectual interests so as not to appear too different from the majority. Nevertheless, there is some evidence of the appreciation of intelligence and school achievement; both tend to show positive, even if low, correlations with sociometric popularity. The anti-intellectual stereotype which adolescents express publicly may be more an expression of their revolt against adult authority than what they, in fact, prefer when choosing their friends. The same picture holds good for peer-group cultures in the UK as in North America, though it may be that British parents are in general somewhat more tolerant of individuality and more appreciative of giftedness in their children than are Americans. (A comparative survey would be interesting.)

Recent changes

After World War II the whole social climate changed in many ways, and this affected educational thinking on both sides of the Atlantic. The pace of technological development accelerated, standards of living rose, but so also did the difficulties of adjustment in a complex civilization, and the instability of international relations. An education designed to maintain the status quo and to pass on traditional culture to the new generation came under question. What sort of world were children being educated for? Did they not require versatility for coping with new conditions in new kinds of jobs, rather than the skills of the past? Moreover, parents generally became more concerned about what went on in schools, and more demanding of improvements. Another notable change was that the generally more permissive conditions of child-upbringing at home meant that the pupils themselves objected more freely to anything they disliked at school, and teachers became less authoritarian, less able to impose their own notions of what should be taught, and how.

In 1957 the Russians succeeded in launching the first satellite, Sputnik, and this had a traumatic effect in the USA (though little in the UK). Apparently America was being beaten in the technological race, and much of the blame was put on the schools for failing to produce as many engineers and scientists as the USSR, and for frustrating rather than encouraging talented students. Some reacted by criticizing the laxity of modern practices and urging a return to the good old grind (cf. Flesch, 1955; Rickover, 1963). But more generally the cry was for greater creativity and less routine conformity in the schools, and better opportunities for the most able. Large funds were put into scholarships such as the National Merit Awards for assisting outstanding students who would have been unable, on economic grounds, to go to college; and varied programmes for helping the gifted were initiated in many school systems. How far these have survived the greater financial stringencies and political pressures of the 1970s is uncertain, and it is very likely that educational fashions are changing yet again. Moreover, such improvements had to compete with a simultaneous concern for the education of handicapped and deprived children, especially blacks and Spanish-speaking Americans. And although these movements were usually funded from different sources, there is an obvious clash between interest in the able few (especially those from middle- and upper-class homes), and interest in the deprived multitudes. It is hardly possible, particularly for non-American writers, to disentangle the threads in so complex a tapestry, but it is probable that the 1960s provided the most favourable climate of the twentieth century for special education of gifted American children, and that we may now be facing another recession. Some of the special programmes of this decade were hastily conceived and poorly executed, and their consequent failure left a legacy of increased hostility towards trying any fresh schemes for the gifted.

Psychologists added their bit to the pressure for change. Criticisms of the static conception of a genetically-fixed intelligence had been mounting since the 1930s, and in 1950 J.P. Guilford delivered a famous address as President of the American Psychological Association on 'Creativity'. His views will be discussed in chapter 4, but briefly his argument was that mental abilities are far too diverse to be indicated by a single IQ. Both psychologists and educationists, he claimed, have largely ignored a whole class of abilities of the imaginative, productive kind. Almost all our tests are 'convergent' in the sense that the testee is expected to converge to, or arrive at, the one right answer to each item, which has been fixed beforehand. He has no opportunity to put forward his own ideas. Nevertheless, there are certain kinds of tests where many answers are possible, and the testee can be scored for the number of responses he produces, and how original they are. These are tests of divergent thinking, and Guilford himself and his followers have devised many such tests which were widely tried out in the 1960s. The implication was that the schools have ignored and damped down this area of man's abilities, and have been dominated by the ubiquitous multiple-choice achievement test which assumes that a person is educated when he knows all the conventional answers. Such claims also require careful scrutiny, before we jump to the conclusion that the creative scientists and artists of the next generation could be picked out by divergent thinking tests, or that the creativity of the population generally could be improved by more innovative education.

At about the same time, Paul Witty's book, *The Gifted Child* (1951) was sponsored by the American Association for Gifted Children; and this promoted wide interest and discussion.

In the UK there was very little sign of a comparable creativity 'craze', and it is likely that the schools, especially secondary schools, are even more tied to examination requirements than those of North America. However, multiple-choice tests are much less used than the old-fashioned essay-type where the pupil has some scope for giving divergent answers in his own words. Nevertheless, British psychologists have shown considerable interest in research with 'creativity' tests. Also, with the 'comprehensivation' of so many secondary schools, concern for the education of the exceptionally able is increasing, as witnessed by the formation of a National Association for Gifted Children. Canadian educationists were also cautious regarding the movement, though there is an active Canadian branch of the Council for Exceptional Children, which includes a section called TAG — The Association for the Gifted.

Currently then, the situation in all three countries is that, in spite of a great deal of talk and of varied activity on behalf of gifted and talented children, the great majority of children (particularly in North America) get no effective assistance. Usually the education system not merely ignores, but is biased against, them. Far too many parents see their bright child, when he first goes to school, already well advanced in verbal and number skills, eager to learn more, bursting with ideas and interests; yet within a few years he loses this enthusiasm, becomes bored and aimless from lack of encouragement, even conceals his cleverness because it makes him unpopular with his peers or with teachers, and he intentionally does inferior work. Occasionally, perhaps by moving him to another school, or exerting sufficient pressure on teachers and the principal, they manage to win some concessions. But often they fear to make a nuisance of themselves in case their efforts rebound, and their child suffers all the more. Such parents are not, in fact, demanding special privileges; like other parents they are paying their taxes for a system which claims, in theory, to provide education adequate to all children according to their needs. Though usually doing a good job for handicapped and retarded pupils, it is manifestly failing to do so for the very bright ones, and is discriminating against them.

The present book is written in an attempt to reduce ignorance and prejudice — ignorance about individual differences and the psychological characteristics of gifted children, and prejudice against organizing special instruction for them, despite the fact that this has proved to be of value in many parts of the English-speaking world.

2 Giftedness and intelligence

No two gifted children are the same in their abilities, talents and personalities. Nevertheless, a very large proportion are distinguished from average children by virtue of superior general intelligence; and this can be measured fairly reliably by an individual test as the Stanford-Binet or Terman-Merrill scales, or by one of the Wechsler scales (WPPSI, WISC or WAIS*). We will comment later on the use and interpretation of intelligence quotients obtained from these or other tests. Some gifted children, however, are characterized more by specialized abilities or talents, for example in mathematics, science, mechanical construction, art or music and so forth (cf. chapter 4) than by very high general intelligence, though this also will usually be well above average. Giftedness then is a good deal broader and more varied than just IQ. But intelligence is such a crucial quality, and so much is known about its origins and development, that this chapter and the next one will be devoted mainly to it.

Growth of intelligence

First let us ask, how early in life can superior intelligence be recognized? It is very natural that fond parents should observe their baby's development intently, and often seize on each new activity or growth as a sign of exceptional ability. But in fact there are scarcely any trustworthy signs of later ability during

*The majority of educational psychologists tend to refer to all the editions of Terman's scales as Stanford-Binet. But in fact the Revised Stanford-Binet Forms L and M published in 1937, and the 1960 Form LM, are as different from the original 1916 Stanford-Binet as the latter is different from Binet and Simon's 1911 scale. Since the distinction is important, we intend to use the label Terman-Merrill scale throughout for Forms L, M or LM, rather than Revised Stanford-Binet, and to retain Stanford-Binet for the 1916 test only.

The full titles of the Wechsler scales are: Wechsler Preschool and Primary Scale of Intelligence, Wechsler Intelligence Scale for Children, and Wechsler Adult Intelligence Scale, respectively.

the first year, and not much that can be relied on in the second and third years. The first couple of years, according to Piaget, constitute the sensory-motor stage during which the child is growing physically, learning to coordinate his senses and movements, learning to recognize and react to objects, people, sounds and words. It is essentially a practical stage in which be becomes remarkably competent in handling concrete everyday situations, e.g. manipulating things and moving around, and in beginning to use speech as a means of communication. But although children vary very considerably in the rate at which these capacities mature, they give virtually no indication of later intelligence. During the second year it is obvious that children are beginning to remember things, and anticipate through some kind of mental imagery; also they can form concepts such as pleasant *v.* unpleasant, or cars, birds etc. But they can hardly be said to be 'thinking', in the sense of considering ideas internally and reaching conclusions by which to direct their behaviour, until around 3 years on average — earlier in some, later in others.

There are a number of developmental tests or scales for 0-2 year olds, such as Gesell's Developmental Schedules, which chiefly record motor development and the beginnings of language. If the scores on these are compared with later childhood IQs, the correlation coefficients are around zero. Nancy Bayley (1955) studied groups of children from birth till 25 years, testing them periodically with tests like the California Preschool, then the Stanford-Binet, and eventually the Wechsler scales.* Though there was fairly high consistency of performance over a few months during infancy, there was no correlation with 12-year old IQ till 2 to 3 years, and even then the coefficients of 0.3 to 0.4 were too low to provide any reliable prediction in individual cases. By the age of 5-6, however, most children had acquired quite a large vocabulary, could comprehend and use fairly complex sentences, and reason out simple problems mentally. that is, they were displaying the same sort of intelligence as older children; and their Stanford-Binet IQs now correlated 0.7 to 0.8 with performance six years later. By 11 years, the correlation with 18-year IQ may reach 0.9. Group test IQs, however, show even

*The work of the Berkeley group of child psychologists on variability in mental growth is described in M.C. Jones *et al.* (1971). Cf. also Dearborn and Rothney (1941), and Bloom (1964).

less stability in childhood, not reaching the 0.7 to 0.8 level of reliability till about 9 years (cf. Hopkins and Bracht, 1975).

Even with individually tested mental ages, there is much more variation in growth curves during middle childhood and adolescence than most parents or teachers realize. A child's developmental and intelligence quotients up to 3 years or so fluctuate wildly, and although there is increasing consistency thereafter, yet mental growth may be rapid at some periods, stationary or even dropping back at other periods throughout the elementary and secondary school years. This arises partly because of differences between the successive tests that are applied; also scores may be affected by the child's attitude and cooperation while being tested. But in addition there are more fundamental changes that probably depend on emotional adjustment and personality development, or on environmental conditions at home or at school, all of which stimulate or depress intellectual progress. Thus the IQ is certainly not as stable or constant as some of the early pioneers like Terman and Burt* led us to suppose. Nevertheless, once a child has settled down in elementary school, his IQ is still the best indicator of his overall brightness, at least for a few years ahead. There is also better justification for testing children who appear to be highly gifted at a younger age than average children, say at 3½ to 4½ years, the reason being that by this time their mental ages on a Binet-type scale may well have reached 5 years and over — that is the level which is fairly highly predictive of later ability.

Early characteristic of gifted children†

It is certainly unwise, then, to take good physical development, or age of crawling, walking or manipulating things, or attending to sights and sounds, as indicators of the future. However, children who do later show mental superiority are generally at least average in these respects. Noticeable retardation in these capacities is more likely to be diagnostic of impaired

---

*Burt (1975) denies that he or Terman claimed anything more than that the IQ is 'relatively stable'. But the figures that he quotes imply much higher reliability than most psychologists have found.

†This section of the chapter is admittedly largely speculative, and is an attempt to pull together available strands of evidence that might be helpful, especially to the 'lay' reader.

intelligence than precocity is of high ability. Margaret Parker (1975) states that gifted children from the start are more active and interested in their surroundings, and sleep less time than normal, as though they didn't want to waste any of their waking time. This may quite possibly be true of some very bright children, but it unlikely to be a general distinguishing characteristic Some gifted children, indeed, may be undersized or sickly, or slow in motor growth, though they are probably the exception. It has been suggested by some child psychologists that certain qualitative aspects of behaviour during the first year, like alertness and social responsiveness are noticeably advanced among gifted children, though these are difficult to pin down, and they too can be deceptive.

Age of beginning to talk is also untrustworthy; for although case histories of gifted children, or later geniuses, often mention very early speech, some others may be considerably delayed and then suddenly seem to make up a year or more's growth in a month. However, rapid acquisition of vocabulary, quick build-up of relatively complex sentences and precision of speech, interest in words and desire to experiment with words between, say 1½ and 3 years, do seem to be more characteristic of later intelligence.

Brumbaugh and Roshco (1959), also Ruth Strang (1960) and Margaret Parker (1975) list a number of other indicators that may be observed in preschoolers, and we will draw to some extent on their books.

Good memory is often mentioned. Bright children recall events, people etc., or pick up stories or verses read to them, and general information, with remarkable ease. They like to examine and manipulate things, take them to pieces, build constructively with bricks or other materials, and tend to show remarkable concentration and purposefulness in such activities. From about 2 years, according to Charlotte Bühler (1935), they should be showing the 'work attitude' — that is, not just flitting from one activity to another, but completing tasks or games that they set themselves. This is something which is essential to later intellectual achievement. Though their reasoning is limited to concrete situations, they often find out for themselves how things work, or what to do to reach some desired goal. Or if they do ask for help or explanations, they quickly understand and apply what they have been told. In their play, they like to copy what they have seen mother, or the mailman, or the dog, doing. In this way, it seems, they are sorting out and reinforcing their impressions of the world and of people. But they are also highly imaginative; for example, they actually appear to see the chair as a car, a boat, a tunnel, or whatever. As soon as language is sufficiently advanced, they show an insatiable desire to know, and ask endless 'why' questions. They enjoy being read to, or discussing picture books, or watching television, and very quickly seem to grasp the point of what is going on even though much of it must be beyond them.

By 3½ or even earlier they may be wanting to read, and can to a considerable extent teach themselves from labels, road signs, TV commercials, picture books etc. Ruth Strang, however, warns us that it is often difficult to distinguish the pseudogifted from the genuinely gifted. The former may have been taught to read or perform other intellectual feats at an early age, but this does not last when they come on to the more abstract reasoning required for a good deal of school work, whereas the latter have discovered things for themselves, without being pressured. This, of course, is helped if adults provide opportunities appropriate to their level of conceptual development.

Catherine Cox's book on *The Early Mental Traits of Three Hundred Geniuses* (1926) reports far more extreme forms of precocity among prodigies such as John Stuart Mill and Francis Galton. A good deal of such anecdotal evidence is, naturally, rather unreliable, and these cases are so exceptional that they should not be regarded as typical of gifted children generally. It is especially difficult for parents to judge their own children since they have little basis for comparison other than casual observations of children of relatives or friends. Hence, a standard scale of tasks given in a standard way, like the Gesell scale or Terman-Merrill, is generally preferable for diagnosis, though, as we have admitted, these may not fully bring out the mental superiorities of gifted preschoolers and, therefore, give low correlations with later intelligence.

While it would obviously be useful if we could identify gifted children early on, so as to be able to provide the most suitable environment for their growth, it is at least as important to remember that apparently gifted youngsters are just ordinary children in most respects. Parents are apt to be disappointed when they are not so advanced in social, emotional or physical characteristics as they are in intellectual development. For example, they may or may not possess the manual dexterity or bodily coordination to match their inventiveness. On the whole they do tend to show above average self-confidence, to make easy social contacts with other children or strange adults, and to accept reasonable parental regulations. They are likely to be more independent and persistent, and maybe more stubborn and self-willed than average. But it would be unnatural if they did not, especially around 2 to 3, display resistances, aggression, temper tantrums, worries and anxieties similar to those in others of the same age.

Characteristics at school

It is somewhat easier to judge intellectual giftedness in the early years at school, since there are plenty of average and dull children to compare with. As would be expected, gifted children learn easily, provided the work is challenging, and provided that they are not put off by boring, repetitive drills, or by being forced to keep in step with slower learners. For them, work is fun, and they can learn far more by independent study than by grind. They are quick to comprehend and see new relations, and they are by now capable of manipulating ideas, not just acquiring concepts and information from others. They need much less explanation of new topics or skills than the average member of the class. They will tend to be better at language, social studies, science, probably maths, than at handwriting or art, though they may show considerably greater talent in some areas than others as they grow older (cf. chapter 4).

The precocity of their speech and vocabulary is one of the most noticeable characteristics. Not only do they know unusual words, but they also employ adult-like sentences. Others who are not so gifted may be equally fluent and loquacious, but do not express the same range of ideas and relationships. The gifted likewise enjoy intellectual problems, puzzles, tests, numbers, calendars and maps. Unusually early they see the need to evaluate and check their solutions, and not be satisfied with any old answer. Since they are accustomed to doing things well and to success, there may be dangers of their becoming supercilious, or over-competitive with other children.

Another group of qualities is often thought to indicate creativity rather than intelligence, though we would question the distinction at this age. Gifted children are apt to produce unusual ideas and questions, unexpected and unconventional solutions to problems, and new ways of looking at things. They show a spontaneous desire to know about all sorts of topics, to explore and discover rather than just accept what parents or teachers tell them. They may show vivid imagination in oral conversation, and later in written stories, or art productions. Also they possess a remarkable range of interests and hobbies. One of the most characteristic of these is making collections — stamps, sea-shells, rocks, wild flowers, cigarette cards, postcards, objects from the past, and so on (though this does not usually reach its peak until about 9 to 12 years). Reading, again, is varied and extensive, and may be preferred to television. But gifted children are by no means just bookworms; they like to play games as much as any normal child, and often show unusual inventiveness and imagination. They are good at planning and organizing and, if well-adjusted socially, tend to become leaders of play or work groups. However, their ideas and language may be too much in advance of their age-peers, so that they frequently prefer to associate with older children. Though often relatively immature socially, they show considerable sensitivity to, and concern about, the feelings of others. Likewise, despite emotional difficulties that may arise from lack of understanding by teachers or peers, they have the advantage of greater self-insight and rationality. Superior ability by no means guarantees superior character development; but though they can certainly be disobedient and troublesome, especially when prevented from doing what seems to them reasonable, they are generally considered as unusually trustworthy and dependable; and they are better able than most to understand the reasons for prohibitions, to appreciate justice and the rights of others, and to express their own attitudes fluently.

Leta Hollingworth (1942) and Terman (1930) have sympathetically described the difficulties of children of extremely high intelligence. Those who, on the old Stanford-Binet or Terman-Merrill, obtained IQs of 170 up are presumably as much removed from the gifted child of 135 IQ as the latter is removed from the average, or the average removed from the highgrade defective of 65. While this statement should not be taken too literally because we have no absolute scale of intellectual advancement and retardation, certainly in some respects the 8 year old with IQ 65 will have the mentality of a 5 year old. One with an IQ of 135 will be like an 11 year old, and at 170 he will be like a 13½ year old. The very highly intelligent may easily be out of touch with average children of his own age, and be bewildered because they tend to reject him. He or she is apt to be more interested in abstract ideas like morality and scientific causation than in football or dolls. With adults too, he can be frightening or threatening. He is apt to be devastatingly rational, to observe and recall inconsistencies in their behaviour, and to brood about them when they resent his criticisms. He asks searching questions about their often facile generalizations, or about topics of which they are ignorant.

As suggested in chapter 1, it is very common for gifted children to play down their intellectual superiority in order to win greater acceptance from peers or unsympathetic teachers, and consequently there is the danger that they may cease to value or to develop their abilities and interests. However, we will return later to such problems of adjustment, and to the ways in which parents and the schools can help.

Sex differences

So far nothing has been said about sex differences, and we have talked mainly about 'he' as an abbreviation for 'he or she'. The average IQ on a well-constructed intelligence test is the same for boys and girls, but there is some evidence — not universally accepted — of a greater range among boys. That is, there are more very bright boys as well as very dull ones. This fits in with the common observation that there are more male scholars and honours students at universities than females, that very few women seem to attain the rank of 'genius', and that there are more males in schools or institutions for the subnormal or defective. But there are many possible sociocultural reasons for such differences; and at least over the 3 to 15 year age range, the numbers of highly intelligent or talented boys and girls are pretty closely comparable. So far as school achievement is concerned, girls tend to get better marks than boys until senior high school or college level, when the position is reversed.

However there are quite considerable differences in some abilities and interests, yet at the same time a great deal of overlapping. For example, girls more often excel in linguistic abilities (though curiously not in vocabulary), in memorizing and retaining what they have learned, and in finger dexterity. Boys more often excel in spatial and mechanical abilities, in mathematical reasoning and physical sciences, in general information, and obviously in large muscle athletic activities. More girls also are interested in domestic and in artistic activities (painting, writing, music, drama, dancing), boys in more practical and adventurous activities. Cultural stereotypes regarding what is proper to the two sexes doubtless account for much of this, although probably not for all; but there is no need to argue here the extent of genetic or constitutional differences.

Even where we find the greatest differences in abilities, the ratio of one sex to the other would be unlikely to exceed 60-40; in other words, if 60 males score above the general average in, say, maths, then 40 females do likewise. Similarly there might be 60 superior female spellers to 40 males. But at the gifted level (say the top 2 to 5 per cent) the odds become greater; probably at least three times as many boys as girls are likely to be specially talented in maths. However, there are no precise figures, and generalizations are dubious since we do not know enough about the effects of cultural pressures. On the whole, gifted children are less likely than nongifted to be affected by these pressures. Thus, very bright girls often show some conventionally masculine interests, and gifted boys show some feminine ones. In most respects, then, we may expect to find very much the same characteristics in gifted children of both sexes.

Terman's studies of gifted children

Most of the chapter so far has been based on rather subjective impressions and generalizations. However, there is a wealth of more objective evidence in the five volumes of Terman's *Genetic Studies of Genius* (1925-1959). This was the most extensive survey and long-term follow up of gifted children ever undertaken.

The first volume was entitled *Mental and Physical Traits of a Thousand Gifted Children.* Actually the size of his sample varied from 643 to some 1500, and they ranged in age all the way from 6 to 12 years (with a few even younger or older). They were selected first by means of teachers' ratings, then through high scores on a verbal group test, and finally by Stanford-Binet IQs. Almost all obtained IQs of 140 and over, though a few went down to 135; thus they represented roughly the brightest 1 per cent of children in the state of California at that time. It should be noted at this point that the method of selecting the group would tend to exclude any underachievers and others who were poorly adjusted in school; also lower-class children and the underprivileged such as negroes would be under-represented. However, though some bias in the sampling must be admitted, many of Terman's results have been confirmed by subsequent surveys, such as those by Parkyn (1948) in New Zealand, and Burt (1962) in England. The average IQ of the gifted group was 151, and 35 of the cases obtained 170 + (on the old method of scoring). Their siblings averaged 123, that is well above average, though usually much below the gifted themselves. There was a small preponderance of boys to girls (55-45 per cent), also there were more first-borns than in the general population. The latter fact suggests higher aspirations for, and greater pressure, and verbal stimulation, of the first than later children.

At the time of the first testing, 85 per cent were accelerated in school and none retarded. According to school grades, their average educational quotient was only 114; however, on standardized achievement tests the mean quotient was 140, showing that the teachers had largely failed to recognize their superior ability and achievement, and were holding them back unnecessarily. When compared with a control group of average children, they excelled particularly in reading (almost half were reading when they entered school at 6 years), language and general information. Also a large proportion were high in arithmetic, and many exhibited talent in music or art. The least difference from the controls was found on practical subjects like shopwork, though the gifted also generally enjoyed such activities and found them easy. Thus they were not onesided, and there was no more unevenness in their performance at different subjects than among the average group.

Their physical health and growth were somewhat superior from birth on, and their vision and hearing good. According to mothers' reports they began walking and talking 1 month and 4 months earlier than average; but, of course, there would be a great deal of overlapping. Thus, the common belief about physical inferiority of the mentally gifted was definitely disproved. Very likely it arose because bright children are (or were in the 1920s) quite often in classes older than themselves, where they would be more likely to be relatively small in stature. Teachers' reports were obtained on nervous characteristics or maladjustment, and these contradicted another superstition: 13 per cent of the gifted and 16 per cent of the controls were 'nervous'. Perhaps this might arise from the natural tendency among teachers to confuse good achievement with good adjustment, i.e. 'halo effect'. But the numbers of stutterers, namely 2.6 per cent of gifted and 3.4 per cent of controls, confirmed it, and this is a relatively reliable and objective index of anxiety.

Ratings by parents and teachers showed them to be, on average, considerably superior in character and personality traits, and to a lesser extent in physical and social. But obviously this could be largely halo effect. Some alleged objective tests of moral and ethical behaviour also gave positive results, but it is difficult to know whether or not the more intelligent would more readily recognize what responses are expected.

A test of three types of interest — intellectual, social and activity — showed the gifted to surpass the controls on the first two. Teachers reported 88 versus 34 per cent as reading 'a lot'; also, the gifted made many more collections, indeed twice as many of a scientific kind. As well as being somewhat less interested in physical types of play, they played alone rather frequently, and often preferred playing with older children.

Volume II in the series contained Cox's study of historical geniuses. The third volume, published five years later, was concerned to show that generally the gifted group fulfilled *The Promise of Youth* (1930). The mean IQ on either the Stanford-Binet or Terman Group Test was now about 133. But one would expect some drop below the initial score on account of so-called regression effect.* The achievements of

*The lower the correlation between two measures, the greater the tendency for those very high on the first measure to 'regress towards the mean' on the second. Likewise, very low scores tend to regress upwards, i.e. to score higher than initially.

those still at school or college were actually more in line with their IQs than initially. There were scarcely any high school failures and three-quarters of all the grades of the girls, one half of the boys, were As. Eighty and ninety per cent, respectively, of those in school were expecting to go to college. Thus, there was certainly no sign of the popularly supposed deterioration of exceptional ability with age. Both health and emotional stability were still superior, though a special study of the 170 + IQ group did suggest that they were more prone to difficulties of adjustment. Terman goes to great lengths to show that, where acceleration (grade-skipping or early entry to college) had been allowed, this produces no ill effects and that such students fully justify their promotion, implying, therefore, that others equally bright should have been given the same advancement.

By the time of the next follow-up, seventeen years later (1947), the mean age was 35. Yet almost 98 per cent of those still living were traced. In addition to a lengthy questionnaire they took a new high-level verbal intelligence or Concept Mastery test. It was difficult to make precise comparisons with initial IQs. There appeared to be an average drop of 10 to 15 points, but much of this could be attributed to the regression effects that would be expected on statistical grounds. In other words, the initial level had been quite well maintained. The average IQ of the spouses of those who were married was also high, and for 364 of their children who were given the Stanford-Binet, the mean was 128 — again close to statistical expectation although obviously much less than that of the gifted parent.

Health statistics were still superior, the death rate low, and only about 5 per cent admitted any serious maladjustment at any time, and their recovery rate was good. Marriage rates were normal, and divorce rate rather below that of the general population. Sixty-eight per cent had graduated from college, which was eight times the current rate in California, and a high proportion had gone on to doctoral work. Their mean income and occupational distribution were superior to the general run of graduates, and many had shown outstanding achievements in the professions or business. For example, they

---

In Terman's data, an interesting, but unexplained, finding was that boys' IQs dropped less often than girls at this second testing.

had produced an impressive total of publications and patents. Yet Terman had to admit that few could be termed geniuses. Another section of the questionnaire showed a wide range of political and social attitudes, though on the whole these tended to the liberal-progressive side. Clearly they were in no sense withdrawn from political and community affairs.

Volume 5, *The Gifted Group at Midlife* (1959), was published after another twelve years, and is of particular interest in showing that they had continued to progress in occupational level. By now (age around 47), some 92 per cent of them were at least in skilled job categories, and 71 per cent in the two highest categories (see table 1). These compare with

Table 1 *Occupational distribution of Terman's gifted group (males and of the general population)*

	gifted group	general population
professional	45.4	5.7
higher business and semi-professional	25.7	8.1
clerical and skilled	20.7	24.3
farming	1.2	12.4
semi-skilled	6.2	31.6
slightly skilled and labouring	0.7	17.8

38 per cent and 14 per cent respectively in the general population. Note too, that the intellectually gifted children gravitate particularly, though not exclusively, to the professions as they grow up. On the other hand, it is interesting that as many as 8 per cent end up either in farming or in semi- and un-skilled jobs. Having a high IQ is not a guarantee of occupational success for every individual, though it creates strong odds for the whole group. Terman agreed that an occasional case may turn out a failure, and he made a special study of the 150 most successful and 150 least successful boys, whom he called the As and the Cs. He looked back through their life histories to see if they could have been detected in childhood. The Cs did average a little lower in initial IQ, but

only five points. There was a more marked difference in the educational and occupational status of their parents. But the first major sign was that they received lower teacher and parent ratings on such traits as prudence, self-confidence, willpower, perseverance, and desire to succeed. The difference was not sufficiently consistent to have made it possible to diagnose the Cs while still at school, but it did suggest that the less successful gifted children possessed certain personality weaknesses. Their scholastic grades also began to decline in high school, though this would seem to be more part of their lack of success than a prediction of failure.

Though Terman died in 1957, his colleagues are still in touch with almost the whole surviving group, and intend to publish further reports, including data on the children of the gifted.

Discussion and criticisms

Valuable as Terman's work was (and there is far more of interest in his volumes than is summarized here), its interpretation is open to serious doubts, and several criticisms should be mentioned. The general impression left by the volumes is what an admirable person in every respect the high IQ child becomes. Actually, Terman never tries to gloss over the wide individual differences among such children. But we pointed out earlier that his sample was somewhat biased from the start. Had he really succeeded in getting a representative group of high IQ children, it is likely that many more of them would have later displayed emotional maladjustment, or undesirable character traits, or failure at school, college or vocation. Thus Terman's conclusions are to some extent over-simplified, and his readers might be pardoned for concluding that the fact of getting a high IQ between 6 and 13 years somehow causes children to succeed educationally and vocationally, to be superior in personality and physique and everything else, for life.

The climate of opinion regarding intelligence and intelligence tests has changed markedly since the 1920s, and many psychologists and sociologists might say nowadays that Terman's results are better interpreted as showing merely that children born in privileged homes are likely to score highly on intelligence tests, also to conform to the values of American white middle and upper classes, and thus to end up in similarly privileged positions.

A less extreme version of this kind of explanation would be that intelligence test items are chosen at least partly for differentiating between academically successful and unsuccessful pupils; and it is, therefore, only natural that there should be quite a high correlation between such tests and school performance. To a large extent schooling draws on the same kinds of verbal and reasoning skills as the tests. Moreover, test performance depends to some extent on cooperation with the tester, just as school performance depends on cooperation with the teacher. In other words the whole of Terman's research might be called a self-fulfilling prophecy.

First let us look at the suggestion that the social class and education of the gifted group's parents were the main factors in their success. Actually 31 per cent of the parents were professional and 50 per cent business or semi-professional, leaving only 19 per cent clerical or manual. In one quarter of the families, at least one parent was a college graduate, and there were many already distinguished persons among close relatives. Also American white and Jewish parents were over-represented in the sample, whereas there were very few negroes or Spanish-Americans.

However, it would be quite untrue to conclude that *all* gifted children, or those of superior IQ, come from 'privileged' families. The *proportion* of children of professional and business parents who are bright is indeed much higher than the proportion of children of lower-class parents. But the actual *numbers* of bright children who come from less privileged families is as large, or even larger, simply because, in the total population there are far more clerical and manual workers than higher-class parents. From data collected in the UK, Vernon (1957a) showed that, among 11 year olds who passed the eleven-plus examination, 61 per cent came from manual class and only 39 per cent from 'white-collar' class homes. Here the IQ borderline was approximately 113. However, if we took a higher cut-off, say IQ 135 (corresponding to Terman's gifted group), the advantage of high social class would be greater. We might expect some 50 per cent of such children to come from Terman's two top occupational categories, 30 per cent from the clerical and skilled manual, and 20 per cent from the semi-skilled and unskilled.* Nevertheless, there are still very substantial numbers of high IQ children who do not come from professional and upper business homes. It is, of course, particularly important that psychologists should endeavour to identify those gifted children who are not favoured by superior home environment.

Much the same conclusion could have been deduced from the fact that the correlation between parental social class and child IQ is quite low, namely about 0.3. Indeed, it is worth recalling that intelligence tests first became popular in educational assessment because it was hoped that they would pick out the able regardless of parental wealth or good home conditions. It is likely that the correlations of parental status with child's school achievement and later occupational status are somewhat higher. For no one would deny that well-off and educated parents are more likely to provide a good education for their children, and be able to pull strings or otherwise help them up the occupational ladder. Nevertheless, the correlation is so far from perfect (probably no more than 0.5, which means that parental status accounts for only one quarter of the variations in offspring status) that it is absurd to try to explain the successful careers of Terman's gifted group purely in terms of social class advantage.

A better case could be made for the influence on children's intellectual development and achievement of a home environment where the parents are not necessarily wealthy, but are themselves well educated, and do much to provide stimulating conditions, training and encouragement. Bloom (1964) and his students have obtained correlations of 0.7 to 0.8 between assessments of such factors and the child IQ or achievement (cf. p.121). In an interesting study in the UK by G.W. Miller (1970) of 480 10-11 year old pupils, parental occupational status correlated only 0.32 with combined intelligence and achievement measures. But, in addition, a number of personality and attitude factors were elicited from the children

---

*These figures are rough ones, both because the total number of children with IQs 135 + is small, and because the distribution of socioeconomic classes in the overall population has altered considerably since Terman's figures were published. However, there is some confirmation for our estimates in the report that 50 per cent of U.S. National Merit Scholars come from professional and business class homes.

by means of questionnaires, including: self-confidence and support by the family; parents *not* regarded as over-authoritarian, over-protective, or indulgent; child given autonomy and freedom to reach decisions; cultured tastes in the home; child's aspirations for higher education and for jobs involving intellectual effort. These are the kinds of values which one might expect to find inculcated by well-educated, usually middle-class, parents; and, in fact, they yielded distinctly higher correlations with the same criterion of ability and achievement.

We would agree with the critics, then, that certain aspects of home upbringing and environment played an important part in the successful careers of the great majority of Terman's gifted group. Indeed Terman admitted this himself, though at the same time the title of his series of volumes — *Genetic Studies of Genius* — strongly suggests his inclination to regard intelligence as inherited from the parents, and to attribute later achievement largely to genetic causes. This issue is so complex, and so controversial, that the next chapter will be devoted entirely to it. Meanwhile, though, it should be pointed out that findings such as Bloom's and Miller's by no means prove that environment is the sole explanation. It is entirely arguable that the parents who provide good upbringing and superior homes are themselves above average in intelligence, and that, therefore, it is the genes that they pass on to their offspring which underlie the children's high IQ.

Furthermore, if a child is born with high genetic potential, he will to a considerable extent create for himself a favourable environment; it is not merely a matter of the environment creating him. Because he is quick to pick up things and retain them, the parents are likely to talk to him more, and to provide superior opportunities and experiences, such as good schooling, books etc. Such a child may also stimulate his teachers at school to bring him on more rapidly; and if they don't he will seek out hobbies, encyclopaedias etc. that foster the growth of his own intelligence.

Before leaving Terman's contributions, two additional criticisms should be mentioned — the first being his apparent confusion of high IQ with genius. The second volume of *Genetic Studies* by C.M. Cox (1926) dealt with an analysis of the characteristics of outstanding persons from history who could reasonably be called geniuses. At attempt was made to assess their child and early adult IQs on the basis of their recorded accomplishments as compared to those of average children. Some of them ranged up to IQs of 200, and the average was reckoned at 135. But others went down to 100, and Terman and Cox admitted that personality and character traits, together with the environment in which the children were reared, were as essential to genius, or more so, than intellectual ability. Nevertheless, it seemed that Terman expected his gifted children to become similar people as adults, and although most of them were certainly highly productive and successful, very few could possibly be classified as even minor geniuses, with international reputations. Terman did realize later that he had been over-optimistic.

Finally, several critics such as Paul Witty (1951) claimed that, by studying high IQ children alone, Terman had missed out a large proportion of children who were gifted in other directions. He wrote that we should 'broaden our definition of gifted and consider any child gifted whose performance in any potentially valuable kind of human activity is consistently remarkable'. This distinction, and the overlapping between intelligence and other talents, constitute a problem which will be taken up in chapter 4.

3 Intelligence, heredity, and environment

Fifty years or so ago it was pretty generally assumed by psychologists and educationists that intelligence was the basic innate capacity of the individual to learn, comprehend and reason. Since this quality was genetically determined, it developed or matured with age, irrespective of the environment in which the child was reared. It reached its maximum by around 15 years and then stayed constant until senility set in. It could be measured fairly accurately by individually administered tests such as the Stanford-Binet, hence the IQ obtained in childhood gave a reliable indication of the educational and vocational level that the person could be expected to attain in his later school career and in adult life. Maybe this statement is expressed in rather extreme terms, but something like it was certainly rather generally accepted, and it still underlies, to some extent, current discussions of giftedness and intelligence.

However, during the 1920s and 30s there was mounting evidence that IQs or scores on intelligence tests were considerably affected by environmental differences — evidence gathered, for example, from the scores of different ethnic or racial groups on the Army Alpha test in World War I, from children who received minimal education such as gipsies or others in remote rural communities, from children who were adopted and reared in superior foster homes, and so on. Most psychologists, therefore, tended to believe that the genes set the limits of an individual's potentiality for intellectual growth, but that the intelligence actually achieved and measured depends considerably on how far environmental circumstances allow him to fulfil that potentiality. D.O. Hebb, in 1949, pointed out that a good deal of the controversy over the nature-nurture issue arose because people were, in fact, using the term intelligence in two very different senses; and he proposed to separate these by calling them Intelligence A and Intelligence B.

Intelligence A is the basic potentiality of the organism, whether animal or human, to learn and adapt to its environment. Thus, man differs from apes, and apes differ from less evolved species, in intelligence. Intelligence A is determined by the genes, but is mediated mainly by some quality of the central nervous system — its complexity and plasticity. Some humans carry better genes than others, and thus have a greater potentiality for any kind of mental development. Intelligence does not, however, develop in a vacuum; the degree to which the potentiality is realized always depends on suitable stimulation from the environment in which the child is reared. Intelligence A is like the seed of a plant: to obtain a flourishing plant one needs not only good seed but also certain environmental conditions such as moisture, light, warmth, and nutriment.

Intelligence B is the level of ability that a person actually shows in his behaviour — his cleverness, the efficiency and complexity of his perception, learning, thinking and problem-solving. This is *not* genetic, nor is it learned or acquired. Rather, it is the product of the inter-play between genetic potentiality and environmental stimulation, whether favourable or unfavourable to growth. Note that we cannot observe, let alone measure, Intelligence A. Even in the early months of life the degree of mental development which we infer from a child's alert and apparently advanced behaviour has been affected by suitable nutrition during and since pregnancy, by birth conditions, and by the parents' handling and other environmental circumstances.

Intelligence B is not any single entity or ability; indeed it is not a 'thing' at all, but a label for the all-round effectiveness of the person's mental skills. No one is consistently able at everything; people vary in their capacities to cope with different kinds of problems, in the concepts they build up, and in innumerable other ways. However, the work of Spearman and his followers (cf. chapter 4) showed that there is sufficient generality to justify talking of a general intelligence. Note also that the skills which make up a person's intelligence must depend on the cultural group in which he is reared, its language, traditions and values. Thus the concepts and skills characteristic of the Intelligence B of a British or North American child may differ considerably from those of, say, an Indian or a Chinese child.

After Hebb's formulation, it was pointed out by Vernon (1955) that we really need to recognize a third meaning for intelligence, which could be called Intelligence C. This refers to the scores on any particular intelligence test. The commonly used tests provide us with only a limited sample of the concepts and skills which go to make up Intelligence B, and the samples differ from one test to another. Thus, the Binet and the WISC Verbal cover quite a wide range of verbal thinking, but the WISC Performance or the Progressive Matrices are based on quite dissimilar tasks. Most group tests of intelligence are different again, since their multiple-choice items are less representative of the whole range of mental skills. Yet a great many psychologists, sociologists, and laymen who talk about intelligence often fail to make it clear whether they are referring to all-round thinking capacities (B), or to scores or IQs obtained from a particular test (C), or the basic genetical potential (A).

The evidence for genetic factors in Intelligence B and C

This formulation of the nature of intelligence, which is commonly called the 'interactionist' view (i.e. interaction between heredity and environment) seemed satisfactory during the 1950s and 60s. However, a considerable body of American writers veered more and more to a strongly environmentalist standpoint, apparently assuming that upbringing and education could account completely for any differences in measured intelligence. They implied also that the low IQs of underprivileged children could be brought up to normal by suitable improvements in their environment and schooling. Then in 1969 the controversy erupted again even more violently than before, when A.R. Jensen challenged this viewpoint which ignored any hereditary differences. Though accepting interactionist theory, he marshalled evidence for the importance of genetic influences, and linked this with the issue of differences in intelligence between American negroes and whites. There is no need to discuss here this emotionally-laden topic. Everyone would admit that there are gifted negro children, and probably many others whose abilities have not been developed or recognized, although the total proportion is smaller than that of gifted white children. What we should look at carefully, though, is the relative importance of genetic and environmental factors in producing individual differences in intelligence. We will concentrate on those arguments which appear to have received the greatest scientific support.

First; there is no doubt that human physical attributes such as height and eye colour depend largely on the genes inherited from the parents (though height is also somewhat affected by diet and healthy living). Thus there is no good reason to think that characteristics of the brain and nervous system which underlie Intelligence A would be any different. Further, by selective breeding, we can produce strains of rats which are superior in learning to run mazes. Thus it seems only logical to allow that when human parents of above average intelligence mate, they are likely to produce children of superior innate ability.

Second; most people tend to accept as evidence of heredity the often observed psychological resemblance between parents and offspring. While this might arise through genetic influence, it does not provide proof, since parents normally bring up their own children; hence, the similarity might equally be attributed to the kind of environment and training they provide. What is much more difficult to explain environmentally is the existence of *differences* between parents and children, or siblings (brothers or sisters). Professors occasionally have average or dull children, and unskilled labourers have very bright ones. The siblings of a gifted child are sometimes 30 to 40 points lower in IQ than the gifted one. Now parents do to some extent treat different children differently, but surely not sufficiently to produce this kind of difference.* Whereas genetic theory does predict that offspring will vary — just as cats have different coloured kittens in the same litter.

Third; the most direct evidence is obtained from studies of foster children. When adopted into good foster homes the IQs of such children tend to rise — pointing to an environmental effect. Yet several studies in the US and in Britain have shown that their IQs correlate more highly with true-parent ability than with foster-parent ability. The

*One possible counter-argument is that some differences between siblings might be produced by factors in the uterine environment, or birth conditions. These differences would be constitutional, i.e. ineradicable, though not genetic.

correlations are lower than those usually found between parents and children brought up in their own homes. Yet the fact that they persist among children not brought up by true-parents must mean some genetic transmission of ability (cf. Munsinger, 1975).

Fourth; although, as mentioned earlier, a child's IQ tends to fluctuate with growth, and on the whole improves with good home environment and schooling, yet it is in fact highly resistant to any direct attempts to train it. Psychologists have not got any recipe that they can pass on to parents and teachers whereby a mentally defective child can be turned into a normal, or a normal one into a gifted child. Certainly it is possible to teach children to achieve in school subjects, or to train some of their mental and motor skills. But attempts to raise all-round mental effectiveness or IQ have been notably unsuccessful. The clearest example of this is provided by the famous Head Start experiments in the United States, which set out to overcome the handicaps of young children from deprived environments by giving them various kinds of kindergarten or preschool training, usually for a few months before they entered first grade. The programmes were designed locally, and were very diverse in conception, methods and coverage. However, in many instances it was possible to follow up the specially trained children in first grade, or later, and to compare them with other deprived children of similar IQ who had not received the training. Performance on an intelligence test was often used as a criterion of improvement. A careful analysis of all the usable results led to the disappointing conclusion that, in most experiments, there was either no difference between the trained group and the controls, or else there was a small gain at first which disappeared after another year. Sometimes the training involved tasks very similar to those included, say, in the Terman-Merrill scale, in which case some improvement was noted, but it did not spread to other kinds of mental performance. Occasional programmes which focused on linguistic drills or other clearly defined study skills did seem to offer more positive evidence of effectiveness (e.g. Bereiter and Engelmann, 1966). It is also possible, though no convincing proof was given, that the children improved to some extent in social adjustment and attitudes to schooling through the additional preschool experience.

In hindsight, it is hardly surprising that the programmes mostly failed to work; they were too little and too late. In other words, a few hours schooling a day, around the age of 5, could hardly be expected to overcome the effects of 5 years' upbringing in unstimulating homes and a deprived environment. In addition, as Jensen claimed, the likelihood of genetic limitations had been entirely ignored. The sponsors of the schemes had indeed set themselves an almost impossible task. Consider, for example, a 5½ year old with IQ 75; he will normally gain 0.375 mental age years in the next 6 months. But if one aimed to push him up to IQ 85, so that he will be better fitted to learn in first grade, he would have to gain 1 year of mental age, i.e. more than twice as much. Nevertheless, the sponsors, together with many psychologists who favoured environmentalist theories, clearly had expected Head Start programmes to be worth while.

The fifth type of evidence, based on IQ resemblances between identical twins, is most frequently cited, but seems in fact to be the most difficult to interpret. The correlations between such twins is indeed very high, over .90, as compared to around .50 between siblings and .60 between non-identical twins, and this is explained by the identicals having identical genes, whereas siblings and fraternal twins share, on average, only half their genes in common. However, it is also clear that identicals tend to be brought up more alike, and to develop in much closer harmony with one another, than do siblings and fraternals, so that again we cannot decide how much of the resemblance would be due to environment. It should be possible to overcome this difficulty by comparing identicals who have been separated at, or soon after, birth and brought up in different homes. Such cases are rare, but 122 have been traced in four different investigations, and the overall correlation now drops to 0.82. Burt's (1958) and Jensen's (1969) analyses of this data indicated that the heritability of general intelligence was approximately 80 per cent leaving 20 per cent attributable to environmental differences between families, or between children in the same family. That is, variations in the genetic constitution were claimed to be four times as important in determining children's IQs as variations in their environments.

However, there are several dubieties: the largest sample of twins reared apart was obtained by Burt (1966), and it now appears that his reported figures are not always trustworthy (cf. Jensen, 1974). Omitting his group, the average correlation for the remainder is .74, which is of course still far greater than the .25 one gets when comparing unrelated children brought up in the same foster home. In other words, same-genes-different-environment is far more influential than different-genes-same-environment. In addition, though, there is evidence to suggest that when one or both twins are adopted they are very likely to be placed in culturally similar homes. Though Burt denies this, it seems quite possible that part of the resemblance indicated by our correlation of .82 or .74 should be attributable to environmental similarity.* Twins are, indeed, a rather peculiar sample from which to reach generalizations about heredity in the wider population. For example, we don't know if their prenatal environments are more similar because they share the same womb, or more dissimilar because they are, in a sense, in competition for the oxygen and food carried in the mother's blood supply. There are disagreements too, as to the most appropriate statistical model to follow in calculating heritability figures: some recent estimates indicate that the heredity-environment ratio may be nearer 60-40 or 65-35 than Jensen's initial 80-20.

Finally, as Jensen himself points out, there is no one fixed universal ratio. The calculations apply only within white British or American samples from which the twins (or other kinds of relatives) were drawn, and all these persons were reared in a fairly homogeneous type of environment. If we could do similar studies involving more extreme environmental differences, such as western whites contrasted with African or aboriginal natives, the environmental component, relative to the genetic, would be much larger. Jensen agrees too, that a large genetic component within one cultural group suggests but does not necessarily imply mainly genetic differences between different cultural groups (such as white and negroes), where it is almost impossible to say how different are their typical environments, or in what respects they differ. The possibility of genetic differences in abilities between ethnic or racial groups is by no means ruled out, but we are not yet in a position to say definitely how far the observed differences are attributable to environment.

*These complex arguments and counterarguments will be examined more closely in a forthcoming book by one of the authors, probably entitled *Intelligence, Heredity and Environment.*

There is other subsidiary evidence, but the points we have outlined are sufficient to show that genetic factors are of considerable importance in determining ability differences between children within a white culture, even if not so overwhelmingly important as Terman and Burt believed, or as calculations based on identical twins seemed to prove.

Evidence for environmental effects

In discussing Hebb's notion of Intelligence B, we pointed out that intellectual or cognitive abilities would not develop at all apart from stimulation by an appropriate physical and social environment. Thus, no one regards environment as unimportant. However, we are apt to forget that much of the environment that stimulates growth is common to everyone within a cultural group. Almost all children see the same kinds of objects, hear similar language, and receive a fairly standardized schooling during the period in which they are building up their perceptual and conceptual skills. However, there are, of course, marked differences between relatively privileged and underprivileged families. Thus, the real question we have to ask is how far do such variations as normally occur within our culture bring about differences in Intelligence B and C; also, how far do any interventions or manipulations that we can introduce (e.g. by improvements in education and child-rearing, or social welfare measures) affect intellectual development? Most people take it for granted that environmental modifications are effective without realizing how difficult it is to prove what kinds of environmental factors affect what kinds of mental growth. Thus psychologists who observe IQ differences between two or more groups of children with different backgrounds are apt to think up *ad hoc* explanations, or just to assume that various treatments will raise or lower mental development without bothering to search for hard evidence. It seems so obvious that children from wealthier homes will have an advantage on intelligence tests over those from poorer homes that they ignore or reject the possibilities of genetic differences. And when faced with the fact that lots of poor children score better than lots of richer ones (as we pointed out earlier, in chapter 2), they are unable to define just what are the crucial background factors that are responsible. Unless this is done, it is impossible to investigate scientifically the efficacy of the factors. Anything, of course, can be explained by something that we know nothing about! This kind of weak theorizing and absence of experimental confirmation were well illustrated by the Head Start programmes.

Nevertheless, it is possible to cite a variety of quite strong evidence. Some of this comes from twin research. In Newman, Freeman and Holzinger's (1937) study of 19 pairs reared apart, it was shown that the greater the differences in home environments and schooling of the two members of a pair the greater the difference in their IQs, ranging up to over 20 points. Among identicals reared in the same home, the average difference is only about 5 points. Further demonstration of the importance of education comes from Lorge (1945) in America, and Husén (1951) in Sweden, who showed that the amount of secondary and higher schooling received made a difference of up to 12 points in adult IQ. Allowance was made for any initial differences in child IQs between those who left school early and those who went on to further education. Similarly, Vernon (1957b) found that the quality of schooling between 11 and 14 years made a difference of up to 12 IQ points between boys who attended the best grammar schools and those in the poorest secondary modern schools in a large English city. Presumably in all these instances the teenagers receiving more or better schooling also obtained more encouragement and cultural stimulation at home. Thus, the effect was not wholly attributable to schooling as such, but it was none the less environmental.

Klineberg (1935) and Lee (1951) found that black children whose families emigrated from the southern states to New York and Philadelphia gained significantly in IQ according to length of residence in the northern cities where negroes experienced somewhat better economic and educational conditions. At the same time it is noteworthy that the maximum rise was limited to an average of about 7 points; negroes did not make up the full 15 points which usually differentiate them from whites. More recent studies of Italian immigrants to the USA (Barron and Young, 1970) and of Jews to Israel (Lieblich *et al.*, 1972), indicate that the descendants of quite backward parents catch up with the local norms of intelligence in a generation or two.

Many investigations of severe deprivation have been

conducted with animals and children. Hebb and his colleagues reared rats and dogs, some of them in the highly restricted environment of a cage, others as pets with a free run of a rich environment. The latter showed greater learning and problem-solving capacities as adults, thus supporting his views on the part played by stimulation in cognitive growth. Similarly, S. Levine (1960) found that the handling, and even painful stimulation, of baby rats increased their later learning ability. The effects of extreme poverty of physical and social environment on infants in institutions have been reported by Spitz (1946), Goldfarb (1947), and Wayne Dennis and Najarian (1957). Such conditions brought about retardation and even regression in motor, perceptual and intellectual development. It is possible, of course, that some of these children might have grown up to be low-grade defectives in any environment; but a long-term follow up by Skeels (1966) did take care of this point. He tested 24 seriously retarded children in a very unstimulating orphanage environment around the age of 1½. Then 13 of them were transferred to another institution where they received more care and attention, albeit from mentally defective girls; and most of them were later adopted into good foster homes. After twenty-five years both groups were traced, and those who had not been transferred — the control group — were all still institutionalized or in low-grade jobs. But the transferred ones appeared to be normal adults, who were self-supporting in a wide range of jobs. Another interesting report by Koluchova (1972), though based on only 2 cases, concerned a pair of twins who were reared until the age of 7 in incredibly deprived circumstances, with virtually no human contacts. When first rescued they were severely subnormal, but after only 4 years of more normal upbringing they were testing at IQs of 94 and 95.

Recently an important study by Heber (1971) in Milwaukee has received a great deal of publicity, though full details are not available, and certain weaknesses have been criticized. Forty children of mentally retarded mothers, whose mean IQ under ordinary conditions of upbringing in the slums would probably have been about 80, were divided into 20 experimentals and 20 controls. The experimentals attended a centre from the age of 3 months and were provided with a specially stimulating environment for 7 hours a day, 5 days a week, designed to develop their cognitive and language skills. Simultaneously their mothers were given an education programme including home-making and child-rearing. On the Gesell scale, the two groups were equivalent up to 14 months, but on various infant intelligence scales between 2 and 4½ it is claimed that the means were 122.6 and 95.2 respectively, a difference of 27.4 points. (It is not explained why the controls were also somewhat superior to expectation.) This has been referred to as a 'total immersion' programme, and Heber agrees that the improved stimulation will have to be continued if the IQ difference is to persist into later childhood. We should await the outcome before concluding that genetic lack has been fully overcome by environmental intervention, also noting that it would obviously be impossible to arrange similar programmes for all deprived children.

Bronfenbrenner (1974) summarizes the results of several recent 'intervention' studies, which were more carefully controlled than the earlier Head Start programmes. The most effective of these involved intervention in the children's homes rather than at school, at an early age; and the most crucial feature appeared to be increasing the amount of child-parent interaction, centred around activities which were challenging to the child. With children in relatively deprived homes it seems possible to bring about fairly permanent IQ gains averaging about 11 points by these means.

One further fruitful line of investigation is the effect of inadequate diet during pregnancy and the first year of life, also of maternal stress and birth conditions on the intelligence of the offspring. The results so far obtained among children in western cultures are somewhat contradictory (cf. Jensen, 1973). But the severe effects of protein deficiency that commonly occur among children in underdeveloped countries are well attested (cf. Vernon, 1969).

Clearly there is a great deal of evidence of environmental effects from many sources, though in most instances the amount of variation in intelligence associated with favourable or unfavourable conditions is fairly limited, and is by no means inconsistent with the conclusions derived from genetic studies. Even Jensen's estimate of 20 per cent for environmental variations in intelligence would imply that the differences between the best 10 per cent of homes in our society and the poorest 10 per cent would bring about IQ differences of some 20 points. This happens to be just about the figure arrived at by

Freeman *et al.* (1928) and Burks (1928) for the effects of superior and inferior homes from their investigation of foster children. If we allow the environmental component to be 35 per cent rather than 20 per cent, the differences would of course be larger. And if we took extreme conditions such as occur in one in a thousand families, even the very large changes of 30 to 40 points obtained in Skeel's, Koluchova's and Heber's studies should be explicable, while still allowing that the genetic component or heritability ratio amounts to some 65 per cent.

Another possibility has been suggested by Jensen (1969), namely that environmental effects may be more severe at the bottom end of the scale than higher up. He regards environmental stimulation as a kind of 'threshold variable', somewhat like diet. Serious dietary deficiencies have marked effects on growth and health, but beyond an average level better diet probably does little to improve a person's physique. The same phenomenon may occur with environmental stimulation of intelligence, though there is not much confirmatory evidence. Also it would probably be untrue to deduce that the extra efforts made by the parents of gifted children to improve their environment and schooling have little or no effects. The analogy is an attractive one, since 'good diet' is difficult to specify, and is obviously a combination of numerous components. Similarly, 'stimulating environment' is difficult to define, and is probably many-faceted. For example, it involves mother-child and teacher-child emotional relationships in addition to appropriately chosen visual and linguistic stimulation.

We would conclude, then, that giftedness and high intelligence do depend largely on heredity, and that gifted children are more likely to be born of intelligent parents. Nevertheless, because of the nature of genetic diversity, a very considerable proportion of those with high intellectual potential will come from average, or even sub-average, families. But such potentialities are only going to be realized in so far as the homes, and society, provide the right kind of environment. Many potentially gifted children will be missed because their environment during the preschool years inhibits optimum intellectual growth, so that by the time they arrive at school or are tested by psychologists, their Intelligence B is considerably lower than it could have been.

The stress that we have laid on genetic differences, as well as upbringing, by no means implies the fatalistic notion of an intelligence fixed at birth. We have noted in chapter 2 the considerable variations that usually occur during development from infancy to adulthood. The evidence in this chapter shows that there is very real scope for improvements in pre- and perinatal conditions, in child care, rearing and education, despite our lack of knowledge of what constitutes a 'stimulating environment'.

We also know that actual achievement, whether in scholastic or other areas, depends even more than Intelligence B on environment, training and on personality characteristics. Twin studies agree in showing that the heritability of school performance, though still quite large, is definitely lower than that of IQ. Yet here too we are clearly very ignorant of the optimum conditions for improving achievement. Over the past fifty years there has been vastly increased expenditure on education, remarkable technological advances, and probably much more widespread concern among parents; and yet there seems to have been little change in overall achievement levels during this period. Somewhat different, and maybe more useful, things are being taught in schools than in the 1920s, and many children are staying on longer; hence, fair comparisons are hardly possible. Thus, we would not subscribe to the common criticism that standards of educational achievement have declined; but equally they do not seem to have improved. The reason is partly genetic, i.e. the pool of genes underlying Intelligence A in the population is unlikely to have altered; and we are still failing to exploit and develop the abilities of the more genetically gifted as much as we should. But the major reason is that we still know too little about how to improve the efficiency of instruction at home or at school, or how to influence children's motivations.

Effects of practice and coaching, and other biases in intelligence tests

At the time of writing, psychological tests generally, and intelligence tests in particular, seem to have acquired a bad public image. This is due partly to the contemporary sociopolitical climate; intelligence tests are said to be culturally biased and to discriminate against lower class or minority groups. This might be justified if it were still believed that intelligence tests really do measure innate potentiality or Intelligence A. But we have seen that they merely provide us with more or less representative samples of Intelligence B, that is the actual overall mental efficiency of members of western society; and there is ample evidence that those who obtain low scores also achieve poorly on educational or other criteria of intellectual capacity within that society.

Secondly, tests have become so widely applied, especially in the USA, to adults as well as children, and used for important educational and vocational decisions, that the public feels threatened by the power of these impersonal instruments, and prefers the traditional methods of general impression, interviews etc. albeit these are generally more inaccurate, haphazard, and open to bias than tests are.

Many other criticisms have been raised (cf. Ebel, 1966), often with justification. One point that aroused particular suspicion in Britain at the time of the eleven-plus examinations was that intelligence, as well as achievement, tests are susceptible to practice and coaching. Children or adults who are sophisticated in tackling multiple-choice items, following instructions and working at speed, have, on average, about a 10-point advantage over those who are quite unfamiliar with objective tests (cf. Vernon, 1960). Even repetition of the Terman-Merrill or WISC within, say, less than one year's gap, produces a distinct practice rise (especially on the performance items). This does not matter much when, as in the US, almost all school children and students are thoroughly accustomed to tests, though some groups from remote rural schools where objective tests are seldom used may still be handicapped. Also, the educational or clinical tester of individual children will generally know, or be able to recognize, when a child has been tested before, and either make some allowance for practice effect or use a different instrument for retesting. But what upsets people is the notion that intelligence as measured by tests can be trained or coached; hence, they cannot, as they are supposed to do, accurately assess children's basic ability for school learning. Often, of course, they do not realize the Intelligence A and Intelligence B distinction, and still believe that tests are supposed to elicit innate potentiality. But apart from this confusion, there is a misconception since training, practice or previous familiarization do not produce a rise in

Intelligence B — that is, all-round mental efficiency. Such training is highly specific to the kinds of items practised and has little or no spread, or transfer, to mental efficiency generally. However, this issue does raise tricky technical problems, of which testers must be aware. They should be careful to avoid comparisons of IQs from children who have had very different amounts of previous experience of tests. With these precautions, there is no reason to think that practice and coaching effects invalidate the conclusions that may be drawn from test scores.

Another problem which tends to be exaggerated is that test scores may be affected if the children are not cooperating with the tester, or not motivated to do their best. Individual testers can usually recognize when there is inadequate rapport, such as may occur with highly anxious, apathetic, distractible, or aggressive children, and discount the results if need be. But obviously there is much less control over children's attitudes to a group test, and for that reason important decisions — at least about younger children — should generally not be based on group tests. However, by the time children have been in school for 3 or 4 years, they are generally so used to classroom tests that little problem arises; and many experiments have suggested that manner of administration and motivation make remarkably little difference. Giving rewards for high scores on intelligence tests tends to make children attempt more items, but not to get more of them right.

A further problem in group-testing highly intelligent children is that they may make intentional mistakes, having realized that beating everyone else in the class makes them unpopular.

However, what chiefly concerns the critics is that lower-class or minority group children may react unfavourably or feel more anxious when tested by a middle-class white tester, or be handicapped by unfamiliarity with his or her speech. Here also there have been many experiments, particularly on the possible effect of a white tester on black children, and the results have been thoroughly contradictory. In one recent very thorough study by Samuel (1976), 208 white and black children were tested, some by whites, others by blacks, with parts of the WISC scale. The overall result was that both groups of children did better with white testers. The author also concluded that good performance depends to some extent on the testees accepting the challenge to do well. As regards the language difficulty, another investigation (Quay, 1971) showed that translating the Binet into negro dialect brought about no improvement in black children's IQs.

One further source of distrust was occasioned by the enormous publicity given in the press to a study published by Rosenthal and Jacobson in 1968. But no publicity was given to later reports by psychologists that the study was technically faulty and did not prove anything, nor to replications by other researchers which entirely failed to confirm the alleged results (cf. Claiborn, 1969). The claim made was that when teachers are told that certain children (actually chosen at random) are bright, and likely to show unusual gains in ability, their IQs rise, presumably because teachers pay them more attention and stimulate them more. In fact, significant gains on retesting after 8 months were obtained only with Grades 1-2 children, not with Grades 3-6; and the authors did not mention (until after the press publicity had appeared) that retests after 4 and after 12 months gave entirely different results. Competent reviewers pointed out various other reasons for distrusting the findings, and the only sensible conclusion is that the various score changes represented merely chance effects. It is, of course, quite probable that self-fulfilling prophecies play a part in children's school *achievements*. For example, many teachers would have higher expectations of nicely-dressed, nicely-spoken middle-class children than of scruffy lower-class children. It may well happen, then, that they do stimulate the former more, and that the children tend to live up to what the teacher expects of them. But the evidence so far flatly contradicts the claim that the same thing happens with intelligence test performance. Considering the lack of success of Head Start programmes which specifically aimed to raise children's intelligence, it is obviously improbable that unconscious biases would be any more effective.

It is not possible, of course, to predict whether or how the climate of opinion regarding testing is likely to change in the next few years. Certainly it will be extremely difficult for educational psychologists to give useful advice to teachers on the treatment of exceptional children — whether handicapped or gifted — if they are debarred from using standardized tests.

In addition to the doubts that worry the layman which we have tried to answer in this chapter, there are criticisms put forward by professional psychologists to the effect that tests have been overdone and are frequently misinterpreted. They tend, it is said, to give an over-static view of the individual as a bundle of fixed abilities and traits, rather than as a growing and changing organism. They measure the end products of his ability development up to that time without throwing any light on the processes whereby he reached this state, or how he will progress beyond it. Again there is more than a little truth in this view, though it is unfair to the trained educational or clinical psychologist who does use tests intelligently and with due caution. He or she does try to find out a lot about the process underlying individual successes and failures, though his methods and insights are, admittedly, more subjective and intuitive than scientific. It is certainly to be hoped that advances in cognitive and motivational psychology will point the way to more effective and more diagnostic instruments. But meanwhile, it would be absurd to discard the instruments which have, in the hands of Terman and countless followers, greatly increased our knowledge of individual differences in abilities, and their causes.

One further line of criticism is that intelligence tests are rather highly predictive of scholastic achievement because of the very inefficiency of our conventional teaching methods. School instruction so often fails to get across ideas and principles clearly that it is mostly the children with good IQs who can bridge the gaps and understand what is being taught. With more 'adaptive' instruction, which works out a clear sequence of 'behavioural objectives' in a particular subject (cf. p.148), finds out just what stage each individual has already attained, and then provides materials for his progress to the next stage, it is claimed that individual differences in intelligence become unimportant. While we would agree that many improvements could be made in techniques for getting across knowledge, understanding and skills, we would be surprised if it were not still found that some children would consistently progress much more rapidly and attain more complex achievements than others. Indeed it is more likely that current or future improvements in educational technology will benefit the bright to a greater extent than the dull, rather than overcoming individual differences. What does seem to be needed is greater diversification of methods and content of school instruction to suit a greater variety of individual talents (whether these be genetic or environmental in origin). This should certainly help to promote better learning and school adjustment among many students who are backward in the kind of conceptual learning that depends so greatly on their Intelligence B, but who are less handicapped in other cognitive abilities. Equally there should be benefits at the top end of the scale. Gifted children already have high conceptual learning ability, but they could use their time more profitably if allowed to develop their knowledge and skills in special areas that interest them, and to employ more flexible techniques of exploration and study than the ordinary classroom encourages.

4 Special talents, statistical factors, and criteria of giftedness

Certain children, we have seen, are gifted chiefly in some special area or type of ability rather than being all-rounders with high IQs. Let us list those talents which occur fairly frequently, concentrating on those for which schools should, if possible, assume some responsibility.

1 *Mathematical* Some children may be much more advanced in this area than in their verbal classwork. They are particularly liable to become frustrated because the arithmetic and mathematics curriculum usually consists of a rather rigid progression. It is presented one step at a time with a good deal of drill and practice before proceeding to the next step. The mathematically-minded child can understand these steps far more quickly and wants to jump on to more advanced mathematical ideas and skills which may not appear in the normal curriculum till four or five grades later. His unusual insights and shortcuts are apt to be particularly unwelcome to the elementary school teacher whose own competence in mathematics is so limited that she (or he) can only teach the conventional sequences of skills.

2 *Science* Gifted children, particularly boys, may develop an interest in some branch, or branches, of science from as early an age as 6. There are nowadays so many good science books for children, together with kits and apparatus, that such a child can usually follow his interest and develop his talents at home. Secondary school courses and school clubs are obviously relevant, though here again the regular teaching may be so uninspired as to put off the exceptional physicist, chemist, biologist, astronomer etc.

3 *Engineering*, mechanical construction or invention, gadgeteering — especially in electronics. Schools seldom recognize or make any provision for these talents, unless they

possess good laboratories or vocational workshops. Here too, though, the really keen and able boy can generally pursue his interest at home, or make his own opportunities.

4 *Visual Arts*, painting, sculpture, decoration, pottery etc. In past years it would have been fair to say that most teachers inhibited rather than encouraged creativity by confining art to accurate still-life drawing and painting. This would not be true today, but, of course, schools still vary widely in the facilities they can provide, and in the qualifications of their staff.

5 *Music* is one of the best developed areas in many secondary, and some elementary, schools, though they tend to overemphasize performance at the expense of appreciation, or composition, of music. The ordinary group activities such as percussion or pipe bands, and choral singing, obviously provide little scope for the really talented child. But he, or she, can sometimes get individual or group instruction in piano, violin, guitar, or other instruments. Because of the expense, many people would expect the home rather than the school to provide; but this would rule out some promising musicians who come from poor homes.

6 *Language* One might expect imaginative writing to find scope in school language lessons and composition. But this is another area where some teachers so emphasize formal correctness that creative abilities are ignored or even suppressed. Also, the evaluation of good English writing is highly subjective, so that one teacher may encourage what another rejects. Sometimes, however, other avenues are available, such as school magazines.

Foreign language learning also deserves mention, though this is already provided in most secondary schools. But attempts to introduce it in elementary schools seem of dubious value, partly because many teachers have little competence themselves. (This is not, of course, intended as a criticism of bilingual schools where much of the instruction is conducted, say in French, by fluent French speakers.) The talented linguist who wishes to learn unconventional languages must usually get them at home, or in special out-of-school classes.

7 *Drama* is often well-provided for in schools with a qualified member of staff; also it can make use of a variety of talents besides acting (e.g. scene painting). Dance or ballet are occasionally found, though the latter is much better catered for in specialist schools.

8 *Sports* There are also exceptional footballers, swimmers and other athletes. Generally these get recognition and opportunities already, so there is no need to argue whether or not they fall in the gifted category.

9 Witty, Havighurst and others claim that some children excel in *social leadership*. It seems unnecessary, however, to classify them as gifted or to ask schools to take special measures on their behalf. If there are some who are consistently talented in this direction, they are likely to make their own way.

10 As pointed out in chapter 1, there is currently great interest in creativity, and it is regarded as a talent (or group of talents) which schools ought to encourage. But presumably it enters into all the previous categories, as does intelligence. Its nature, and detection are discussed in chapters 5 and 6.

The overlapping of talents, and their origins

There is very little evidence regarding the numbers of gifted children who are talented in one, or a few, areas as against those who are outstanding generally. Cox and Terman looked into this point in their study of 300 geniuses from history, and concluded that versatility was more common than specialization. Many of them, it seemed, could have made their mark in several areas, Leonardo da Vinci being a supreme example. Cox notes too, that in about one quarter of the group the particular area in which they became famous as adults was foreshadowed in the interests and activities of childhood. This suggests that a great many had explored other areas before they took up their main one. Likewise, Anne Roe's work indicates that eminent living scientists often ranged widely in their abilities and interests during their school days. Some eventually found their chief forte almost by accident, for example through the influence of an inspiring teacher.

Although De Haan and Havighurst (1957) strongly emphasize the diversity of talents, they also state that general intelligence is basic to all of them. In other words, children with a special talent or talents would probably be of above average intelligence, though not necessarily as high as the generally academically talented. Also, most children of high intelligence would show this particularly in certain talent areas. As Terman's results showed, high IQ children would probably include most of those outstanding in writing, science and mathematics. But intelligence correlates less highly with mechanical-constructional, visual-artistic, musical or dramatic talents, and only slightly with athletic talents. Thus, some first-class athletes might well obtain IQs below 100, though they would be more likely to average around 110. Branch and Cash (1966) mention that ballet schools demand good intelligence and academic achievement among the girls and boys they train. Outstanding dancers need to be able to think, not merely to control their limbs.

It is appropriate to consider here the applicability of the conclusions reached in chapter 3 to special talents. Do special talents depend more on home influences, training and practice, or more on genetic factors? Again, the answer is that both are necessary, though we have even less conclusive evidence than in the case of intelligence. As regards musical ability, it is clear that some children possess an exceptional aptitude from too early an age to be attributable merely to the musical experiences that the parents provide. Occasionally such talent runs in families for several generations (e.g. the Bachs); but in other cases it appears despite lack of interest and encouragement from the parents, even when there is discouragement on their part (e.g. Handel). Most often, however, the parents are to some extent musical and do introduce the child to good music from early years and, when he appears talented, encourage him to learn an instrument. It is obvious, also, that great devotion to, and practice and training in music are essential to the formation of a gifted composer or performer.

Number is another talent which tends to appear rather early, and to be highly predictive of later achievement; this would lead us to suspect that it has a considerable genetic component. It would be more difficult to make a strong case for the genetic origins of talent in the visual arts, or the sciences. They seem to necessitate a good level of intelligence and of some form of creativity, but also to be more dependent on family and other environmental influences; and they may be less predictable from early interests, sometimes not manifesting themselves until well into adolescence. However, our knowledge is too fragmentary to allow any definite generalizations.

The bearings of factor analysis Charles Spearman

Many of the questions about the nature or content of abilities, and their interrelationships, have been studied by the method of factor analysis. Such analysis involves quite complex statistical techniques, but we will attempt to provide a relatively simple introduction (cf. Vernon, 1961). It dates from the work of Charles Spearmen, at the University of London, in the early decades of this century. He was concerned with the generality of cognitive or intellectual abilities. Do they all reflect a single underlying capacity, or is there a limited number of distinct faculties, e.g. reasoning, memory, etc., or instead is there a whole host of specialized abilities for particular tasks? Spearman realized that the answer could not be obtained from casual observation or armchair speculation. It was necessary to measure the actual degree of overlapping or correlation between scores obtained on various ability tests. Researches carried out by Spearman and his students indicated that quite diverse abilities, such as sense of pitch, reaction times, and vocabulary, do usually ᵥyield positive, though far from perfect correlations (e.g. between about $+0.2$ and $+0.6$). There was a tendency for people who scored above average in any of them to be above average in others, though at the same time considerable unevenness could be found in some people's abilities at particular tasks.

Spearman's interpretation was that there is a general underlying ability or 'factor' running through all performances to a greater or lesser extent. He called this 'g', rather than general intelligence, since intelligence is difficult to define unambiguously, whereas 'g' is a mathematically determined highest common factor. In addition, every different performance involves a specific ability, or 's' factor, peculiar to that task alone. The more intellectually complex the task, the more it depends on 'g'. For example, Latin or mathematical reasoning have much higher 'g-loadings' than rote memory or sensory acuity. Spearman's analyses indicated that the main essential feature in 'g' is the grasping and application of relationships — what he called eduction of relations and correlates. He pointed out also that by combining the scores on numerous different items (as in the Binet scale), or subtests (as in most group intelligence tests) one should get a purer measure of 'g'; since the various specific elements involved in, say, Analogies, Digit Memory, Similarities etc. would tend to cancel one another out.

Although Spearman (1927) produced a good deal of evidence to support this Two Factor theory, it did not stand up to later research. Burt in England, Thurstone in the US, and others demonstrated that there are many additional distinctive types of ability, which Burt called group factors, and Thurstone called multiple or primary factors. These were neither general nor specific, but occurred in quite a wide range of similar tasks. For example, Burt showed that some children are better than might be expected from their 'g' or intelligence scores in all kinds of verbal performance, such as vocabulary, reading, spelling and English composition; and others might be inferior in all kinds of number work. The former were said to be high on 'V' or verbal factor, the latter poor on 'N' or number factor.

Thurstone and Guilford

Thurstone's investigation (1938) included more than fifty tests. He claimed, initially, to find no general factor running through all the tests. Instead, the patterns of intercorrelations could be explained in terms of seven or eight primary factors, namely:

V (Verbal)	P (Perceptual Speed)
N (Number)	W (Word Fluency)
S (Spatial)	I (Inductive Reasoning)
M (Rote Memory)	D (Deductive Reasoning)

However, he was working with highly selected college students, and when he applied similar tests to younger adolescents and children, who would be more heterogeneous, the primary factors did tend to correlate among themselves. There was a super-factor (or factors) running through all the primaries, and this he called a Second Order Factor. Obviously it corresponded to Spearman's 'g'. Although the presence or absence of 'g' is still a matter of contro- versy, the crucial condition is that of heterogeneity.* In

*Many psychologists hold that there is increasing differentiation and specialization of abilities as age increases. This seems plausible; for example,

heterogeneous groups such as a whole age-group of children, or a representative sample of adults, correlations among abilities tend to be so high as to yield a strong 'g' or general intelligence component. Thus, when we try to pick the most gifted children in an elementary school grade, most of those showing special talents will be high in intelligence, and vice versa. However, in senior high schools, or still more in universities, where the range of ability is more restricted, the specialized abilities stand out more strongly. For example, the best mathematicians may be only average in foreign languages, and the outstanding painter may be quite poor at mechanical tasks.

It will be asked, why does not Thurstone's list of primary factors — supposedly the basic dimensions of human abilities — correspond more closely to our own list of the main types of human talent? Only the V factor is similar, since Thurstone's N actually represents routine arithmetical operations, not mathematical reasoning. The answer is that Thurstone's tests represented only a fairly narrow range of abilities; they were the sorts of tests commonly used in psychological investigations, and they did not attempt to cover all the abilities and achievements of everyday life. For example, Thurstone had no music, mechanical, or art tests, though his S (Spatial) ability does play some part in mechanical and in visual art abilities. The fact is that human abilities are tremendously varied, and they can be classified and subdivided in all sorts of ways. Hence, the factors that emerge depend on what tests one chooses to include, and on the kind of people who are tested, i.e. their age, sex, and particularly their degree of selection or homogeneity.

Now Terman began his work with gifted children at a time when Spearman's theories were most influential, and this helps to explain why he regarded general intelligence as the preeminent ability which would be basic to any form of genius. But we need now to broaden our conception of giftedness, while still allowing that general intelligence, preferably measured by verbal tests (i.e. Thurstone's V and reasoning

---

the good general scientist at secondary school may specialize in atomic physics as an adult, and lose most of his knowledge of chemistry and biology. But the published evidence for differentiation is far from convincing, and psychologists seldom realize the pervasive influence of heterogeneity.

factors) is a major component, especially among children, in all kinds of mental superiority.

The factorial work of Thurstone and his students was further expanded by J.P. Guilford (1967) in the 1940s and 50s. He emphasized even more the richness and multiplicity of mental functions, particularly among high-grade adults, as against the notion of a single global intelligence, or a limited number of Thurstonian factors. On the basis of intensive correlational studies of a wide range of thinking abilities, he arrived at a threefold classification of factors:

I   5 kinds of *Operations* — Cognition, Memory, Convergent Thinking, Divergent Thinking, Evaluation
II 4 kinds of *Contents* or test media — Figural (nonverbal), Symbolic, Semantic (verbal), Behavioural
III 6 kinds of *Products* — Units, Classes, Relations, Systems, Transformations, Implications

This implied the existence of $5 \times 4 \times 6 = 120$ different kinds of abilities or factors, and his investigations have confirmed some two-thirds of these. However, this scheme, or 'model', of intellect seems too elaborate to have much practical application; one could never give the tests required to measure all 120 factors to any individual or group. But he did take a particular interest in the creative side of intellect as mentioned in chapter 1, and listed some 8 of his factors which he regarded as particularly necessary for creative production. Several of these involved what he called divergent as opposed to convergent thinking operations, and we will describe the kinds of tests which he initiated, and their uses, in chapter 6. It may be noted that, as with Thurstone's primary factors, Guilford's do not help us to differentiate different kinds of talent. One study (Hills, 1955) tried to show that mathematicians are characterized by a particular pattern or profile of Guilford's factors, but without success.

Who are the gifted?

We have now arrived at the point of defining gifted children as those who are outstanding in general intelligence, and/or in one or more areas of special talent. They also tend to show unusual personality characteristics, interests etc., as described in chapter 2. But how outstanding? Where do we draw the borderline, and what proportion of children fall in the category of gifted?

If we asked a teacher of an average class to make an estimate of his pupils' abilities, he would be quite likely to answer that about half the children are around average; about one quarter are noticeably dull and backward, and about one quarter are superior in ability and easy to teach. But the proportions might vary considerably according to the neighbourhood of the school. Also he would be well aware that there are not three distinct groups. There is a continuous distribution all the way from the very dull to the outstandingly brilliant or gifted. Though he may sometimes talk about A, or B, or F children, he knows that one cannot draw strict dividing lines. Those just above the A borderline will be very little different from those just below, at the top of the Bs. Similarly giftedness is a matter of degree; one cannot fix any precise point above which children are gifted and below which they are not. And, of course, the higher up the scale one chooses the cut-off, the fewer will be included in the gifted category.

We will first discuss this borderline in terms of intelligence quotients, preferably as measured by a reliable individual test such as Terman-Merill, or one of the Wechsler scales. This does not mean ignoring the other kinds of abilities, or personality traits; but we will come to them later. Although giftedness certainly cannot be determined from an intelligence test alone, the IQ makes a useful starting point.

Inevitably the topics and arguments in the rest of this chapter will seem somewhat technical and abstract to the ordinary parent or teacher. But many discussions of gifted children contain a great deal of 'waffle', which could be avoided if people were better acquainted with the relevant psychological and statistical principles.

The normal distribution of intelligence

Very early in the history of mental testing it was suggested by Quetelet, a French mathematician, and by Sir Francis Galton, the British pioneer of studies of individual differences, that mental abilities — like many physical attributes — tend to be distributed according to the 'normal', or bell-shaped curve. If we plot the number achieving various scores on a test, the majority will fall around average, and then tail off symmetrically as we approach the extreme high and low scorers. A similar tendency can be observed in school or college examination marks, though the percentages or grades that teachers award on the basis of subjective judgments of merit are often more skewed or irregular than scores on objective tests. There is not, in fact, any natural law which says that human attributes are always normally distributed. The heights of people at a given age do conform quite closely, but weights do not. In the case of mental tests, the items are often initially selected in such a way as to yield normality, so this doesn't prove anything. However, when Binet and Simon devised the first test of general intelligence in 1905, they scored it on the basis of the age level of items that a child could pass, i.e. in terms of mental ages. Then L.M. Terman, who developed the Stanford-Binet and Terman-Merrill intelligence scales, suggested that by taking the ratio of mental to chronological age, an index of intelligence could be obtained which would be fairly stable regardless of age. This was the Intelligence Quotient or IQ, and IQs did appear to approximate to a normal distribution. Hence, many tables have been published, like the following, which purport to show the numbers of children or adults falling at different levels on the IQ scale.

Table 2 *The distribution of IQs*
(assuming normality and a standard deviation of 15)

130 and over	very superior		2.3
120-29	superior		6.7
110-19	above average or bright normal		16.0
90-109	average		50.0
80-9	below average or dull normal		16.0
70-9	dull		6.7
40-69	highgrade feeble-minded or moron	mentally defective	2.3
20-39	lowgrade, imbecile		
0-19	idiot		

The overall range or spread of a normal distribution is defined by its standard deviation, and Stanford-Binet IQs yielded a SD of about 15. This meant that only 2.3 per cent of an ordinary group of children should obtain IQs 2 or more SDs above the average, i.e. 130 and over. Likewsie 2.3 per cent should be below 70; and only 1 in a thousand individuals (0.14 per cent) should exceed 3 SDs, i.e. 145 upwards or 55 downwards. Only 32 per million should reach or exceed IQ 160. These calculations appear, then, to provide a means for deciding what cut-off to apply in selecting any desired percentage of gifted children. Thus Terman, in his study of 1000 gifted children, desired to include as many as possible of the brightest 1 per cent, and used 135 to 140 IQ as his borderline.

However, the problem is a lot more complex than suggested so far. Different tests of intelligence, and even the same test applied to different age groups, do not yield the same standard deviation. The figures can range from about 12 points to 25 points, and this would mean that the same IQ of 130 might cut off 0.6 per cent when the SD is low, but 11½ per cent when the SD is high. The reason for such variations is partly that growth with age is more rapid on some kinds of intelligence items than on others; and partly because we have no guarantee that a year's growth in mental age represents the same amount at different points on the scale. Maybe a child builds up intelligence more rapidly from 2 to 3 than from 12 to 13; there is no means of saying. But we do know that, on tests like the Terman-Merrill, growth slows down from about 13 or 14, and probably ceases after 20, so that various, quite arbitrary, subterfuges have had to be adopted in calculating late adolescent and adult IQs.

Indeed, constructors of mental tests have, since about 1960, abandoned the use of mental ages and the so-called 'classical' IQ. Instead 'deviation IQs' are generally used nowadays. The obtained distribution of raw scores or items passed in each age group is converted to a normal distribution with a fixed SD, usually 15. This means that IQs obtained at different ages, or on different tests, now represent a constant level of superiority or inferiority to the mean of the age group. Deviation IQs (which are not really quotients at all) are roughly comparable to classical ones over a fairly wide age range, but tend to be somewhat more restricted. Thus, the WISC or Wechsler Intelligence Scale for Children adopted an SD of just about 15, which means that IQs scarcely ever range much above 140 or below 60. On the Terman-Merrill, with a somewhat larger SD of 16, it is still possible to range from about 40 to 160. But with the classical scoring, as used up to 1960, IQs of 160 to 200, or 0 to 40 used to turn up fairly frequently. The advantages of greater consistency of present-day IQs are to some extent offset by poorer discrimination among the extremely bright and the extremely dull.

Another difficulty in interpreting IQs is that standards can alter over the years. According to R.L. Thorndike (1973) the average IQ obtained by English-speaking American children aged 2 to 5 years rose from 100 to about 110 by 1970, and smaller rises were found in other age groups. He suggested that the stimulus provided by television was largely responsible among young children, and that 12 to 18 year olds had improved, on average, because of more extended secondary education. Unless, therefore, Thorndike's corrected norms are employed, children recently tested with the Terman-Merrill (and quite possibly other tests) will obtain larger numbers of above average IQs than in the past. The new version of WISC, called WISC-R, has also been made more stringent, because the original WISC norms were becoming too lenient. Another factor in the upward swing may be that children in general have become more familiar with taking tests. In Britain there was a marked rise in group intelligence test performance among 10-11 year olds from about 1945-1955, which was probably attributable to the coaching and practice they were getting on the tests used in the eleven-plus examinations (cf. Pilliner *et al.*, 1960). Consequently, it was found that mental age norms for older group tests published before World War II had become too lenient to be usable.

A third difficulty arises because it is doubtful whether the distribution of classical Stanford-Binet or Terman-Merrill IQs ever was strictly normal. When large samples were tested, there often appeared to be an excess of IQs around 90, and fewer than expected around 110, so that the curve was noticeably skewed. Almost certainly, again, there was a kind of bump in the distribution curve below about IQ 60, though the exact shape is not known because of the tiny numbers available. But an excess might be anticipated because, in addition to those with very low IQs from ordinary genetic and environmental causes, there are the pathological defectives attributable to rare genes (e.g. Mongols), to biochemical abnormalities (e.g. cretins and phenylketonurics), or to birth injuries (cerebral palsy etc.).

The existence of excessive numbers at the top end was hardly suspected till Burt, in 1963, published an analysis of 4523 Terman-Merrill (classical) IQs, and found that the distribution curve approximated more closely to what is called a Pearson Type IV than to a normal distribution. This implied about twice as many IQs of 145 and over as previously supposed, namely 27 *v.* 13 to 14 per ten thousand, and an even greater discrepancy at higher levels. Thus, Burt claims 77 per million with the extremely high IQs of 175 and over, where normal curve calculations had allowed only 3.3 per million. So it becomes more understandable why Terman and Leta Hollingworth were able to study quite sizeable numbers of children in the 170-200 range.

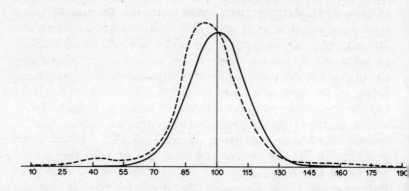

Figure 1 *Approximate distribution of (classical) Terman-Merrill Intelligence Quotients:* — — — — — *Normal distribution with standard deviation 15:* _____

A rather exaggerated indication of the true distribution of 'classical' IQs is given in figure 1, compared with the conventional normal distribution. Note that the curves cross around IQ 130-35, which means that if we are concerned with the 'very superior' group rather than the extremely high IQ children of say 160 up, there is not much difference. Both Burt's and the normal distribution yield close to 2¼ per cent of 130 upwards. Nowadays, however, the extremely bright of over 160 just do not occur, not because of any decline in the proportions of very intelligent children in the population, but simply because of the way modern tests are standardized. Thus it is essential to realize, when reading books or articles that refer to gifted children with IQs of 160 up:

(a) that these existed in considerably greater numbers than would be expected from conventional statistical expectations;

(b) that if they were tested with present-day Terman-Merrill or WISC-R, they would score within the range 140 or below up to a maximum of 166.

Setting a borderline

Where then, on the modern IQ scale, should we say that a child becomes so intelligent that he probably needs special educational provision? There is no single answer to this, any more then there is to the question — how many inches tall is a tall man? However, the figures shown in table 3 will help us to see the approximate numbers cut off by different borderlines on a test such as Terman-Merrill (Thorndike, 1973) or WISC-R, which yield deviation IQs.

Table 3 *Numbers of children at high IQ levels*

IQ	approximate numbers
150 and over	1 in 1000
140 and over	½%
130 and over	2½%
120 and over	10%

These figures refer to a total school population and, as mentioned earlier, they will vary considerably between better — and poorer — neighbourhood schools. They will vary also through chance fluctuations. Thus while, on average, a class of 40 children should contain one with IQ 130 or over, the numbers might easily range from zero in many classes to perhaps half-a-dozen in a few classes.

Different writers have advocated different proportions as falling within the category of gifted. Thus Terman was concerned with the top 1%, whereas De Haan and Havighurst (1957) think in terms of the top 10% (i.e. roughly IQ 120 upwards). And they suggest that if provision can also be made for the top 10% in different talent areas, the total might rise to 20%, or one fifth of the pupils or students in an average school. Interestingly, 20% was the average proportion of 11 year old English children selected in the 1930s to 50s for secondary education in the academic type of grammar school, though the figure varied considerably in different areas of the UK. If there was any rationale for this proportion, other than historical accident, it was that the 20% provided a sufficient pool of all students who stood much chance of getting to university, or becoming teachers, or entering other white-collar jobs.

However, this proportion seems inconveniently large when considering truly gifted children, and few school systems would be able to afford special educational measures for so many. Moreover, if we did include IQ 120 up, the really exceptional child of say 150 + would still be so much in advance of the 120s that he might be held back and prevented from progressing at the rate that suited him. If, on the other hand, we considered only, say the 140s and over, there would be so few in most schools that it would be difficult to make special arrangements; and a great many other very able children in the 130-40 range would be omitted. For example, in an average school of about 400, we might expect to find only 2 such children.

Thus we agree with the majority of authors who suggest 130 as the approximate borderline. This level, cutting off the top 2-2½ per cent is also recognized by many teachers (cf. Ogilvie, 1973). Also one can justify it fairly well by the following argument: it has become widely accepted that IQ 70 is a useful borderline for denoting the lowest 2-3 per cent in ability who usually fall so far below the average that they cannot really keep up, and are, therefore, sent to special classes or schools. This is not an absolute figure; there are some children between, say 60-9 who can adjust pretty well, and some others of 70 to 80 who are so maladjusted, troublesome, or otherwise handicapped that they are better placed in a special class where they receive more individual attention. Similarly, we are suggesting, that IQ 130 be regarded as a rough borderline above which children become too different from the average to adjust well to standard schooling, and too different for most teachers to be able to look after their special needs. But this too should be flexible. Many children with IQs of 120-9 show similar qualities, if in lesser degree, and might, therefore, benefit greatly from some form of enrichment of their normal curriculum. And others even of 140-5 may manage well in an average class, if they 'click' with the particular teacher. But satisfactory adjustment and progress become less likely the more they exceed 130. Much also depends on the general IQ level of the school. Thus in a good school in a middle-class area, where the average IQ is about 110 or more, the 130-9s might already be well catered for, and the outstandingly gifted would mostly score 140 and over. Contrariwise, in a school where the mean IQ is only 90, pupils with 120 and over might be considered exceptional.

All the above discussion of borderlines may distract us from realizing that it is preferable *not* to specify or segregate one small group of a certain IQ level as 'gifted', and all those below this level as 'ungifted'. All those whose abilities are much superior to the average of their classmates should come under review, and arrangements made according to individual needs.

Finally, how about those who are distinguished more by special talent or talents than by high IQ? Obviously any decision here must take into account the facilities the school possesses, or can acquire, for developing such talents. One would hope that some help could be given at least in the areas of mathematics, science, language, art and music. If IQ 130 is regarded as the approximate borderline for the generally gifted, then all those who appear outstanding in any of these talents (again, say, in the top 2½ per cent) might be considered, provided their IQs do not fall below about 120. As already pointed out, we do not know just how many additional cases this would entail because most high IQ children are also talented, and most highly talented also have high IQs. But a reasonable guess would be that the inclusion of those gifted in a particular area might raise our 2½ per cent to about double, i.e. 5 per cent.

We will return to the procedures involved in identifying gifted pupils in chapter 7.

5 The nature of creativity

Creativity is generally associated with the work of outstanding artists, scientists, inventors and others. They need not necessarily be geniuses, but their productions do show sufficient originality or importance to win considerable acclaim or recognition. However, in recent years creativity has become somewhat of a catchword, and we hear of creative toys for children, creative meals, creativity in advertising and so forth. And perhaps there is continuity between the productions of a Leonardo da Vinci and those of the householder who designs his garden, or his wife who makes new dresses. Certainly children show creativity and imaginativeness in their play, or in constructing things; they do not merely follow the rules or imitate others. Even puppies and kittens invent new things to do with balls or spools which could hardly be called just instinct. However, we shall be looking in this chapter mainly at the creativity of outstanding adults, since we presumably hope gifted children will grow up to resemble them, even if their creative accomplishments during their school years are relatively trifling.

Clearly then, creativity covers a wide range of phenomena. Irving Taylor (1959) has suggested distinguishing five levels from the simplest to the most advanced. These are:

1 Expressive, as exemplified by imaginative play which may show little or no skill or originality, but is an independent expression of the individual concerned.

2 Productive, e.g. games, crafts etc. where there is some control or technique in addition.

3 Inventive, showing originality and flexibility, not merely imitative.

4 Innovative, embodying a significant departure from the conventional in art or science.

5 Emergentative, that is, discovery of a new and fundamental principle (e.g. relativity).

Another useful idea put forward by Burt (1943) is that creativity is quite unlike most human abilities, which seem to follow the normal distribution curve fairly closely. It conforms rather to the exponential equation which Pareto, the Italian sociologist, applied to human output, or to pheno- mena like income. Much the greatest number of people obtain quite low incomes, or show little creativity. Quite a lot have middling incomes, while a very few obtain incomes out of all proportion to the rest. Similarly a few geniuses, e.g. Shakespeare, Mozart, Freud, are vastly more productive — millionaires as it were; and there are quite a lot of minor figures who also make substantial and lasting contributions, though they probably do not total more than about 1 per cent of the population.

Defining creativity

Creativity is traditionally something mysterious, and only fairly recently has there been much attempt to study it as a natural phenomenon. We have not even got a satisfactory definition which would embrace all the examples mentioned above, though a good many definitions have been put forward (cf. Ghiselin, 1963). A recent attempt by T.P. Jones (1972) reads: 'Creativity is a combination of flexibility, originality and sensitivity to ideas which enables the thinker to break away from usual sequences of thought with different and productive sequences, the results of which give satisfaction to himself and possibly to others.' (The word 'thought' would have to be taken rather broadly if it is to include Pavlova's dancing, and Namatjira's paintings.) One of the present writers has suggested: 'Man's capacity to produce new ideas, insights, inventions or artistic objects which are accepted as being of social, spiritual, aesthetic, scientific, or technological value'. Most authors emphasize novelty or the production of new combinations, but temper this by pointing out that schizo- phrenic drawings, or children's mistakes in arithmetic, may be novel without being creative. However, the addition of 'acceptability' or 'value', or 'appropriateness' as a criterion, gets one into difficulties, since it is notorious that scientific discoveries (e.g. Mendelism), or new art forms (e.g. Sur- realism), or religious movements (e.g. Christianity) are often rejected or ignored at the time, though recognized later. The value of an invention can generally be assessed fairly easily, since people want to buy or use it, even if it is as potentially harmful as the atomic bomb. Likewise the value of a scientific theory, e.g. Einstein's theory of relativity, is fairly objective because competent scientists agree — to use Ghiselin's phrase — that 'it restructures our universe of understanding'. In the case of the arts, however, evaluation is inevitably more subjective and unanalysable. Presumably the impact that a work of art makes on connoisseurs is more important than its appeal to the multitudes; but this would hardly be true of creative social leadership.

Rather than trying to pinpoint the essence of creative thinking or activity, it will be instructive to consider two major dimensions or continua of mental activity:

1 Reproductive *v.* productive
2 Thinking to a logical or utilitarian end *v.* fantasy or emotion-based thinking.

Reproductive and productive thinking

All thinking can be regarded as solving problems, or trying to adapt to life's situations. Most simply this is done by calling up past relevant experiences. Instead of learning by trial and error, or conditioning, the organism can put together and sort out past learnings internally and choose the right one to guide his action. We say 'the organism', since thinking certainly evolves below the human stage. Rats, according to Tolman, build up internal representations or 'cognitive maps' of mazes; even hens, it is claimed, can acquire some sort of concept of 'darker or lighter than ...', which they then apply in a new situation.

Probabaly the greatest proportion of human thinking is reproductive. We recall the best route for driving from A to B, or a child recalls number combinations in doing his arithmetic sums. It also enables us to carry out internalized mental trial and error much more rapidly and effectively than by actually performing each alternative course of action. For example, a young child who wants to reach something from a high shelf thinks that he would not be tall enough even standing on a stool, but he would be on a chair, and goes straight for the chair. Note too, that we can use a variety of 'media' for carrying out such thinking; sometimes it can be done through visual images of the possibilities, though more often (among older children and adults at least), verbal or other symbols are more precise.

At a more advanced stage thinking becomes productive when we grasp relationships between our ideas, and come up with effective solutions to new problems. Instead of reproductive trial and error, we jump the gaps as it were, provided we are sufficiently intelligent. This, too, can be discerned in a rudimentary form in subhuman species. W. Köhler, in his famous studies of apes, had a chimpanzee in a cage and a banana outside and out of reach. The animal was already able to rake in food with a stick, but there was no stick around. However, there was a tree growing elsewhere in the cage. After a period of frustration the ape suddenly seemed to realise that he could get a stick by breaking off a branch of the tree. Köhler attributes this to a sudden 'insight' into the problem. The ape had restructured or reorganized his perceptions; instead of seeing branches just as parts of trees, he saw them as potential rakes. And thereafter he could deal with the same situation without hesitation, i.e. reproductively.

Further investigation of problem-solving in humans have been described by Köhler's colleagues, Wertheimer and Duncker. For example, Wertheimer (1959) asked a child, who knew the area of a rectangle was length × height; what was the area of a parallelogram? After a considerable thought the child realized that by snipping off the triangle A and moving it to B, one had a rectangle, and this gave the answer. Another series of studies by N.R.F. Maier (1930) brought out the extent to which ingenious solutions depend not merely on grasping connections, but on breaking down older concepts and attitudes; productive insight is, in a sense, the opposite of habitual, reproductive, thinking. And this is certainly an important element in creativity. The musical composer makes use of the standard sounds of European instruments and

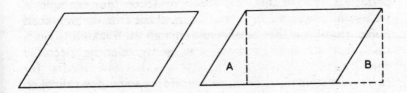

voices, and the relations implicit in the ordinary scale; but he departs from conventional usage to arrive at new combinations, that is, themes and harmonies (or discords) that have not been thought of before.

Quite a different approach to creative thinking is based more on Stimulus-Response theories rather than on Gestalt theory. Mednick (1962), followed by Wallach and Kogan (1965), conceive of thinking in terms of associational processes, and point out that, for most people, the initial associations to any stimulus or situation are quite conventional ones. But some people have more abundant associations than others and are capable of producing more remote or unusual, though still relevant and appropriate, associations; and these are what we call creative. There is, of course, more to the theory than this, and it has proved fruitful for research, as in Wallach and Kogan's study described later. But we find it less satisfactory in that it seems to make productive thinking an extreme form of reproductive thinking rather than distinguishing them.

Reality and fantasy thinking

As described so far, thinking has led to solutions or decisions which adequately meet practical needs or, at a more complex level, are logically valid. But a good deal of thinking is not tied to reality in this way. It arises from feelings and needs, or expresses our desires or fears, without necessarily issuing in effective action. Day-dreaming is the obvious example; but as Peter McKellar (1957) points out, there are several other kinds of nonreality thinking such as night dreams, hallucinations, and hypnogogic states. While we cannot explore the minds of young infants, it seems entirely likely that, as Freud has claimed, they have intense feelings and desires for comfort, food, mother-contact etc., which constitute the beginnings of conscious states or images. Freud calls these 'primary process' or Id thinking, and believes that it persists in the repressed Unconscious of the older child or adult; whereas reality thinking is 'secondary process' — thinking under the control of the Ego.

Day-dreaming, together with children's imaginative play, seems to be a kind of interplay between primary and secondary. They arise largely from conscious emotions and unfulfilled wishes, and they may express unconscious needs;

but also they constitute a kind of trial and error process of trying out various solutions or imaginary gratifications. The small girl playing with her dolls is exploring and sorting out her experiences of family life and child-rearing, while also expressing her wishes for love and care, for conformity to adult standards, and so on. She is learning to handle her fantasies, to draw on primary process and yet to advance to rational thinking. And this element of fantasy is, in our view, what differentiates creative thinking from intelligent and productive thinking, though no doubt they often merge into one another; there is no clear dividing line.

Freud in 1908 first drew attention to the resemblances between the work of the artist or poet, day-dreaming, and the play of childhood. All of these involve expression of one's personality, including repressed tendencies; we are trying to refashion the world to fit our inner needs. But the artist cannot do this as directly and openly as the uninhibited child. He has to disguise his fantasies to make them more acceptable. In Freud's later writings on Leonardo da Vinci, Dostoevsky, and other artists he argued that artistic and scientific creation arises from sublimation of repressed sexual and aggressive tendencies. This, of course, is high speculative and unverifiable; and it has been criticized by many psychologists, such as Carl Rogers (1954), for the implication that creativity is a kind of neurotic defence mechanism. Plenty of neurotics are far from creative. Hence, later followers of psychoanalysis, such as Kris (1952) and Arthur Koestler (1964) have modified the theory, particularly to allow more scope for the critical function of the Ego. The artist, or other creative person, is more open than most of us to primary process fantasy; he is less inhibited by conscious controls, and retains some of the spontaneous imaginativeness of the child. Hence, he can disregard conventional learned associations and produce original syntheses. But having found his inspiration or creative idea, the Ego functions again take control and elaborate it so that it ends up as a finished work of art or discovery. As Wordsworth phrased it — 'emotion recollected in tranquillity'. Creation is a kind of interplay between the conscious and preconscious levels, indeed an interplay between the deeper personality trends, the intellect and — as we have seen — the society which accepts it. The appeal or impact that it makes on others arises because the artist has deeper insights and more imagination than most of us; he helps to solve our conflicts and tensions too by converting his inner promptings into pictures, words or sound patterns.

Inspiration

Obviously this is very vague and imprecise as a theoretical explanation but it does fit in with what we have learned from the introspective, often anecdotal, accounts that great artists or scientists have given us about their methods of working. And it accords with psychological investigations of their personality characteristics.

Many extracts from the writings of highly creative persons, or observations of them by their contemporaries, have been published (cf. Ghiselin, 1952); also R. Harding's books, *An Anatomy of Inspiration* (1940), gives a fascinating overview. A much briefer, yet widely quoted, summary is provided by Graham Wallas's (1926) outline of four main processes or stages that seem to occur very frequently in both artistic and scientific creation:

1 *Preparation.* The artist must be thoroughly skilled in his profession, and the scientist expert in the particular area for anything of value to emerge. The latter particularly will know what the problems are in this area, what relevant work has been done by others, what techniques (e.g. instruments) could be adapted from other areas. In other words, inspiration and innovation are no use without a large body of knowledge and skills to be creative with.

2 *Unconscious cerebration.* The scientist is usually highly motivated to achieve some progress in his area, and has formulated the crucial problems, but may put them aside because no solution is forthcoming. Many writers and musicians are described as being possessed, as it were, by a strong emotional urge to create, and suffer an agony of frustration. Although we cannot observe what is happening in the mind, particularly at preconscious levels, it seems as though a kind of fermentation takes place; the drive and the ideas go on churning around in the back of the mind.

3 *Inspiration.* Often quite suddenly, when doing something else, or awakening from sleep, the third stage of inspiration or illumination comes, accompanied by great emotional excitement. It may be the germ of an idea, or at least the outline of a solution, a new synthesis has been achieved.

4 *Elaboration and/or verification*. Almost always a further lengthy process of working out, checking, following up implications, occurs before the creative product is finished. This, of course, is largely a secondary process, and like Stage 1, depends greatly on skill and expertise.

As it stands this scheme is too rigid. Often the stages are mixed up or, in the case of a lengthy piece of work, repeated. Wagner worked on *The Ring* at various times over 26 years. Obviously this was not one inspiration, nor was he in a state of white heat throughout; yet the final pages are at least as inspired as the opening. It would be difficult also to apply it to many painters — to Turner perhaps; but was not Velasquez also 'creative' in a different way? It might be thought that scientists and artists are entirely different, and obviously the latter tend to rely more on emotion and fantasy, to be more sensitive and open to impressions from their environment. Yet the former also experience the thrill of creative fever even if, to use Edison's phrase, genius is 1 per cent inspiration and 99 per cent perspiration. They work on hunches or 'inspired' guesses, not always according to textbook accounts of scientific method. The scientist's aims are usually more convergent, the artist's divergent — to use Guilford's distinctions; but not necessarily. For the creative scientist is breaking new ground and may open up a whole field (Freud, for example); while the writer or painter or musician may decide quite precisely on the ideas or main theme, and converge all their resources of talent to express this in the most satisfying aesthetic form. Convergent-divergent corresponds rather loosely to our dimension of reality *v.* fantasy thinking, but as we shall see in the next chapter, it is quite inadequate as a criterion of creativity.

Some further comment may be made here regarding 'unconscious cerebration' — naturally an unpopular notion among behaviouristically inclined psychologists. In the present writer's view it is quite a common phenomenon in problem solving, let alone creative inspiration. When attempting to write an article or lecture he frequently finds it difficult to progress because there are so many complex points to try to organize into lucid form. On such occasions, he studies these points again and then puts the task aside. Almost always, next morning, they seem to have sorted themselves out, and writing this section comes quite easily.

The abilities of highly creative individuals

Cox's (1926) study of nearly 300 geniuses, referred to earlier, indicated that such outstandingly creative individuals were mostly superior in intelligence, sometimes very superior, though others were not much above average. Philosophers and writers obtained the highest estimated mean IQs, followed not far behind by scientists. Musicians were intermediate and graphic artists rather lower, though still averaging 122. More recent studies based on actual tests such as Roe's, Cattell's and MacKinnon's likewise show quite a wide range of ability. But MacKinnon, who studied living members of several professions (e.g. architects, writers, scientists, inventors) and contrasted those who were recognized as highly creative with others who were also very expert but less creative, found that the former were not distinguished from the latter by IQ or scores on conventional intelligence tests; nor, incidentally, did Guilford's divergent thinking tests show any promising differences. Different professions often showed different patterns of abilities. For example, writers were generally very high in verbal ability, physical scientists in spatial and non-verbal abilities, as might be anticipated. But the most successful objective test was the Barron-Welsh art judgment test, based on preferences for unconventional, simple, and symmetrical designs. Some mean scores are quoted below:

artists	39	architects generally	26
highly creative archi-tects	37	low-creative scientists	19
		normal student sample	18
research scientists	30½		

Barron (1969) claims that this fits in with the neo-Freudian type of theory, outlined above. In his view, the creative person, particularly the artist, thrives on disorder, and yet manages to produce ordered sequences of ideas.

Another common finding is that creative persons are often not highly qualified academically (though many are). Hudson (1966) showed that Fellows of the Royal Society, which includes most of the outstanding research scientists in Britain often obtained second- or even third-class Honours degrees at university, rather than first-class. In Roe's investigation, many outstanding scientists lighted on their particular area of creativity quite late in their student careers, after a fairly humdrum record of achievement in other subjects. However, one would expect that many potentially creative individuals would not settle kindly to a regular curriculum and conventional teaching at school or college, and might better develop their own interests elsewhere. Heist (1962) claims that many students who were considered to show high creative promise in their secondary schools dropped out of college early. Nevertheless, this does not mean that achievement is irrelevant. Creative scientists and writers must be highly accomplished in standard concepts and skills even if they rebel against them, and other artists must develop their talents, whether within or without the academic environment.

As in the case of gifted children, the question may be asked: how much does socioeconomic class and environment contribute to the production of genius? Both Galton and Cox admit that most eminent persons or geniuses in history benefited from upbringing in cultured, often wealthy homes. Of Cox's group, 18% of the fathers were nobility, gentry, professional or upper business; but 13% were skilled working-class or lower business, and 5% semi- or unskilled. Particularly during the fourteenth to eighteenth centuries it would have been difficult for creative artists and scientists to make their mark without such advantage. Nevertheless, a proportion did come from relatively poor homes, or were of peasant stock, or were largely self-taught, for example, Kepler, Gauss, Faraday, Burns, Pasteur, Luther, Kant. Among Roe's scientists more than half were the sons of professional men, and none the son of an unskilled labourer.

Not long after Galton was writing on hereditary genius, others such as De Candolle in France and J. McKeen Cattell (1906) in the US were pointing out the importance of environmental influences: that eminent scientists mostly came from professional and upper- or middle-class families, and lived in countries, or states, where there was a good education system, universities, libraries and laboratories, and where there was political and religious freedom to publish. For example some eighty times as many American scientists were found in Massachusetts as in Mississippi.

We would still conclude that genetic factors are of importance since numerous geniuses did make good despite poor environment; but we can also infer that, in all probability, many other individuals whose abilities were potentially as great as those of Galton's and Cox's geniuses were lost to society because of environmental handicaps.

Emotional stability and personality

Probably the medicine man in primitive societies was a terrifying figure; and the creative genius is still looked on with some awe and suspicion. John Dryden in the seventeenth century wrote: 'Great wits are sure to madness near allied.' And Lombroso, an Italian psychiatrist, in 1891, devoted a book to the theme that genius is a manifestation of the diseased mind. Even Kretschmer (1931) believed that it involved a psychopathic component, though he was also concerned to show that different types of genius were associated with different bodily physiques and temperaments. For example, empirical scientists tended to be pyknic cyclothymes, idealist philosophers to be asthenic schizoids. Naturally it was easy to pick cases to fit the theory, by ignoring those that don't. Many examples of highly unstable writers, painters, musicians, even some scientists, readily come to mind; but others appear to have lived richly and fully — Shakespeare, da Vinci, Rabelais, Rembrandt, even if they sometimes got into trouble with the authorities.

The first attempt at a scientific survey by Havelock Ellis (1904) covered over a thousand eminent British men and women. A fair amount of ill-health, and minor emotional difficulties like stammering, shyness or melancholia, were noted, but only 4 per cent could be classified as insane. In 1926, Cox reached substantially similar conclusions.

Obviously it is unsatisfactory to rely on biographical data from the past, and Anne Roe's (1952) investigations of living American scientists in the 1940s are of particular importance. She succeeded in obtaining the cooperation of 22 physicists, 20 biologists, and 22 social scientists, who were among the most eminent and creative in their professions. Though she employed a few ability and projective tests, most of her data were obtained by lengthy clinical interviews in which they freely discussed their upbringing, interests and methods of work. She seems to have been commendably unbiased by any doctrinaire theory, e.g. hereditarian, or psychoanalytic, and admitted that her cases varied tremendously in personalities and backgrounds. Yet certain common features, and differences between the subgroups, tended to recur.

In boyhood they had shown a good deal of independence and isolation; family relationships had been rather impersonal, though there were usually high expectations of achievement and encouragement of learning, and of the development of intellectual interests. Several came from broken homes, or had suffered prolonged illnesses when young, which further increased their solitariness and self-sufficiency. Some had been more strongly influenced by another relative, or an outstanding teacher, than by either parent. The social scientists differed noticeably in having more stormy backgrounds and conflicts with parents. As adults all groups tended to be rather detached as though they had sublimated their social and sexual needs into an intense interest in objects, animals, or people. They were imbued with the scientific attitude that, through research, one can master certain aspects of the environment and find out for oneself. Their outstanding characteristic was their intense absorption in, and utter commitment to, their work (which they hardly regarded as work), and their disinterest in conventional social affairs and recreations. Though the physicists and biologists often appeared rather undersexed, they were usually happily married, enjoyed family life, and spent what time they could spare with their children. Thus, despite many unusual features in their personalities and daily living, they could hardly be called maladjusted. The social scientists, however, were again rather different, being more gregarious, and more likely to live turbulent lives. Over 40 per cent of them had been divorced, as against 10 per cent of physicists and biologists.

Further studies of scientists have been reported by R.B. Cattell, Gough and MacKinnon, and McClelland* (1962). These tend very largely to confirm Roe's findings. Cattell (1968) obtained scores of 140 eminent researchers on his 16 Personality Factor test, and found that they differed from general adult norms chiefly in being more schizothymic (reserved, critical), and more desurgent (restrained, non-social), highly dominant and high in Ego strength (self-control) and self-assurance, highly self-sufficient, yet at the same time high in artistic sensitivity, somewhat radical, and, of course, highly intelligent. Other studies stress the scientists' avoidance of interpersonal involvement, and their preference

*McClelland provides an interesting attempt at psychoanalytic interpretation of the scientist's motivation.

for abstractions and things, their emphasis on order and structure, and their hardworkingness. They are also strongly masculine in their attitudes, while artists show greater femininity. Almost all are males, and they tend to come from radical, Protestant backgrounds. However Gough (1961) warns us not to overgeneralize by pointing out that there are many different sub-types, with different attitudes and working methods, e.g. the Initiator, the Scholar, the Methodologist etc.

Let us move on to the work of MacKinnon and his collaborators, at the Institute for Personality Assessment and Research (Berkeley, California). Numerous groups of creative people were studied extensively, using a variety of ability and interest tests, personality instruments, ratings, observations of behaviour, and interviews by experienced staff. Whenever possible, these subjects lived in at the Institute for a three-day period, and — as already mentioned — their characteristics were compared with those of control groups of less creative individuals in the same professions. Only the results for architects have been published in detail (MacKinnon, 1962), though a general survey of all groups is provided by Barron (1969). However, architects are particularly interesting since their work combines mathematical and technological skills with aesthetic judgment. .

The creative architects, as contrasted with the noncreative, showed, on average, stronger interests and values of a scientific and aesthetic type, and were less attracted to business careers. They were also somewhat more feminine than masculine in their responses, which MacKinnon interprets as being more emotionally sensitive, not accepting the American stereotype of the extroverted, aggressive male. A majority scored on the introverted side of the Myers-Briggs inventory; but there were also big differences on some of the Jungian functional types; thus they favoured perception or receptiveness rather than critical judgment, and intuition rather than sensation. The self-ratings and personality scales gave a picture of self-sufficiency, belief in themselves, individualism, dominance and determination, and holding radical progressive and nonconformist views. The non-creatives more often stressed the conventional virtues of responsibility, reliability, sincerity, good-naturedness. However, the creatives were not usually Bohemian, or unconventional for the sake of being different;

their rebelliousness was more in intellectual and cultural matters. Architects in particular were self-assured and businesslike, whereas mathematicians were more 'up-in-the-air', less dependable and socially ill-at-ease. Scientists on the whole seemed to be the best balanced group, as one would expect from Cox's, Roe's and Cattell's studies. In so far as their creativity is more controlled by reality, they probably do not, like artists, express their personalities to the same extent in their work. However, all the groups could be said to be greatly concerned about personal adequacy, and at the same time they were all intensely task-oriented, or living for their work. It is as though they are motivated to prove themselves through their creative productions.

The group of writers was similar to the architects in many respects, but they were particularly noted as being interesting and fluent talkers, much concerned also with philosophical problems and values; and they tended to think, and associate ideas, in unusual ways. More than any other group they raise the problem of mental health. Barron* has discussed this issue at length, and admits that many creative individuals might rate rather low on such conventional criteria of mental health as good social adjustment and responsibility, absence of neurotic symptoms, accurate perceptions of reality etc. Indeed when the Minnesota Multiphasic Personality Inventory was applied to the writers and architects, they showed more psychopathology than the non-creatives or the general adult norm. But at the same time they were remarkably high on the measure of Ego strength, showing personal effectiveness and control. This would suggest, then, that it is not inner conflicts and repressions that underlie creativity, as indicated by Freud's original theory, but the capacity to draw on these and to convert them into works of art and discovery.

Two noteworthy studies of outstanding living artists have been published by Roe (1946) and Eiduson (1958), though they give rather little biographical information and are based more on interpretations of projective tests — Rorschach and T.A.T. Both authors agree that there is no single distinctive type of personality. The common stereotype of the effeminate, Bohemian artist is rarely justified, and there seemed to be as much variation as in almost any group of professionals. Many of them had unhappy childhoods, were lonely or isolated, or

*Cf. also Lytton's excellent discussion (1971).

experienced rejection. Their artistic talents were recognized early, but though some had talented and encouraging parents, a few had parents who strongly opposed their choice of vocation. Roe's group all studied at art school for a period, but she emphasizes the extent to which their talent was self-developed. Like her scientists they were very hard-working and persevering. Eiduson contrasted three groups: (i) 25 artists who had received psychiatric treatment for neurotic problems; (ii) 25 in business occupations, also neurotic; (iii) 15 artists who had not sought treatment. There was little difference between (i) and (iii), but significant differences between both groups and (ii) on the projective responses, suggesting that neurotic disability as such was irrelevant.

Chiefly the artists were distinguished by unusual ways of perceiving and thinking, by their greater sensitivity and imaginative originality; while the business group were more down to earth, practical, and disliking indecision.

Dudek (1968) also gave the Rorschach Inkblots to 3 contrasted groups: (i) 41 genuinely creative and successful painters and writers; (ii) 19 other less successful artists (according to experts' ratings); (iii) 22 non-artists. On the basis of Kris' view that creativity arises from preconscious and primary process levels and is then fashioned by the Ego, Dudek hypothesizes that creative artists would give responses indicative of primary process, i.e. crude, direct or primitive expression of sex and aggressive drives. This was confirmed by finding mean scores of 7.3, 4.1 and 4.2 primary process responses in the three groups. The first group also gave more Wholes, or synthetic responses (13.0, 10.6 and 8.7), but were slightly lower in Movement and Colour responses, which are often interpreted as inner creativity and emotional ability respectively. Yet another comparative study of highly creative and less creative art students was carried out by Götz and Götz (1973), using the Eysenck Personality Inventory. Those regarded by their teachers as gifted were significantly more introverted and more neurotic than the ungifted; and the difference was further exaggerated when only the most highly gifted were compared with the rest.

Relevant in this connection is a study by Golden, Mendel and Glueck (cf. Taylor, 1962) of a group of typical, well-adjusted American males. They point out the absence of all the qualities which tend to characterize creative artists —

richness of personality, intropsychic tension, breadth of interests, imagination and spontaneity. In a sense, then, artists and writers are abnormal or different from the accepted social norm, though not necessarily neurotic, and very rarely psychotic.

Barron's book (1969) mentions two other interesting groups — business managers, and creative women. The former were studied by him in Ireland, using most of the IPAR methodology. They included many who had shown outstanding innovativeness, originality, and leadership in social change. The most creative were strongly masculine and assertive, tough, and low in such traits as pleasant, mild, understanding. Staff observations and interviews confirmed that they were independent, unconventional and sure of their own ideas, yet also stable and highly intelligent. Though there are a few resemblances to creative scientists and artists, it seems that social and executive creativity emanates from a very different kind of personality.

The much smaller proportion of women than men who are recognized as outstandingly creative has often been noted, and generally attributed simply to the strength of cultural conventions. However, Helson (1966) and the IPAR staff followed up over a hundred graduates of women's colleges, many of whom were nominated by faculty as having high creative potential. Most were married, and some were continuing their creative careers, but others had clearly experienced severe frustrations and disappointments. Many reported having emotional difficulties, feelings of isolation, and depression, due to the conflict between preserving their femininity and their intellectual or artistic ambitions. In other respects they quite closely resembled the male groups described above, showing mistrust of personal relations, rebelliousness, independence of thought, and high levels of aspiration. They were more intelligent, and secured better college grades than the non-creatives; also they scored highly on the Barron-Welsh art test (but not on divergent thinking tests). There was no tendency towards greater masculinity, though a considerable number had displayed tomboyish characteristics as children. This contradicts Lombroso's and Kretschmer's conclusion that the only women who are creative geniuses are essentially masculine in temperament. Their own reports, and reports from parents, indicated that the creatives had been highly gifted as children, and that there was a considerable continuity in the development and maintenance of their interests. Unfortunately the report does not state how many were attracted to writing, to other arts, or to science; and there was no attempt to compare proportions of creatives with those obtaining among male graduates.

Creativity in the normal adult and child

How much light does all this work throw on creativity in the ordinary adult, or the gifted child? Not very much: for obviously they seldom undertake the prolonged, emotionally-driven, productions characteristic of highly creative individuals. An occasional adult may spend years making a model ship out of matchsticks, or building up a new kind of business enterprise. More apposite would be the adolescent scientist who plans and carries out an elaborate research for a Science Fair. Creative writers and musicians can also be recognized among high school students. The creative accomplishments of students and adults have been assessed, for example, by Wallach and Wing (1969), Nichols and Holland (1963), and Torrance (1969b), using self-descriptive questionnaires. But no detailed enquiry seems to have been made into their methods of work, or the nature of any inspiration they may show; and little is available on the personality characteristics of the more and less creative.

Nichols and Holland followed up National Merit scholars at the end of the freshman year, and assessed their scientific, literary, dramatic, musical and graphic art accomplishments, as well as their academic grades. They compared these criteria with various types of information collected in high school. Generally the best predictors were similar activities carried out at school, and vocational aspirations. For example creative scientists had carried out science projects at school, and were already strongly motivated to become professional scientists. Personality and parental attitude measures gave few consistent correlations beyond the 0.2 level. Another limited but interesting study by Parloff, Datta *et al.*, (1968) compared secondary school boys who had produced creative research projects with other less creative though high achieving students, on the California Psychological Inventory. The creatives scored particularly high on a personality factor termed Disciplined Effectiveness. Their studies were well-organized and efficient, and they showed initiative and self-direction. Apparently, at this stage the more creative did not show the non-conformist or rebellious traits characteristic of MacKinnon's high-creative adults, nor the isolation described by Roe.

Though these authors did not investigate creative boy writers or artists, Schaefer and Anastasi (1968) did include these as well as scientists in constructing a Biographical Inventory for identifying creative male students in senior high school. A large number of items dealing with home background, interests etc., were included which had been shown to differentiate significantly between students nominated by teachers as creatives, or non-creatives, on the basis of original science projects or imaginative artistic or literary productions. The creatives also scored highly on divergent thinking tests. Both groups of creatives came largely from professional families, and their parents provided models of creative interests and productivity, and of effectiveness; their homes encouraged cultural and intellectual orientation. The boys already showed pervasive and continuing enthusiasm for their chosen field; they devoted much of their leisure time to relevant activities, and were relatively uninterested in sports. The artists particularly showed a diversity of unusual background experiences; e.g. their families had moved frequently; the boys described many odd hobbies; some claimed eidetic imagery, and some were given to a great deal of day-dreaming. The creative scientists, however, were more conventional, and appeared to be below average in social participation during childhood. In general these characteristics seem to support Roe and MacKinnon, though of course at a less intense level. A further study of adolescent girls (Anastasi and Schaefer, 1969) showed a very similar picture among creative artists and creative writers (scientists were not included). There was substantial evidence that the girls had been more influenced by their fathers, boys by their mothers.

Still less is known about younger children aged, say, 5 (or less) to 15, though obviously some do produce far more creative games, paintings, compositions, stories or poems, handwork or models, novel ideas, and so on, than others. Probably there is more variability, or less consistency over the years, than there is in general intellectual ability or in-school achievement. But it is also more difficult to assess the creativity of their productions because of the immaturity of their technical skills. Even such exceptionally talented and creative childhood works as Daisy Ashford's *The Young Visiters* do not necessarily presage similar productivity later. On the whole, it would seem as though children's interests — what they like doing on their own initiative — are better indicators. Do they prefer to write, paint, or make things, to more conventional activities, and do they enjoy music, literature, science etc. beyond their years? Many who do not grow up to be recognized as creative scientists or artists may nevertheless show considerable aesthetic sensitivity and creativity in their leisure time activities. But such 'amateur' creativity should probably be distinguished from the creativity of those who make worthwhile and lasting contributions to the arts, sciences, or in social or other areas. Productions such as these probably do require something like the dedication and absorption, and the personality characteristics we have described, together with advanced technical skills, which the amateur usually lacks.

6 Divergent thinking tests

Guiford's work on 'divergent' tests as measures of creativity was not the first. Binet and others had experimented with inkblots as tests of fluency of imagination at the beginning of the century. And Burt (1926) included the *Consequences* test of creative thinking in his battery for vocational guidance. For example:

> If everyone in the world suddenly doubled in height, what consequences would follow?

Answers to such problems can be scores (as described below) on the basis of number of different ideas, and their unusualness or imaginativeness.

Thurstone and his students established a number of fluency factors in the 1940s. For example, Ideational Fluency (F) was measured by such tests as:

> Write as many names of animals, or as many round things, as you can in 1 minute.
> Think of a man climbing up a ladder. Write as many ideas as you can that come to mind.

This factor was distinguished from Word Fluency (W):

> Write as many words as possible that begin with C, or end with TION.

But relatively little progress was made until the middle fifties, when the trickle of psychological publications on creativity became a flood. Tests such as these, and others devised, e.g. by Guilford (1950)* and Torrance (1965), which called for an

---

*Guilford in fact set out to measure some eight factors which he regarded as different, though all contributing to creativity. These included Ideational Fluency, Originality, Spontaneous Flexibility, and Sensitivity to Problems. However, most subsequent writers have contented themselves with one factor — a combination of fluency and originality. Torrance scored most of his tests for four aspects: Fluency, Originality, Flexibility, and Elaboration. But in practice these intercorrelate so highly that there seems little point in trying to distinguish them.

unrestricted flow of unusual ideas, were thought to elicit unconventional, original thinking, either among children, college students, or adults.

Other examples of commonly used tests include:

Alternate uses Think of unconventional uses for a brick, a newspaper, a paper clip, an empty tin can.

Plot titles Guilford presents a number of short stories, and asks for titles which are then assessed for cleverness and originality.

Similarities Write as many ways as possible in which the following are alike: CAT and MOUSE.

Remote associations (Mednick) Three words are given, e.g. mouse, cottage, blue. Think of a word which links them all (ans. cheese).

Multiple vocabulary (Hudson) give as many different meanings as possible for BIT, POST etc.

These two latter tests are in fact found to depend more on convergent verbal ability than on divergent ability.

Obviously children of elementary school age could not readily write responses to group tests such as these, though they have been used down to about 10 years. Wallach and Kogan (1965), and Vernon (1966) have given some of them orally and individually. But Torrance (1965) attempted to reduce the verbal element by drawing and other more concrete tasks. For example:

Circles A series of one inch circles (or other meaningless figures) is provided, and children are asked to develop each one into a different, meaningful drawing.

Picture, or design, construction Children are provided with pieces of coloured paper, and arrange them into a design or picture.

Product improvement The child is shown a toy, e.g. a dog, and asked to suggest ways it could be improved to make it more fun to play with.

Patterns (Wallach and Kogan) A number of simple, meaningless line drawings are shown, and the child is asked what each one makes him think of, or what it could be.

Rorschach Inkblots (Vernon, 1966) Though this was initially developed as a projective test of personality, the responses can readily be scored for number (productivity) and unusualness. The writer has found blots nos. 6, 3, and 8 are sufficient to give a good range of scores. Above age 12 they can be projected on a screen and the children write their own responses on outline diagrams. Similarly, pictures can be used (as in the Thematic Apperception Test), and stories elicited orally or in writing, and scored for fluency and unusual ideas.

While these all involve nonverbal stimulus materials, the responses are verbal, except for tests like Circles. Free drawings of, e.g. human figures or other themes can likewise be scored for originality and imagination. But nonverbal response tests generally seem less reliable, and do not correlate well with verbal-response scores. However simple, they depend to some extent on technical skill in drawing.

Scoring

One of the drawbacks of these tests is that the scoring is excessively tedious and time-consuming — so much so that they could hardly be applied routinely to large numbers of children. Even counting numbers of responses given in a certain time is difficult, because one cannot readily define just how different they have to be. If a child is asked what to do with an empty tin can, and says: keep marbles in, keep pencils in, keep nails in … are these different?

But quantity, or speed, of responses is not enough. One way of assessing quality is by rarity. Thus, Wallach and Kogan simply counted unique responses — those not given by any other testee in a large group of childen, or adults. Torrance (1965) and Cropley (1967a) suggest graded scores, e.g. 4 points for responses given by less than 1%, 3 for responses given by 1-2%, 2 for those given by 3-6%, 1 for 7-15%, and zero for over 15%. But here too, responses can be unique or rare in some respects, yet similar to those given by other testees in other respects. Moreover, an entirely bizarre or eccentric, yet quite trivial or inappropriate, response can be unique or rare; though psychologists who advocate this criterion claim that a bizarre answer turns out to be appropriate if one asks the child why he gave it. And if one does try to take account of appropriateness, this introduces a subjective element into the scoring. Nevertheless, the writer (Vernon, 1971) advocates scoring responses 2, 1 or 0: 2s being those which are unusual and appropriate or clever, and given by not more than 5 per cent of subjects of the same age; 0s are common responses given by 10 per cent or more; and all the rest are 1s. By totalling these scores one covers the quantitative and qualitative aspects simultaneously. Where possible, it is preferable to have two or more markers score independently, though in several studies inter-scorer agreement has been high. Even this simplified technique is lengthy since all the responses of a considerable group of the same age, say 200, must first be tabulated and classified as 2s, 1s, or 0s, and only then can each individual testee's responses be compared with the list, scored and totalled. However, if additional new, or partially new, responses turn up in another group, it is fairly easy to assign them 2s or 1s. It is undesirable to take over some other psychologist's list, obtained from a rather different group. For example, Torrance publishes lists for his Minnesota battery of tests, but these would certainly not be suitable for English children, and doubtfully for Canadians.

Administration and instructions: reliability

A lot of evidence (cf. Vernon, 1971) indicates that the performance of children or adults on divergent thinking tests is affected by the conditions of testing, the way the instructions are phrased, and the frame of mind of the testees. Torrance (1969a) has generally administered his tests in much the same way as convergent tests, with time limits and instructions to 'think of as many ideas as you can ... that no one else will think of'. But Wallach and Kogan argued, quite plausibly, that more creative ideas would be produced in a 'game-like' rather than a 'test-like' situation, where there is no pressure or competition. Each child in their group of fifth graders was asked individually to play games with a friendly observer — not a teacher or tester. Vernon (1971) arranged for seven classes of eighth grade children to do a battery of divergent tests under normal testing conditions, and another parallel seven classes to do them in a much more permissive atmosphere, with virtually no timing, and freedom to change from one subtest to another. The second group produced considerably more responses of higher quality than the first. However, it is difficult to standardize such conditions, and to prevent permissiveness from degenerating into bedlam. Adolescent and adult subjects often treat the test as an opportunity for obscene or macabre jokes, and naturally this will depend a good deal on whether they think the tester will keep their shocking responses to himself, or pass them on to teachers or parents. Hudson (1968) found that students produced more responses than usual when asked to think of what a Bohemian artist might say, and even when asked to respond like a pedantic Scottish engineer. All this means that divergent tests cannot readily be standardized, since the degree of fluency and unconventionality can vary with the attitudes of the testees, and how they conceive the task. However, one should not exaggerate this weakness; if the instructions and general approach are kept constant, minor variations between different testers can generally be ignored, as in Binet testing.

One might anticipate that such attitudes might fluctuate from one occasion, or one tester, to another, and it is in fact found that when divergent tests are repeated after a few months or more, the correlations (reliability coefficients) are lower than those usually obtained with convergent tests. Haddon and Lytton (1968) gave the same set of six tests at 11 and 15 years; and the correlation of total scores was 0.62. Moreover, the second-occasion scores were predicted as accurately, or inaccurately, by a verbal intelligence test as by the first-occasion divergent tests. We do not know how far the lack of stability is due to changes in creative abilities and divergent thinking with growth, how far to variations in testing conditions or attitudes.

Factorial consistency

The crucial considerations are whether a number of different divergent tests correlate sufficiently with one another to show that they are measuring the same factor (cf. chapter 4), and whether their correlations with convergent tests of, say g or V, are low enough for us to conclude that the factor is a distinctive one. Here the evidence is extraordinarily contradictory; but the variations in findings are mostly attributable to the following:

1 The diversity of the divergent tests. Wallach and Kogan's tests were all much alike (oral response), whereas Getzels and Jackson's were quite miscellaneous, and intercorrelated with one another no higher than they did with intelligence tests.

2 The difference in conditions of administration. The special conditions imposed by Wallach and Kogan, as described above, led to a minimal correlation of only 0.104

between their divergent and convergent test scores.

3 The heterogeneity of the group of testees. In one study by Hasan and Butcher (1966), which included a whole age group of Scottish 12 year olds, the correlation between divergent total and IQ was as high as 0.743.

4 The ability level of the group. It has been suggested that divergent thinking and verbal intelligence are closely inter-dependent among average and dull children. A child who lacks good vocabulary and verbal comprehension is unlikely to produce many unusual verbal associations. But above, say, 120 IQ, these capacities become increasingly independent. A 125 IQ child may produce almost as many good-quality divergent ideas as a 155 IQ child. The evidence for this so-called 'threshold hypothesis' is far from conclusive, but it seems quite plausible.

Cropley (1966) suggests that divergent and convergent abilities are distinctive, yet overlapping, types of ability (to use the factorist's terminology, they constitute oblique factors). This fits in with Vernon's results, where nine divergent tests and four convergent were given to a moderately heterogeneous group of Canadian Grade 8 students. A substantial common factor, with 33 per cent variance, was found to run through all the divergent battery. However, approximately one-third of this could be attributed to convergent $g + V$, and two-thirds were distinctive. The actual overall correlation between the two batteries was 0.30, implying that many students might score considerably higher on divergent tests than intelligence, or vice versa. But it is important to remember that there is no one final figure; the degree of overlap will vary with the age and ability of the children, the kind of tests, and the conditions of testing. Probably with younger children who are given individual (e.g. Binet) intelligence and oral divergent tests, the correlation is a lot higher, since in both types of test the children supply their own answers. Thus, the statement commonly made, on the basis of Getzels and Jackson's (1962) results, that intelligence tests fail to discover 70 per cent of creative students is definitely misleading.

Validity

Most psychologists who write about divergent thinking tests call them creativity tests. But this implies that they are valid measures of the psychological characteristics which we have tried to specify in the preceding chapter — a claim which is certainly not justified. Because divergent tests involve giving unusual associations, this does not mean that they are measuring the same kind of originality as that shown by the creative artist or scientist, or even the normal child or adult who produces something constructive. The lack of satisfactory evidence is not entirely the psychologist's fault, since clearly it is extremely difficult to specify just what is meant by creativity in daily life or in the work of outstanding professionals. The latter can hardly be identified with any certainty until the age of about 30, and no-one has yet attempted to test children at, say, 10 and follow up sufficient numbers for twenty years to see if the highest scorers do turn out to be highly creative. It is more feasible, of course, to assess creative accomplishments at school or college, but this usually means asking teachers to rate pupils' or students' creativity; and it is only too likely that they will designate as creative those whom they regard as good scholars, who produce the sort of work that they favour, and will often downgrade those who produce more original or unconventional work. However, considerable ingenuity has been used in getting around this kind of difficulty of finding criteria with which to compare the tests.

Another problem is that when a divergent thinking test correlates positively with some criterion, this could be due to the verbal intelligence component rather than the specifically divergent component of the test. And as verbal intelligence is much more conveniently and efficiently measured by standard tests, it would be stupid to use divergent ones until they are proved to add significantly. Getzels and Jackson, and Wallach and Kogan, in their classical studies of divergent thinking tried to overcome this by contrasting children who were high in divergent with those who were high in convergent performance.* Cronbach (1968) pointed out that this was a statistically inefficient technique, and that multiple regression analysis, which first allows for convergent prediction and then isolates divergent, is much preferable.

*In Wallach and Kogan's study, comparisons were also made with those high on both types of ability, and those low on both.

Studies with children

To summarize some of the main findings: Torrance (1965) and Yamamoto (1963) claim that children rated as showing 'curiosity', or as having most original ideas, score highly on divergent tests; the same holds for pupils nominated by their peers as having 'wild and fantastic ideas'. However, other studies yield correlations of less than 0.3 with ratings, and even lower when intelligence is held constant. Torrance also arranged for small groups of high, medium and low-divergent pupils in elementary school to discuss and demonstrate scientific toys, and observed that the high scorers contributed the most ideas.

Getzels and Jackson's (1962) study has been criticized on several grounds, including the unrepresentativeness of their sample. However, they did show some interesting characteristics as differentiating the most divergent from the most convergent. Both groups were good achievers, though the divergers were not much liked by their teachers, and the children themselves were aware of this. For their own friends, they preferred such qualities as wide range of interests, and sense of humour, to the more conventional signs of ability and success; and they were unusually adventurous in their vocational choices. They showed more imagination and humour in projective story-telling. Finally, they came more often from entrepreneur families, whereas the most highly intelligent were more often children of professionals (cf. chapter 8).

Wallach and Kogan's (1965) carefully designed study of fifth graders showed, among other findings, that children high on divergent *and* convergent tests were generally the best adjusted to both teachers and peers. They were mature and intellectually flexible. Those high on divergent but low on convergent were more often in conflict with the school and with themselves; they felt inadequate except in nonacademic subjects or activities where their imagination could blossom. Those with the reverse pattern of scores were devoted to intellectual values, intolerant of unconventional ideas, and were often cool and aloof to other children. They felt threatened by more permissive teaching or unstructured school activities. Finally, the below average in both types of ability were intellectually bewildered, and apt to indulge in compensatory behaviour, but tended nevertheless to be more sociable and confident than the two preceding (unbalanced) groups. Many other complex findings are quoted which are difficult to follow since they often differed for the two sexes. But Cronbach's reworking of the data by multiple regression analysis indicated that divergent tests seldom added much of significance to the information provided by convergent.

Numerous investigations of correlations between divergent thinking and school achievement have given somewhat contradictory results; and there seems to be no consistent difference between different school subjects, presumably because the relevance or irrelevance of divergent thinking depends more on the way a subject is taught and examined than on its content. Thus Haddon and Lytton (1968) found higher average divergent scores in more progressive English primary schools, which emphasized self-initiated learning, than in more formal and conventional school (though the two sets of schools were matched for IQ). These differences persisted to some extent when children from both types of school were retested in various secondary schools four years later (Haddon and Lytton, 1971). However, Lytton and Cotton (1969) were unable to confirm that type of teaching approach in the secondary school affects divergent test performance.

In Australia, Dewing (1970) gave four Minnesota divergent thinking tests to twelve-year-olds, and developed a criterion of the children's creativity in daily life from teachers' and peer ratings, gradings of imaginative compositions, and two questionnaires dealing with leisure time interests and attitudes to creative activities. The overall correlation (actually a contingency coefficient) between the scores and the criterion reached 0.39, when IQ was held constant, showing a moderate degree of validity. Similarly Vernon (1972), working with some 400 Canadian eighth graders, employed a composite criterion of ratings, marks given to compositions for creativity and maturity, leisure-time artistic and scientific activities, and drawings. His total divergent thinking battery correlated 0.51 for boys and 0.63 for girls with this criterion, suggesting that a shorter and well-standardized battery could be of diagnostic value to educational psychologists or school counsellors. However, much of the prediction was attributable to verbal intelligence, and when this was held constant, the validities dropped to 0.29 in boys and 0.42 in girls; thus it became more doubtful if the tests are worth the trouble. Note too that these figures represent concurrent validity; for longer-term predictions of creative capacities, the superiority of the intelligence tests to available divergent thinking tests might well be greater.

In relation to personality, Vernon's study provided no confirmation that high-divergent children are disliked by teachers or peers. Indeed the girls were distinctly above average in sociometric popularity, though there was some indication from personality questionnaire responses that they were strong in qualities of leadershp and independence, and showed more cultural, athletic and especially artistic interests, and fewer conventional feminine and social interests. The highly divergent boys gave a somewhat different picture, being more nondescript socially, but particularly likely to show strong science interests and achievement. In the personality area they showed a strong need for achievement, methodicalness, and positive self-concepts, and to conform to school and adult standards rather than expressing rebellious or independent opinions — a finding which fits in neatly with Parloff and Datta's study of talented boy scientists (cf. p.82). Torrance (1965) and Lytton (1971) have suggested that high-divergent thinkers are more popular in schools which place more value on creative learning than in highly formal schools.

Studies with adults

Turning to studies of college students and adults, the evidence is very patchy. Some investigations do report positive correlations of divergent scores with assessments of creative achievement among research scientists (Shapiro, 1968), university Ph.D. students (Torrance, 1969), airforce captains (Drevdahl, 1956), public relations men and advertisers (Elliott, 1964) etc., yet no-one seems to have sufficient faith in the tests to advocate their regular application in selecting creatively-talented workers. Presumably most psychologists are put off by the difficulties of standardized administration and scoring. Both Cropley (1967b) and Hudson (1968) report small-scale follow-up studies where divergent tests were given to university students on entry and showed no agreement with first-year academic performance, but did appear to be more predictive of third- or fourth-year achievement. The obvious implication would be that, during the first year, courses and examinations tend to be highly factual and rather rigid, whereas later on at least some university staff begin to welcome more originality among their advanced students. But here, too, no-one has followed up this lead.

Earlier (1966) Hudson had found a marked tendency for divergent males, in English secondary schools and university, to specialize in arts subjects, convergers more frequently in science subjects. He argues strongly that divergent thinking should not be identified with creativity (and we agree with him), but that divergent and convergent thinking represent contrasted cognitive styles or defence mechanisms, which different students adopt for coping with ideas and people. The converger tends to avoid personal relations; he likes a settled, conformist, world, together with school subjects or jobs where he knows where he stands (cf. Wallach and Kogan's findings). He is somewhat of an authoritatian, or at least respectful of authority. The diverger is more flexible and easy-going in personal relations (though not in fact more extraverted). His fluency does not mean that he is more creative, except perhaps in literary composition; rather he uses a flow of words to avoid hard thinking. But although Hudson presents considerable evidence for these ideas, the situation is far from simple. In countries other than England, where specialization in arts and science subjects is more likely to be postponed to age 18-20, instead of taking place at 15-16, the same association with divergent-convergent does not seem to occur. Also, it is mixed up with sex differences, since girls are less likely than boys to choose science; and Hudson has shown that adolescents tend to regard the scientist as masculine, the artist as feminine. In Vernon's study, described above, divergent thinking seemed to have quite a different significance in the two sexes. Relevant here, also, are Ausubel's critical comments (1968). He writes: 'Creativity is one of the vaguest, most ambiguous, and most confused terms in psychology and education today ... Scores on measures of divergent thinking are indeterminably contaminated by such factors as fluency and glibness, uninhibited self-expression, impulsivity, and deficient self-critical ability.'

Although divergent tests seem to tell us little that is useful about adult abilities, they give rather more consistent predictions of cultural interests. Wallach and Wing (1969) gave much the same tests as Wallach and Kogan's to 503 freshmen, together with a questionnaire covering their accomplishments in various extracurricular fields — music, science projects, student leadership etc. A general intelligence or Scholastic Aptitude test failed entirely to correlate with such activities, though it did give moderately good predictions of freshmen grades. However, divergent test performance was related to accomplishments in the visual arts, writing, science, and student leadership. It did not work as well in the social service area, nor in music and drama presumably because good achievement in the latter depends more on executant skills than on creative artistry and interest. Torrance (1969b, 1971) has gone a stage further by testing two groups of students in Senior High School and then following them up, one group after seven years, and the other twelve years later. As adults they filled in a questionnaire about their careers and avocational activities, and their responses were rated for creativity. The original test scores gave correlations of around 0.40 with this follow-up criterion. If this finding were confirmed, it would suggest that divergent tests possess quite useful validity for some purposes. However, another long-term follow-up of tests given to seventh grade Canadian pupils showed that they did not contribute significantly to the prediction of either academic or non-academic accomplishment six years later (Maslany, 1973).

Possible improvement in tests

In general, then, divergent thinking tests are disappointing. They do elicit some kind of 'imagination', and are related to certain personality traits and interests, but too inconsistently to be of much practical value. Why should this be so? One reason may be that they do not, like convergent tests, supply the testees with any clear task. The subjects can, and do, interpret what the tester wants in all sorts of ways. Another is that the tasks are mostly so superficial: why should anyone bother to think creatively, or to express their full potentialities, in suggesting uses for a brick, or saying why a cat and a mouse are alike? In contrast, they have to use their brains to the utmost in tackling difficult intelligence test problems. Certainly there is no resemblance to the emotional drive, the dedication and lengthy labour involved in works of creative genius, or even in the research of a moderately talented Ph.D. student. A third mistake that appears to have been made by 'creativity testers' is the assumption that all manifestations of creativity require the same kind of verbal fluency and unconventionality. Surely the scientific imagination is very different from the literary-artistic, and probably other types, even apart from the technical skills that they involve. At secondary and more advanced levels it should be possible to pose more realistic problems, providing scope for imaginative solutions, in, say, scientific, literary, and social (understanding of people) areas. An analogy might be drawn with the Thematic Apperception projective test, where 'focused' pictures such as those involving achievement, affiliation, or other explicit needs seem to give more worthwhile results than the original version, which was too ambitious in trying to give scope for the expression of both conscious and unconscious aspects of the 'total personality'.

In other words, a worthwhile test of any aspect of creativity should be as nearly as possible a sample (or set of samples) of the kind of behaviour or thinking it is supposed to measure or predict. This, of course, is true of almost any test, whether of aptitude, achievement, or personality, though it is often forgotten by psychologists who hope to devise miraculous shortcuts.

Consider, for example, the selection of graduate students for Ph.Ds. It is hoped that they will do creative research work, largely on their own initiative, as well as reaching a high level of academic achievement in their area. Staff selection committees have the greatest difficulty in choosing good students, usually on a basis of previous academic grades, and references from previous teachers. (Sometimes good references from another university seem to be written because the staff there are anxious to get rid of the student.) Occasionally scholastic aptitude or intelligence test scores (e.g. the Miller analogies) are taken into account. So far as we know, no university department is giving divergent thinking tests in addition, though Torrance implies that they would be valuable for the purpose. Would it not be better to obtain a set of relevant worksamples before committing the student, or some grant agency, to the expenditure of $10,000-15,000, and two to three years of his working life, as well as keeping out some other student who might have benefited more? In his undergraduate, and still more in Master's level courses he could be required to prepare literature surveys of fields that interest him, and to carry out minor pieces of research which should be certified by his supervisor as representing his (the student's) ideas and efforts rather than other people's. This kind of thing is commonly done in many departments, though usually rather haphazardly, especially when the student applies from another university.

An obvious difficulty is that it involves a lot of subjective judgment; it is by no means a standardized test. Nevertheless, in the writer's experience, the assessment of work of this kind reaches quite a high level of reliability. When faced with concrete evidence like a literature survey or a report of an experiment, independent staff members do tend to agree rather closely on its merits and defects.

Some implications of these ideas for the assessment of gifted children will be discussed in the next chapter.

7 Identification of gifted pupils

Any plan for identifying gifted pupils must, of course, depend on the type of programme that is envisaged. For example, does it involve removing the children who are picked out to another school, full- or part-time, or to separate classes or small groups within their present schools? Schemes of this type, as we will see in chapter 10, can often work successfully; and selection of children for such schools or classes is a fairly straightforward task. However, these schemes are often criticized as 'élitist', and nowadays there is a general preference for arrangements which avoid labelling any particular group as 'gifted'. Various alternative terms have been coined, e.g. AcTal (academically talented), HAP (high academic potential), MGM (mentally gifted minors), MPH (matriculation programme honours) etc.; though any of these, of course, will be seen through by parents who are jealous at some children apparently getting more privileged treatment than their own. A more acceptable aim is to diagnose, and work out more individualized programmes within the school, for any who need them. Alternately, optional interest groups may be formed where an element of choice is left to pupils and parents, but which, in effect, cater for different ability levels.

Obviously, testing policies will have to be geared to these contingencies. However, in this chapter we will be concerned mainly with selective identification. If that is the situation, decisions will have to be reached on how many gifted children can be catered for with the available staff, what facilities are available for the specially talented; is the focus to be more on upgrading or enriching the instruction of gifted children in the core curriculum, or on providing more scope for pursuing special interests during the children's free time? Then there is the point already mentioned (p.65): Do we apply a fairly uniform borderline of ability in all schools, e.g. mostly in the 130 + s? Or do we think more in terms of those who are much above the school average, whether this falls at IQ 115 or so, or at 90 or below? We emphasized at the end of the same chapter the need for a flexible rather than a fixed borderline of ability.

Age range

The first problem to be discussed in more detail is the age range of children who are most likely to benefit from any special provision. Obviously it is desirable to recognize and encourage the development of talent from as early an age as possible. But in the light of the variability of intelligence with growth (chapter 2), it would be most unwise to rely on tests, or to try to make educational decisions before the age of 5 or 6.* Although many children attend nursery school or kindergarten from 4 years or earlier, and the exceptionally gifted ones may already score mental ages of 6 years up, most psychologists would be reluctant to put much trust in the stability of their IQs. It would be advisable to wait until children have had at least six months in an American or Canadian Grade 1, or an English second year Infants Class, though with occasional exceptions, and many would prefer to postpone till third grade or 8 years of age. Another reason is that, in more progressive school systems, the kindergarten and early grades are becoming more flexible, and are catering fairly effectively for the brightest children by individual and small-group work. Thus it seems unnecessary to introduce special schemes until the more rigid régimes commonly found in third or fourth grade begin seriously to frustrate the highly gifted. (This does not imply that parents who can afford it should not send younger children to high-ability private schools, though there is little evidence as to their advantages.) Too early classification of children into bright, average and dull, or A, B and C categories, as frequently happens in English primary schools, is positively disadvantageous for the reasons discussed in chapter 10.

Nevertheless we must admit some disagreements on this matter among educationists and psychologists. It seems that bright and apparently mature children who are admitted to first grade before the regular age generally maintain their lead

*Musical talent is exceptional in sometimes showing itself definitively at much earlier ages, though here too the promise observed at, say, 3 years may not develop.

(cf. chapter 9). Martinson and Lessinger (1960) claim that reliable identification of gifted children is possible at 4½ because of their advanced mental age. And they mention a study in California where kindergarten children took the Pinter-Cunningham test and Goodenough Draw-a-Man in group form, and were rated by teachers; and that about one-half of the high scorers were subsequently found to have Terman-Merrill IQs of 130 up. It would seem then that a rough screening is possible before the age of 5; but later retests would be essential for discovering those whose ability had previously been either over- or under-estimated.

At the other end of the age scale, say 16 years up, there is also less urgent need now that so many senior high schools, and English sixth forms, have courses at different levels for more, and less able students, or arrange programmes geared to individual abilities and interests. In addition, school clubs often provide scope for special talents. By this age, also, the student, his parents and teachers, have a pretty realistic notion of what he is capable of doing. Thus, the most important age range, from our viewpoint, is from 8 or 9 to 15, that is the period when education tends to be conducted by the cheapest mass methods. It is unfortunate also that in most school systems there is a break at 11-12 years, between elementary and secondary schooling, since there is not much point in encouraging students in, say, Grades 4 to 6 to progress in their own rate, and then regrouping them simply by age, and reimposing a standard curriculum for all in Grades 7 to 9.

Intelligence tests

It has already been stressed that we should not rely on any rigid IQ borderline for defining the gifted. Nor will any combination of scores from several standardized tests suffice to provide a mechanical diagnosis. Nevertheless, especially in trained hands, the intelligence test can provide the single most important predictor, particularly over the age range of 7 or 8 to 15. Intelligence continues to grow beyond 15, but at higher ages Intelligence C (test results) seems to become less representative of Intelligence B (all-round ability), presumably because the short items, usually given at speed, provide a poorer sample of the complex mental processes involved in academic or vocational tasks. And there is no satisfactory evidence to suggest that the breaking down of intellectual functioning, along the lines Guilford pursued (chapter 4), yields any higher validity.

At any age a single test is to some extent unreliable, both because of its limited sampling of intellectual functions, and because of its tendency to be affected to some extent by conditions of administration, rapport or by chance factors. Thus it is preferable for a school system to apply appropriate tests every two years or so and enter the results on a cumulative record card. Consistently high scores or IQs, or a rising trend, provide a much surer basis for predicting future ability.

The best available instruments at the time of writing are the Terman-Merrill (or Revised Stanford-Binet), with 1972 norms, for 4½-8 year olds, and the WISC-R Verbal or Full Scale for 8-15 years. It should be remembered that the SD or spread of IQs on the former is rather larger than the latter; i.e. IQ 132 on the former would be equivalent to 130 on the latter. Individual testing is, of course, time consuming and therefore expensive, since specially trained personnel must be used. Such testing therefore becomes a major component in the costing of any scheme for the gifted. Hence, the possibility of substituting group tests, at least for initial screening, should be explored. For older children, say from 10 onwards, an up-to-date group test, e.g. the Lorge-Thorndike, will do quite a good job. It is an advantage to include verbal and non-verbal sections in such a test since the nonverbal part will give a better chance to budding scientists and mathematicians. However, entirely nonverbal tests like Raven's Progressive Matrices have quite low predictive value. Again the largely pictorial group tests for quite young children, e.g. from 5-8, are almost useless and apt to be very misleading, since their scores or IQs have quite low correlations with any kind of scholastic achievement or with later IQ (cf. Hopkins and Bracht, 1975). What would be better would be an orally administered verbal group test for 6-10 year olds, which does not depend on having to read complex instructions. Unfortunately, although one or two of these have been published (e.g. Cornwell, 1952) in England, there seem to be none that have been widely applied, or standardized in North America.

We would also advise against factor group tests such as Thurstone's PMA, or Differential Aptitude Tests like the Bennett D.A.T., even at the junior high school level. These provide profiles of scores on several factors or abilities which might appear to yield more information than a single global IQ (or verbal and nonverbal IQs like the Lorge-Thorndike). But a lot of follow-up evidence is available, especially on D.A.T., which shows that such tests simply do not differentiate effectively. Whatever the criterion, the same subtests tend to show the highest validities — usually the verbal and non-verbal reasoning, while the other scores such as spatial, number etc. add very little. Being fairly short, the separate subtests are low in reliability, and Spearman's 'g' factor (or Thurstone's V + R) is too prominent for other more specialized talents to be diagnosed. However, if school psychologists or counsellors trained in testing can conduct and interpret the tests, they may find certain advantages in differential batteries.

Especial care is needed with the norms or score distributions of group tests, since they vary considerably from test to test. Many of them have insufficient ceiling to yield IQs much above 125. Thus the tester who is trying to identify, say, the top 2½ per cent (corresponding to 130 + on WISC-R) would do better to collect norms from his own school, or school district, and find which score is in fact obtained by the top 2½ per cent. It is perfectly possible to obtain group test IQs differing up to forty points from individual test IQs at about the same time, partly because of norm differences, and partly because the group and individual Intelligence Cs are far from perfectly correlated. Pegnato and Birch (1959) attempted to compare the efficiency of several different techniques for picking out gifted 14 year olds. In a school of 781, 91 students were found to be in the top 1 per cent with individual test IQs of 136 and over. Nominations by teachers of those whom they considered to be gifted, identified only about half of these high IQ students; and a group intelligence test identified much the same proportion when 125 IQ or over was used as a cut off. However, the group test was distinctly more efficient in that it identified fewer 'false positives' — i.e. students diagnosed as gifted whose individual test IQs were below 136. Each method gave about the same number of 'false negatives' — i.e. failures to identify students who were in the high IQ group. Any other test employed and student nominations were even less efficient. In interpreting these findings we should, of course, remember that the individual IQ itself is an imperfect criterion. We have no means of determining all those who should have been singled out as gifted; nor do we know whether all the 91 merited this description. Thus the chief lesson from this investigation is that different indices of giftedness do not correlate very closely, and probably several such indices should be used rather than relying on any single one.

Group tests certainly have some value in preliminary screening, especially among students aged 10 or more; but clearly it is necessary to allow rather wide limits. For example, if we are hoping to catch the 2½ per cent with 130 + individual IQs and the majority of 120s + with special talents, we should probabaly take all the top 10-15 per cent on the group test for further consideration. It would not be necessary to test all the 15 per cent individually, only those who exhibited one or more other signs of giftedness such as teacher nomination or evidence of special talent.

Coming back to WISC or WISC-R: particular caution is required in interpreting Performance IQs. These do not (like paper-and-pencil non-verbal or spatial tests) relate highly to scientific-technical aptitude. Thus, the Verbal IQ alone is likely to be a better predictor of most scholastic abilities than the Full Scale, which incorporates verbal and performance. However, when the Performance IQ greatly exceeds the Verbal, say by 15 to 20 points or more, this may be suggestive of some linguistic handicap such as coming from a foreign language-speaking, or highly deprived, home. If other evidence backs this up, more credence can be given to the Performance IQ as an indicator of the child's intellectual potential. It is quite possible, for example, that an immigrant child to Britain, the USA or Canada may be potentially very brilliant, though handicapped temporarily by language difficulties.

If individual testing is to be attempted before the age of 6, it would appear that the Terman-Merrill scale, or the McCarthy Scales of Children's Abilities are the best choices. Wechsler's WPPSI for 4-6½ year olds does not correlate as highly as one would like with later IQs.

Any of these individual tests give the tester useful opportunities for observing fluency and quality of verbal expression and reasoning, breadth of interests, perseverance at intellectual and constructional tasks, concentration of attention etc. No one has investigated how reliable and valid these judgments are; but sometimes the tester can discern giftedness better than the child's teachers. Conversely, he may recognize that some of the high achieving pupils recommended by the school are merely of good average intelligence but lacking in any vital 'spark'. We do not recommend any particular score profile on the WISC subtests as particularly indicative; all the verbal subtests, including Digit Span, should be high, and the Block Design is the most useful subtest in the performance section.

Creativity testing

We return to this topic once more since several writers such as Gallagher (1965) and C.W. Taylor (1962) urge that reliance on convergent-type intelligence tests picks out the wrong kinds of students. The modern world, they claim, particularly needs Guilford's divergent, creative and innovative thinkers. Taylor points out that intelligence tests are almost useless in separating more effective and productive professionals, such as scientists or doctors, from the less effective. While we have already admitted above that these tests are less useful for predicting any kind of adult achievement, this criticism is unfair in that any test applied within a highly selected group tends to give low correlations. Intelligence tests still have considerable validity in more heterogeneous groups (e.g. for allocation of personnel in the armed forces). Children who later become professionals would almost all have obtained much above average IQs if tested between, say 10 and 15 years. Another point worth repeating is that the individual tests we have mentioned for selecting gifted children are much less convergent than the conventional group test, and therefore more likely to pick potentially creative individuals. Finally, we concluded, in the previous chapter, that divergent-thinking tests are too troublesome to score, and yield too little significant information about creative capacities to be worth using on any large scale.

However, it may be conceded that, when a psychologist is concerned with identifying small numbers of candidates for special programmes, scores on a divergent battery might occasionally help to show whether some of them are capable of more original thinking than their teachers give them credit for; or conversely whether others are too prosaic to benefit much from the programme. The Minnesota or the Torrance Tests of Creative Thinking might fulfil this need, but a better collection of subtests could be put together; and the psychologist who wants to use them should prepare his own local list of common and unusual responses, rather than relying on lists from a somewhat different cultural group.

Another approach which has shown more promise than divergent tests is the Biographical Inventory. Possibly it works because it focuses more on personality characteristics than on abilities. The instruments devised by Schaefer and Anastasi for diagnosing creative boy scientists and artists, or girl artists and writers, at senior high school level, have been described earlier (p.83). The long-term predictive value of these instruments does not seem to have been followed up, but they did show moderate validity when tried out on additional high school samples.*

Another inventory by Taylor and Ellison (1964) was built up of items which discriminated between more and less creative adult research scientists. This covered a wide range of childhood, adolescent and current interests, creative school or leisure activities, favourable factors in the home background etc. In cross-validating successive versions of the test with various groups in creative-type occupations, Taylor claims consistent correlations with supervisors' ratings of around 0.5. Unfortunately, similar instruments are not available at junior high or elementary school levels. Consequently, in discussing the identification of children with creative talent, below, we have to fall back on the 'work-sample' approach which was recommended at the end of chapter 6.

Special aptitude tests

Before discussing other types of test, let us try to clarify some of the frequently used terms:

Achievement refers to performance in any defined field of human ability, such as reading comprehension, running one

*Actually the scoring keys were obtained by analysing the responses of 4 groups of 50 boys, and 4 groups of 50 girls. These keys were then applied to additional groups of 50 who had been similarly rated by teachers. The following cross-validation coefficients were obtained:

| Boy scientists | 0.35 | Boy writers and artists | 0.64 |
| Girl artists | 0.34 | Girl writers | 0.55 |

mile, painting a picture, or grades in mathematics. Clearly these depend on the instruction and training given as well as on the person's aptitude, motivation and interest. Often they can be assessed by objective (e.g. multiple choice) tests, though some types of achievement are more complex, or qualitative rather than quantitative, and must be evaluated by subjective judgments from teachers or experts.

Aptitude refers rather to the capacity to achieve well in the future, given suitable training. *Talents* are the same as aptitudes, though the term usually implies exceptionally high ability. A musically talented child, for example, is probably in the top 5 per cent or less on any measures of musical capacity. We have already shown in chapter 4 that aptitudes and talents are neither innate potentialities, nor acquired skills, but resultants of the interaction of genetic tendencies with environmental stimulation and practice — much like Intelligence B. Thus one cannot tell whether a child has considerable aptitude for music unless he has had plenty of opportunity for learning music, and developing skills in singing, instrumental performance, composition, or listening etc.

Does this not mean that aptitude is identical with achievement to-date? Not quite, since one can use other more indirect signs in predicting future achievement. For example, one may judge that a child has an aptitude for learning Spanish before he has actually learned any Spanish, on the basis of the observation that he has done well in English and French, and shows interest in language learning.

Psychologists are popularly supposed to possess a whole arsenal of tests for measuring aptitude for any and every vocation or talent area. Unfortunately this is far from true, and there are very few tests which are likely to be of much help in diagnosing the kinds of talent listed earlier. Those that have been published are intended mainly for 16 year to young adult level, and even these tend to have disappointingly low validities when compared with subsequent criteria of achievement; that is, they seldom contribute much more than ordinary intelligence tests, or previously administered achievement tests.

The area in which most test development has occurred is that of mechanical ability. Although included in our list of talents in chapter 4, it is, of course, of rather minor interest in the present context. Only rather rarely would special arrangements be made in a school for a talented boy to spend free time on mechanical or constructional activities. However, a brief review will be given.

There are various practical tests based on assembling mechanical objects, or on formboards (cf. Paterson and Elliot, 1930). These are time-consuming and expensive, and do not possess up-to-date norms for 9-15 year boys. The Block Design in WISC is relevant, though it is more a 'g' or general ability test than a spatial-constructional one. Much more widely used are group tests based on pictures of mechanical and physical operations, such as Bennett's (for Grade 9 upwards). This is of moderate value, e.g. for vocational counselling of older boys, though one doubts if it adds much more than would a ten-minute conversation with the boy regarding his mechanical and technical interests and information. What sort of things has he actually made (specimens might be asked for)? What does he know about materials, tools, electrical and other terms etc.?

In the visual and decorative arts, there are some tests of appreciation or taste, based on judgments of pictures of artistic objects. These have little relevance for predicting artistic skills, and are again standardized mainly for college students and adults. De Haan and Havighurst (1957) and Havighurst *et al.* (1955) mention a series of informal tests devised for talent identification in a scheme at Portland, Oregon. For example, several drawings or paintings done by promising children were rated for talent by art teachers or consultants. Similar methods of screening were used in the areas of creative writing, music, drama and mechanical aptitude, and social leadership was assessed from sociometric nominations.

In music there are several possibilities. The best known tests are Seashore's Tests of Musical Talent. However, these are based on the out-worn theory that by testing sensory capacities such as sense of pitch, time, rhythm, intensity etc., one could assess the capacities basic to musical aptitude. In fact, they contain so little musical content that they are quite poor predictors. The tests also tend to be too difficult for younger children. More up-to-date tests such as Drake's Musical Aptitude tests and Bentley's Measures of Musical Abilities do make use of musical materials. The best validated battery is Wing's Standardized Tests of Musical Intelligence. This contains seven subtests on records or tape, covering auditory recognition and appreciation of harmony, rhythm etc. Norms are available (for English children) between 7-15 years. Though lengthy to apply, the battery can be particularly useful when there are doubts as to whether a child is sufficiently musically talented to benefit from music lessons.

School Achievements Marks or grades given for classwork, or scores on standardized achievement tests, can be of value in areas like mathematics, possibly science, and social studies. Gifted children will usually score well above their age or grade level. But tests and examinations can also be misleading since they may not provide scope for advanced talents. For example, the teacher who is trying to teach his class long division is unlikely to give credit to the pupil who has taught himself algebra. Likewise, English and Language marks tend to be given for qualities other than those shown in imaginative writing. As pointed out in chapter 1, a considerable proportion of the most gifted do not shine in ordinary class work, since they have not received the opportunities to develop, or to display, their real talents. They may be poorly motivated to achieve well on conventional skills as taught by conventional teachers. Thus, it would be unwise to insist on a high level of all-round achievement before admitting a child to a programme for the gifted. This might cut out the very ones most in need of help. On the other hand, there are likely to be many children with IQs around 120-28, who are achieving straight 'A' grades, but who are better left to continue their successful progress in a conventional curriculum, since they might react adversely to a more flexible environment.

Parental information

One might expect that parents should be more aware of their child's gifts than is the school, since they have much more opportunity to observe his intellectual capabilities and leisure-time activities when he is following his own inclinations. True, many of them pester the school to accelerate him or to make other special arrangements. Their observations and suggestions should be considered carefully, but unfortunately they do often exaggerate and indulge in wishful thinking, having had little chance to compare his accomplishments with those of others of his age. Still worse, they may be pressuring the child by giving extra tuition at home so that temporarily he is achieving quite well, and yet he lacks the general intelligence or other talents needed for future progress. Such a child might well do poorly in a class for the gifted where much depends on his individual initiative.

On the other hand there are, of course, many families where the parents are too uneducated or unconcerned to observe anything unusual in their child's abilities. Not only do they provide no encouragement at home, but also resent suggestions from the school. If we did rely rather largely on parental diagnoses and aspirations, the tendency to favour middle-class over lower-class children in programmes for the gifted would be increased.

The attached questionnaire was devised for circulation to parents in a Canadian city school system, in order to provide background data on the need for special provisions. Obviously it could be modified or much expanded to meet local needs. The school, or the psychologist, should be able to make some judgment of the genuineness of the case from the answers to Question 10, and then to follow-up, or perhaps interview the parents if they appeared already to be doing their best on the child's behalf.

SCHOOL BOARD ENQUIRY INTO GIFTED CHILDREN

Parent's name and address _____

The _____School Board is aware that there are, in the city's elementary and junior high schools, a considerable number of children with exceptionally high abilities or talents. Some of these, who are capable of much more advanced work than most of their classmates, may not get as much encouragement or opportunities as they deserve. It is hoped, therefore, to introduce a scheme for identifying such pupils, and helping the schools to provide better opportunities. Information from parents would be valuable in planning any such scheme. Either father, mother, or guardian, should fill in the questionnaire with respect to each child whom they believe to be exceptionally able or talented, and return it to the school.

1 Child's name _____
2 Boy/Girl 3 Age (years and months) _____
4 Name of school _____ 5 Present grade _____

6   What are the characteristics of this child which make you think that he or she is much above average in ability? Please check any of the following that apply, and add others if you wish.

a   Spoke fluently, and used difficult words, by 3 years old   _____

b   Learned to read at 4 to 5 years   _____

c   Showed an intense, continuing, interest in some special area from an early age
Which area? _____

d   Shows exceptional understanding of advanced topics and ideas   _____

e   Shows remarkable knowledge of many topics, and very good memory   _____

g   Shows unusual imagination and original ideas in his leisure time activities   _____

h   Show exceptional initiative and independence in games or hobbies, or doing things for himself   _____

i   Says that his school work is boring because it is too easy   _____

j   Always gets very high grades at school   _____
Others: please specify _____

7   Estimate the number of hours per week (outside school hours) that he or she spends on reading   _____

8   What are his main reading interests (types of books, magazines, newspapers, comics, encyclopaedias, travel, science, literature etc.? _____
_____

9   What are his or her special hobbies and interests (e.g. collections, making models, photography, drawing, and painting etc.)? _____
_____

10   What do you do to encourage him or her to develop their talents and interests? (Check any of these that apply)

a   Supply more advanced books   _____

b   Supply scientific, model-making, painting, or other equipment   _____

c   Encourage use of the local library   _____

   d Arrange for music lessons   _____

   e Family excursions to museums or other places of
interest   _____

   f Encourage him to watch serious TV programmes
rather than popular crime, sport, or comedy
programmes   _____

   g Give help with school homework   _____

   h Teach him or her more advanced maths, science,
foreign language etc. than is available at school   _____

   i Go to concerts, theatres, or good films   _____

   j Discuss political or world news with him or her   _____

      What else? _____

11 Have you yourself (or your wife/husband) got a
special interest or talent which you would be
willing to share with a group of gifted
children? _____

Teacher nominations

Since neither tests, school marks, or parental information
provide sufficient evidence by themselves, a good deal of
responsibility devolves onto the school for recognizing the
gifted. True, Pegnato's research (p.103) showed that teachers'
evaluations are also frequently inaccurate; and many
psychologists who write on creativity testing claim that
teachers tend to disapprove of the unconventional, creative
child. However, it is possible to draw their attention to
characteristics of gifted children which they should be on the
look out for. The following description was included in a
questionnaire to elementary and junior high schools in a
Canadian city, asking for information about gifted children in
their own classes:

   Please note that gifted children are not necessarily those who
   always get high grades, nor always the most attentive, docile
   and cooperative in the class, though they may be so. More
   important indicators include:
      They are either so much more intelligent than the rest of
   the class, or so talented in some particular area (e.g. mathematics, art, science etc.) that it is difficult to keep them
   busy and interested.
      They are quick learners, who understand advanced topics
   easily.

They are fluent and grammatical in speech, and have a large vocabulary.

They may have a remarkable range of general (or specialized) knowledge in one or more areas.

They often ask unusual (even awkward) questions, or make unusual contributions to class discussions. They display great curiosity.

They may produce original and imaginative work, even if defective in technical accuracy (e.g. poorly spelt compositions or poetry).

They show much initiative and concentration in working on topics that really interest them.

Several rating scales have been devised for use by teachers in elementary schools which have programmes for the gifted, and these cover much the same qualities as listed above. One that appears to be soundly constructed and easy to use is J.S. Renzulli and R.K. Hartman's *Scale for Rating Behavioral Characteristics of Superior Students* (1971, cf. also Syphers, 1972).

Further improvements in ratings or nominations would result if schools provided more opportunities generally for talents and high intelligence or creativity to display themselves. One cannot reiterate too often that abilities do not develop in a vacuum. They have to interact with relevant environmental experiences in order to become recognizable. Thus schools do not exist solely to train children in standard skills; they should also provide experiences which will make possible the diagnosis of future promise.

A useful analogy may be drawn from the world of sport. Keen adults keep a look out for promising tennis players, swimmers, footballers etc., and the community and the school provide many opportunities for budding adolescents to practise and improve their skills (e.g. swimming programmes). Coaches are often available, and they can select the most promising for further help and training. One wishes that something similar could be made available for young electrical engineers, or artists.

To some extent diagnosis by providing opportunity is carried out in everyday classroom questions and answers, and discussions. These should provide many opportunities for observing superior comprehension, reasoning, vocabulary and information, and expression of unusual viewpoints. However, a research by Gallagher, Aschner and Jenné (1967) brings out some of the limitations. Records were made of oral interchanges in junior high school classes, and these were classified under Guilford's five types of operations (cf. chapter 4). The enormous majority of teachers' questions and student replies were found to fall within the categories of Cognition, Memory and Convergent Thinking, plus a miscellaneous category including classroom management, routine affairs, praise, censure etc. Only about one twelfth of interchanges, on average, were classified as Divergent Thinking or Evaluative Thinking, i.e. open-ended questions which allowed scope for a variety of individual opinions and judgments. But there were wide individual differences between teachers and classes, and with better training teachers could surely expand such categories. In written assignments and homework, also, opportunities could be introduced for superior abilities to find expression, though these would, of course, be much more troublesome to mark and evaluate than multiple choice or simple completion tests.

Handwork, drawing and painting, unless very rigidly organized, do allow more freedom for individual effort. But the work that children produce, especially in elementary school, is apt to be very variable. Few of them will have acquired sufficient technical skill to display real talent. Yet if a child consistently creates apparently talented drawings or other art objects, it would be worth showing them to a qualified art teacher, or some specialist outside the school, who could judge whether additional facilities should be provided.

Many secondary schools have introduced optional subjects in Grades 7-9 (English forms 1 to 3 or 4), which aim to encourage individual interests, though the range of choice is naturally limited, and children may choose for the wrong reasons. School societies can also flourish at this age level and thus bring out talented actors, artists, photographers etc.

It is in project work that the gifted child has the greatest scope for displaying his abilities, interests, creativity and drive, his enjoyment of research and reading to obtain information, and his capacity to organize his materials. Moreover, this approach can be used profitably in many school subjects (or can cut across several subjects) at almost any age from about

Grade 4 on, given imaginative teachers who can think up appropriate topics, help children to follow their own ideas and evaluate the results. In effect such teachers are giving a psychological test to their students — a test which is a good deal more powerful and indicative than those which psychologists have at their disposal, though naturally more difficult to interpret because it is quite unstandardized and open-ended. It is more powerful also since it gets away from the notion that giftedness consists simply of exceptional abilities which can be diagnosed by intelligence, aptitude and achievement, and perhaps creativity, tests. It recognizes that the child's personality and interests play a major part in the production of a successful project; it is diagnostic because, more than any other scholastic activity, it makes him 'ego-involved'. The same, of course, is true of the miniature researches which were recommended in chapter 6 as the best approach to selecting able and creative graduate research students.

Personality tests

Some psychologists would favour giving personality questionnaires (like Cattell's High School Personality Quiz), or projective devices (e.g. the Children's Apperception Test or Rorschach Inkblot's), or interest inventories (e.g. the Kuder Preference Record), in diagnosing the gifted. Cattell and Butcher (1968), for example, claim that in the prediction of scholastic achievement, cognitive, personality and motivational tests are far more effective than cognitive tests alone. But we feel very dubious as to whether the results obtained in a few experimental studies would be borne out by routine administration. Not only is personality testing time-consuming and expensive, but also teachers could not be expected to administer, score and interpret personality instruments correctly. Interest inventories are indeed useful to school counsellors who provide guidance on educational and vocational careers, but they are not generally applied until after the age of 15 years.

Projective devices have their clinical uses in studying the emotionally disturbed child, but no one has shown that they help to identify the highly gifted. Even the 'need for achievement' apperception test developed by McClelland and

Atkinson gives very irregular and generally low predictions of actual achievement, although one would have expected achievement motivation to be highly developed in all gifted children. A more promising approach to TAT interpretation is described by M. Arnold (1962).

Discussion

Whatever techniques for identification are used, we should realize that it is not a single, once-and-for-all assessment. Rather it should be regarded as an ongoing process, and many pupils who may show insufficient promise when first considered should be reconsidered if their superior abilities become more apparent later. It must be expected, also, that there should be quite a number of drop-outs. These may have been mis-diagnosed, perhaps because their parents turned them into 'pseudogifted' (p.18). But others fail to fulfil early promise, sometimes for health reasons, lack of home support, decline in motivation, e.g. through unstimulating schooling, or from adolescent personality changes (cf. Burt, 1975). It is much better to withdraw from a programme any pupils who are found not to be benefiting from it.

We have no further advice to offer regarding the problem of recognizing giftedness despite poor background, linguistic, or other handicaps. De Haan and Havighurst suggest that the most frequently missed children are: 1 Those of low occupation status, or from deprived minorities, e.g. negroes and Indians; 2 Children in rural areas; 3 Girls. One might add that we are probably not doing the job properly if more than two-thirds of the children identified come from professional and upper-business-class homes.

Summing up: It is possible for an elementary or junior high school to run its own scheme, and pick out most of the 5 per cent or so most gifted or talented pupils. The principal or head teacher would need to be thoroughly keen and knowledgeable, and to be backed by his staff, the administration and parents. A fair degree of accuracy could be obtained, say from Grades 5 to 9, by applying a well-chosen group test (given recently, with precise adherence to instructions), obtaining ratings from teachers and consulting with parents.

However, it would be much more satisfactory if trained psychologists were involved in the selection. The recommended procedure would be quite closely analogous to that used with the seriously retarded or maladjusted, i.e. with other exceptional children. Teachers of classes within the relevant age range should keep a look out for the extremely bright and talented, using a rating scale such as that already mentioned. Such children would be referred through the principal to the school psychological service. A psychologist would give individual WISC-R or Terman-Merrill, and other tests if needed, interview the child, obtain fuller reports from the teachers, and enquire into home conditions and parental attitudes. He or she could then advise whether the child would benefit from an already existing programme, or plan in consultation with the school what other special measures might be feasible.

The main difficulty with such a scheme is, of course, expense, since it might involve roughly doubling the current number of school psychologists. However, a compromise might be possible whereby the school was responsible for group testing, and screening the most clearcut cases, and the psychologist was brought in to advise on the more borderline ones.

8 Home upbringing of gifted children

What has the psychologist to offer on the home upbringing of gifted children, and the conditions that foster or inhibit the growth of their talents? There are a number of useful books, simply written for parents, such as Ruth Strang's *Helping Your Gifted Child* (1960), F.N. Brumbaugh and B. Roshco's *Your Gifted Child: A Guide for Parents* (1962), and M. Parker's *The Joy of Excellence* (1975). We will summarize the points that they make later, but should first admit that there is very little solid evidence to back their arguments and recommendations. As already mentioned in chapter 3, it is very difficult to prove that any particular environmental factor affects mental development. Thus, we have no psychological recipe for bringing up children to be more intelligent, nor for moulding their personalities as we would wish. Very often they do absorb much of the values, interests, attitudes to work etc. of the parents and so to some extent turn out as the parents had hoped or intended. But we all know how often they prove to be different, or rebel against parental influence, especially during adolescence. Some who appear to have had a sound and sympathetic upbringing become wastrels or criminals, and it is seldom if ever possible to pin down what went wrong. Their gene patterns may have predisposed them to be temperamentally different; school experiences and the influence of friends may have affected them; or parental handling either in infancy, later childhood or adolescence may have been less appropriate than it seemed on the surface. They are more likely to rebel against society when society has thwarted them. Thus, the development of talent, or scholastic achievement, or creativity, are far less predictable, or explicable in terms of environment, than we commonly assume. It is possible to enunciate a number of rather platitudinous general principles which on the whole tend to foster good ability and a sound personality, but one can never be sure how they are going to work in any individual case.

We have dealt earlier (chapter 5) with the favourable effects on many of Galton's and Cox's geniuses of cultured and stimulating homes, and showed that some did not have such advantages, and even developed their abilities in the face of great obstacles. For example, Handel's desire to become a musician was strongly opposed by his father. Others, such as John Stuart Mill, were severely over-pressurized towards intellectual achievement from early childhood, and discouraged from mixing with other children or from indulging in normal play activities. Mill later admitted his lack of motor and practical skills, resulting from his upbringing. Likewise young Mozart's father trained his musical capacities intensively from about 3 years, and by 6 was exploiting him by travelling around Europe and displaying him to royalty and the public. True, Mozart had such exceptional talent that he took to this life like a duck to water. But it could hardly be regarded as suitable upbringing for a young child. Norbert Wiener (1953) has described his own unhappy childhood and education as a mathematical prodigy. It could, of course, be argued that these and similar creative geniuses would not have achieved as they did had they not been so strongly stimulated by their parents. We have no means of judging how beneficial or otherwise was the type of home upbringing, particularly in the case of persons who lived long ago.

The most illuminating researches in this area are those of Anne Roe into the personalities and background of eminent living scientists, and MacKinnon's work on highly creative and less creative architects, scientists, and other groups. Both have been described in chapter 5.

Most of Roe's scientists came from professional or other higher-class families, where there was a strong emphasis on intellectual values; and they were all of Protestant or Jewish background, no Catholics. More of them than one would normally expect were firstborns, usually with a long gap before the next eldest. This, together with the rather distant, impersonal family relationships would tend to encourage their self-sufficiency, isolation and concentration on developing their own interests. Many of them seem neither to have received nor given a great deal of affection. However, the social scientists were much more likely than biologists or physicists to show disturbed relationships with parents, and to be more dependent. Many had conflicts with their fathers and still felt rebellious; in other cases the mother had been dominating and the father inadequate. As with Terman's geniuses, the childhood interests of Roe's scientists often foreshadowed their later specialization, but they showed considerable versatility, and they might sample and do well at a number of diverse areas during their schooling before finally choosing their main field as adults.

MacKinnon provides relatively little detail on childhood background. But he notes that several of the architects did not experience favourable life circumstances in happy homes. Those whose fathers were cruel and unsympathetic were no less creative than others who identified with adequate father figures. The most frequently observed characteristic was that either the father, or mother, or both, were themselves artistically inclined, and encouraged the boys in such activities as drawing and painting.

In Nichols and Holland's follow-up of National Merit scholars (described in chapter 5), the correlations of creative achievements with parental variables were rather low and irregular, though this is to be expected in highly selected groups. However, a number of them were psychologically meaningful and statistically significant; for example, the level of parental education showed positive relations with several of the criteria, father's education being more important in male students, mother's among girls. Generally the parents (particularly the father) of the most able students seem to have been more permissive and democratic, less authoritarian, than those of the less successful. They encouraged self-reliance and ambition in their children, and were less concerned with conventional, socially-conforming traits.

This fits in with the observed tendency of highly authoritarian societies (e.g. Sparta) to be less productive in the arts and sciences than more democratic societies (e.g. Athens, Renaissance Italy). But it would, of course, be extremely difficult to define precisely the nature of these political régimes or social climates, or to assess them objectively.

Quite a different approach is to investigate the relations between environmental factors and children's IQs, or scores on divergent thinking or other tests. There is so much literature in this area that we can merely select a few examples. R.M. Wolf (cf. Bloom, 1964) interviewed the mothers of sixty fifth-grade children, and assessed the following home variables:

Parents' intellectual expectations of child
Intellectual aspirations for child
Information about child's intellectual development
Rewards for intellectual development
Emphasis on the use of language
Opportunities for enlarging vocabulary
Emphasis on correct usage
Quality of language models available
Opportunities for learning in the home
Opportunities for learning outside the home
Availability of learning supplies
Availability of books and periodicals
Assistance in facilitating learning

These combined variables gave a multiple correlation as high as 0.76 with the children's verbal group test IQs. As pointed out on p.30, the result by no means proves that a stimulating environment produces high intelligence. Also we do not know at what ages, or in what ways, the above kinds of stimulation were applied.

A somewhat similar study by Fraser (1959) of 408 12 year old Scottish children, and their families, yielded a multiple correlation of 0.687 between home variables and IQ, and 0.752 with school achievement. Apparently the most influential of the variables were:

Parental encouragement
Parents' own education
(Small) family size
General family atmosphere
Newspaper and magazine reading

A useful indication of the relevance of family atmosphere and discipline is provided by Kent and Davis' (1957) investigation of 118 8 year old children, who were given the Terman-Merrill and the WISC performance tests. Social workers visited the homes and interviewed the parents, classifying them under four headings:

Demanding, i.e. high expectations of intellectual achievement and behaviour (124.2, 113.4)
Over-anxious and protective mothers (107.3, 100.7)
Unconcerned or laissez faire (97.0, 103.0)
Normal, with tolerant but firm discipline (109.9, 110.4)

The average verbal and performance IQs are given in brackets. Clearly children from demanding homes scored most highly, especially on the verbal Binet test. The 'normal' children do well on both tests, but those with over-anxious mothers are good verbally and drop considerably on performance tests. Children of 'unconcerned' parents show the opposite pattern, being lowest on the verbal side. Again, of course, we cannot take such results at their face value; we do not know the parental intelligence levels, or whether intelligent parents are more apt to be 'demanding' and seldom 'unconcerned'.

A great deal of further research has been done purporting to show the effects of parental behaviour and attitudes on children's personalities and abilities (cf. Hoffman, 1964-6; Moss and Kagan, 1961; Schaefer and Bayley, 1963). Too much of it, however, is based on parents' statements regarding child upbringing, and it is well known that the views they are willing to express may bear little relation to their behaviour in practice, still less — in all probability — to the way their children perceive and interpret their behaviour. One relevant study might be mentioned, where the home 'atmosphere' was assessed by direct observation by social workers, namely that of Baldwin, Kalhorn and Breeze (1945). On the basis of their ratings, homes were classified as democratic, acceptant, indulgent, rejectant, autocratic, casual etc. (or mixtures of these). By retesting the children's IQs, it was found that greater intellectual growth took place in the democratic and acceptant homes than in the rejectant, casual or autocratic homes.

Schaefer and Bayley (1963) carried out a long-term follow-up of children from early infancy to adulthood, using observation, testing and interviews. Both maternal and child behaviour were assessed on a number of variables, and the mothers' characteristics were classified under two main dimensions: Love *v.* Hostility, and Autonomy *v.* Strict Control.

The results are too complex to be summarized easily, but considerable correlations were found between maternal characteristics and the children's (especially the boys') social, emotional and intellectual characteristics, even into adolescence.

Weissberg and Springer (1961) studied thirty-two high-IQ children, who also took divergent thinking tests, and interviewed both parents. Parents of the more divergent or 'creative' children appeared to encourage their child's independence, did not dominate them, but recognized their individuality. Generally they were more relaxed, and were tolerant of 'regressive' behaviour, such as childish play and fantasies. The fathers tended to be in autonomous, i.e. self-directing, jobs themselves, and the families were not closely knit; each member tended to go his or her own way.

The best known study of this type, that of Getzels and Jackson (1962) also contrasted high-IQ, but low divergent children, with low-IQ but high divergent children, as already described (cf. chapter 6). One of the major home differences was that the fathers of the high-creatives were more likely to be in business occupations, those of high-IQ — low-creatives, in professional jobs such as teaching. The parents of the latter were less permissive, and more apt to pressure the children towards conventional social behaviour and academic achievement.

A more extensive study in Australia by Dewing (1970) tended to confirm these findings. She selected 12 year olds for high *v.* low creativity, both on the basis of divergent thinking tests, and on 'creative performance', i.e. teacher and peer ratings combined with check lists of creative leisure-time interests. The parents' answers to questionnaires sometimes related to one, sometimes to the other criterion, and often differed between the sexes, so that it is difficult to generalize. However, it appeared that the mothers of the highly creative were better educated, more egalitarian and less authoritarian, allowing children to choose their own friends and make their own decisions, and encouraging them in artistic interests and activities outside the home. They themselves were more independent in the sense of being less satisfied with the conventional home-making role. The fathers of the creative children tended to be more independent, original, less sociable, and the author claims that they had more influence on boys, the mother on girls. She refers also to Schaefer and Bayley's dimensions, and believes that her results confirm the importance of Autonomy, though not of Love *v.* Hostility, in the development of children's creativity.

One more experimental enquiry will be outlined, that by Coopersmith (1967), since it contradicts the rather common belief among psychologists that permissiveness and 'democracy' are the most desirable conditions for bringing up children in general. The author was concerned with self-esteem, confidence, and positive self-concepts among 10-12 year old boys. This characteristic was assessed both by a personality questionnaire and by teachers' ratings of the children. Though not directly relevant to giftedness (the correlation of self-esteem with IQ was only 0.28), Coopersmith argues that creativeness requires belief in one's own capacities; and a substantial correlation was found between positive self-concept and the Unusual Uses test of divergent thinking. From mother interviews he found greater acceptance and affection among the H than L parents (i.e. parents of boys with high and low self-esteem); but he disagrees with Schaefer's autonomy *v.* strict control dimension. His H parents were less permissive, and maintained high standards, though they were neither rejecting, punitive, dominating or authoritarian. Firm control was combined with recognition of children's rights and privileges (appropriate to their age). They encouraged freedom within established guidelines, and they preferred to resolve conflicts by discussion or reasoning rather than by arbitrary discipline, or giving in. It is under such conditions, Coopersmith maintains, that children can best build up strong internal controls. This conclusion appears to fit in with Barron's finding of high Ego-strength in creative architects, Roe's reference to high standards, Kent and Davis' 'demandingness', and other studies which mention encouragement of independence.

However, it is clear, from Cox and Terman's, Roe's, MacKinnon's and other writings that no one family pattern is ideal, and that there can be exceptions to any generalization about family 'climates'. There is no one best way of child rearing. Moreover, such terms as 'control', 'warmth' etc. are extremely vague, and liable to many different interpretations. Now let us try to survey the suggestions for bringing up gifted children, partly based on the research just described, but more often derived from general psychological theories of child development which, as we have seen, must be regarded with considerable caution.

The variability and unpredictability of children's development has been stressed already, but should be reiterated, as also the warning against placing reliance on intelligence tests given before the age of, say, 5 years. Parents are far too apt to seize on some early skill or interest, and expect this to grow into a major talent, and then to be disappointed.

Parents, again, may observe incipient scientific interests and buy the child expensive chemistry sets, models, a telescope etc., which he plays with perfunctorily and quickly drops. Much simpler materials often do more to stimulate his imagination, and provide more scope for him to develop scientific, artistic, or handwork talents. On the other hand, the common indications of later ability may be lacking in early childhood. For example, children who show no particular promise in language acquisition sometimes bloom later and become excellent writers or linguists. It is particularly important for parents to avoid projecting their own interests and talent aspirations onto the child. If both parents are scientific, or musical, the child may follow their bent, partly perhaps through genetic causes, more likely because he grows up in an environment where these activities are fostered. But in many cases he may be entirely disinterested in them, or show high capability in something quite different. It may often happen that children of parents who were frustrated in obtaining a good education, or following their own choice of career, do do well academically and vocationally and thus realize the parental ambitions. But they are less likely to achieve such success if they are constantly pressured towards scholastic or other achievements than in a family where it is taken for granted that children enjoy learning and trying their best, i.e., where the 'need for achievement' is built up indirectly. Those who feel ever-driven by parental wishes are quite likely to fail; or if they realize that their parents are making exceptional efforts on their behalf, they are apt to develop guilt feelings because they cannot live up to their expectations. Neurotic defence mechanisms may result, or they may compensate by delinquent behaviour. More generally, attempts to plan a young child's whole career on the basis of early accomplishment seems at least as likely to lead to rebellion during later adolescence as to fulfilment.

The dangers of over-pressurizing are constantly emphasized by psychologists though it is obviously difficult to draw the line between this and the encouragement of serious interests, of the 'work attitude' (cf. p.17), and the maintenance of high standards. The child should not be told that he is exceptional, nor get the impression that the life of the family centres around him, particularly if he has older or younger siblings. They may be less gifted than he is, but they are sure to show abilities in other directions; each should receive the same care and affection and be valued for what he is. Relatives and visitors should likewise be dissuaded from drawing invidious comparisons between the gifted and other children in his hearing.

Undesirable pressuring often involves overscheduling the gifted child's time, for example, insisting on his doing extra homework, practising the piano, or other skills, thus leaving insufficient time for relaxation and independent play. Young prodigies do sometimes 'burn themselves out', perhaps through being over-stimulated during childhood, though it must be admitted that others seem to thrive on parental direction of most of their activities, and to fulfil their early promise as adults. But as Dr. Spock has stated, more mistakes are made by parents who try too hard than by those who are more relaxed. Regarding homework, parents can take a reasonable interest and indicate that they are always willing to help, without insisting on completely accurate arithmetic and spelling, or extreme neatness before the child is sufficiently mature. Quite a lot of otherwise able adults are remarkably weak in mathematics or spelling, the most likely reason being that they have built up a 'complex' regarding the difficulties of these skills in childhood.

While the parents of a gifted child can reasonably expect that he should do well at school, and should praise him for his success, they should also be tolerant of inconsistent achievement. Being top of his class throughout his school career is not necessarily desirable, since it may mean that he is becoming unduly 'convergent', and losing his initiative.

Exploitation or showing off to admiring relations and friends is particularly to be avoided. Some parents, finding their offspring quick in picking up scientific facts, try to train them to become walking encyclopaedias, or put them in for TV competitions. Others get them to memorize and recite poetry in public. Things acquired by rote learning or enforced drill (as distinct from the reinforcement of arithmetical and language skills by constant use) seldom last. Also, encouraging a child to use his talent to show superiority to others is likely to rebound by making him unpopular at school or when playing with other children. It is better to try to build up the idea that his talents should be used to help others, rather than for his own and their benefit.

Another point constantly made is that gifted children are children first and foremost: they should be valued and treated as such, rather than just for their achievements. Their frequent precocity in, say, speech or reasoning sometimes leads others to respond to them as though they were far more mature than their age, and thus to forget that — physically, emotionally or socially — they are much more childlike. Brumbaugh and Roshco give a good example, namely the 6 year old boy who for his birthday wanted both an atlas and a cuddly toy. John Stuart Mill at 7 years was intellectually an adult, yet at the same time a child who believed in Santa Claus. Similarly Norbert Wiener, entering Harvard at 12 years, was still a child in social relationships.

Treating the gifted as normal children

What are the main needs of children over the preschool and elementary school period — needs which are as important for the highly gifted or mentally retarded, as they are for the average child? The following should certainly be included.

1 The bodily needs for food, shelter, health and physical security generally.

2 Psychological security — the need to feel wanted and accepted by parents, and other significant persons; to receive sympathy and help when distressed or in difficulties; to be provided with a stable structure for his existence.

3 Social needs — to be accepted by and cooperate with other children of about his own age; to identify and conform with their interests and activities.

4 At the same time there is the need, even from 2 years or earlier, for individuality and independence. He is not merely dependent on the family and peer group, but wishes to venture out, explore and establish his own competence and achievement.

5 The need for play — both physical play for exercising and perfecting his bodily skills, constructive play for gaining mastery over objects, social play with others, and fantasy or imaginative play for acting out his emotional conflicts and anxieties (cf. chapter 5).

If there are differences in respect of these needs between the very bright child and the average, they are likely to arise because he may receive less acceptance from peers, and sometimes from school teachers, who do not understand his level of thinking. Moreover, he is probably more sensitive than usual to the attitudes of others towards him. Hence, he requires greater help and understanding, and support, at home. This is all the more true of the exceptionally intelligent, for example, those with IQs over 160, since they are so different from the majority; whereas the 130's and 140's are usually better able to adjust to the interests and ideas of others.

While all these needs are important — more important indeed than intellectual stimulation — we are not implying that they should always be gratified freely, or that the gifted child should get everything his own way, any more than should ordinary children. He should not be shielded unduly from difficult tasks or experiences of failure. He has to learn to live with restrictions or rules which are appropriately geared to his age, and to cope with frustrations, disappointments and obstacles. Besides such obvious things as teaching him to avoid dangerous objects, and to respect the rights and property of others, he will benefit from having regular duties, such as clearing up his toys, helping mother with chores, and so forth. He will not necessarily be any quicker than other children in building up 'good' habits, though he is more likely to accept rules as reasonable if they are explained in terms he can understand. But intellectual advancement does not mean that he is capable of much greater responsibility, or maturity of judgment, than other children of his age. Both during the preschool stage, and as a school child, he is likely to be normally resistant and disobedient, to show occasional tempers or aggressive behaviour, and to test out his parents or teacher to see how far he can go, and whether he can get around them. Probably he will be more ingenious than usual in this kind of manipulation, and possibly more strong-willed. And because he is so successful in many accomplishments, he may all the more resent failures or criticism either at home or at school.

How much pressure adults should apply, and at what ages, or what blend of permissiveness and control must be an individual matter to be judged in the light of their understanding of his personal development. As the gifted child grows older, he should increasingly be treated as an autonomous person, with views of his own which are taken into account in family discussions and planning. By considering him as an individual in his own right, he is more likely to learn consideration for others. For example, more than most children he is apt to become absorbed in some intellectual, constructive or play activity, and to dislike being interrupted as much as adults do. It is reasonable, therefore, to give plenty of warning of meals, bedtime etc.

Difficulties can also arise with gifted children because, with their vivid imagination, they may suffer more from anxieties and conflicts or become over-dependent, or shy and withdrawn. What might, for example, appear to be overelaborate or morbid fantasies, such as persistent imaginary playmates, or 'tall' stories of incredible adventures, are by no means uncommon, and may well arise from some unsatisfied need. In general parents should be advised not to worry themselves about troublesome periods or minor maladjustments. Practically all children experience these at some time, and the great majority grow out of them without any special treatment. Only if there are persistent or severe problems which are also observed by teachers at school should parents seek help from the school psychologist or child guidance clinic. Such disturbances certainly can occur in very bright children, though on the whole less frequently than in the average or dull, possibly because they have a better understanding of their own and other people's motives. They can comprehend the reasonableness of adult advice and reassurance and to some extent work out their own solutions to problems. Psychologists, indeed, are very apt to underestimate the resilience and adaptability of children. True, a lot of people grow up to be neurotic, partly through unsympathetic handling during childhood. But far more achieve a fair degree of adjustment in homes where parents know nothing of Freud, but just rely on good sense, sound values and affection.

Fostering the development of talent

On the more positive side, the general principle of rewarding desired accomplishments applies at least as much to gifted as to average children. If constructive or creative behaviour is recognized and praised, it is more likely to recur in future; though at the same time it is unlikely to be trainable unless there is some predisposition in his genetic equipment and personality. Sometimes the parents of a gifted child, being themselves of above average ability and education, are apt to be unduly perfectionist, criticizing the weaknesses in his drawings, models, speech etc., or laughing at his childish writings or inadequate concepts. Nevertheless, careless or crude productions should not be praised to the same extent if there is good reason to suppose that he could do better.

One must remember that the child's self-concept, including his confidence and motivation to try, is built up largely from the way parents, other adults or children, respond to him (cf. Coopersmith, 1967). If he is told that he is stupid, timid, weak, and his attempts to learn or produce are denigrated, he will come to regard himself as inferior and behave accordingly (or else rebel and compensate by aggressive behaviour). Creative and highly talented persons are successful because they believe in themselves. Indeed, however high a child's IQ or his potential aptitude, he may accomplish very little unless he has also acquired motivation to learn and achieve, first of all at home, and later at school. Likewise, self-criticism of inferior productions can be instilled at home by giving discriminating praise or rewards only when they are deserved, and by constructive and helpful criticism of shortcomings. Obviously this self-evaluation is a fairly advanced acquisition; Piaget's writings would suggest that scrutiny of the adequacy of one's own ideas is not reached till the formal developmental stage at around 12 years, even in quite able adolescents. We would have thought that much younger children can begin to introject standards of adequacy in many everyday activities much earlier; for example, being properly dressed for some social occasion, completing an exercise carefully at elementary school, making neat cut-outs or model aeroplanes, completing tasks rather than just flitting from one whim to another, and so on.

Children learn at least as much by imitation, and

identification with a loved or admired person or group, as they do by direct experience. Thus it is important for parents to realize that what they *do* will have more effect than what they say should be done. In other words they should provide good models of the kind of qualities they wish their child to display, e.g. conscientiousness, orderliness, honesty, tolerance, courtesy and generosity to others, and respect for their rights.

Many other qualities are acquired incidentally through modelling on the parents, rather than by direct teaching: that a rational approach to problems is more effective than an emotional one; that one can best gain one's ends by resourceful effort, not by whining, temper tantrums or aggression; that education and cultural activities are of value — or alternatively that they are useless and boring. It has frequently been noted that the drop-out and failure rates at college are much higher among students whose parents have not themselves attended college, than among those in whose families there is a tradition of higher education.

It is accepted by many psychologists (even if not satisfactorily proven) that children acquire their basic sense of trust, confidence and outgoingness from warm relationships with the mother in the first year or so of life. Also she tends to be the major influence in the building up of speech and linguistic understanding. But the role of the father, particularly among boys, has been somewhat neglected by clinical and child psychologists. Since he is usually the central or dominant figure in the family, boys are strongly influenced by his attitudes and behaviour, e.g. good or bad-temperedness, his interest in cultural pursuits or lack of it etc. And if he is neglectful, unwilling to play with or take an interest in the children, they are less likely to achieve good adjustment. There is substantial evidence of his influence in the development of scientific and mathematical, spatial and constructional talents. Besides trying to teach his son practical skills in the home, he should let him know as much as possible about the nature of his own job, and his place of work.

It is important also that parents should share the same values and aspirations. Conflicts between them are apt to cause childhood anxieties which tend to be hidden or repressed. But we should remember Roe's findings on eminent social scientists. Distant, or discordant parents sometimes seem to stimulate certain kinds of creativity. Once again, parents should be warned about worrying too much, being too analytic about themselves or how they should treat their gifted child, or seeking guidance from psychological (especially psychoanalytic) theories. Within the kind of limits that we have tried to outline, it is much better for them to behave as their natural selves.

M. Parker (1975) makes some interesting suggestions regarding behaviour towards adult acquaintances who are not used to being contradicted by a gifted child, or being shown that they are wrong. Such a child will eventually have to learn respect for others and acceptance of social conventions, even if irrational; also to realize that other children and adults may be uninterested in the kinds of things that interest him. Without relinquishing his own standards of truthfulness, he will need to acquire 'survival techniques' for coping with the wider social world.

Interests and activities

While it is obviously desirable to encourage, and to provide opportunities for special talents, it is equally important to achieve a good balance of activities, for example, social and physical, not merely intellectual or artistic. Some gifted children avoid athletic and muscular achievements because they do not learn them so easily, or show the same superiority as in mental development. The body needs exercise as much as the mind, and childhood is preeminently the time for active, vigorous play. Caution may be needed against pressuring the child to play with others of around his own age; some gifted children seem to be natural isolates. At the same time, it is only through social experience that he will learn to cooperate and share with others. Even if difficulties occur because his ideas and interests are more advanced than theirs, he has got to learn to live with them some time. If he is very much more intelligent than average, it is better to seek out companions who are also superior; e.g. the 160 + IQ will fit in more readily with 130s + than with those of average ability. Parents should not be surprised if gifted girls appear excessively masculine or tomboyish in their preferred activities; and likewise gifted boys may like sewing, cooking or other conventionally feminine activities. Neither of these characteristics is invariably present, but gifted children seem less affected than others by the common sex-stereotypes.

Terman's study drew attention to the wide range and versatility of gifted children's interests. Reading and collections are the most common, but by no means the only ones. Constructional activities are popular, and involve concentrated thinking on how to achieve the desired object or model. Also they provide a sense of mastery over things when completed, and an enhancement of the self-concept. Piaget's theory of mental development is relevant here. He believes that preschool and preadolescent children build up higher-order schemata or more advanced concepts and understanding more by doing things and by practical experience, than by verbal means such as having them explained by adults. However, other psychologists such as Vygotsky and Bruner lay more stress on verbal symbolization and abstraction of experience; and probably there is an inter-play between the practical and the linguistic. Evidence has accumulated recently that the two sides of the brain have rather different functions, the left side being particularly involved in verbal and temporally organized activities, the right side in more spatial and practical activities (cf. Hebes, 1974). We may infer that it is important to stimulate both and to try to integrate their functions. Piaget also stressed that, while it is very difficult to accelerate the grasp of new concepts and principles — the child tends to find them out for himself when he is sufficiently mature — yet he can be provided with tasks, problems, experiences which are ahead, but not too much ahead, of his current level of thinking. He may become bored if activities merely require schemata that are already fully established, and frustrated if they are too far beyond his comprehension, but be maximally motivated if he can see and achieve some new competence. The more gifted a child, the more he is likely to be a 'self-starter', i.e. to seize on some challenging task and persist till he has accomplished it. (Hence his boredom with easy, routine, classroom activities.)

One of the reasons for questioning the somewhat secondary role that Piaget ascribes to language is the intense curiosity that the gifted child shows in everything around him, and the way he continually seeks verbal information. He asks not only about practical things, including scientific and geographical questions, but also about abstract matters of morals, sex, life and death. It is natural that parents should sometimes get tired of trying to answer, though in all probability their willingness to explain things in terms appropriate to his level of intellectual development and expand his primitive or half-formed concepts have a lot to do with fostering his development; and that answering by arbitrary statements, or refusing to be bothered, inhibits his growth. At the same time the opportunity should be taken whenever possible to show both that adults are not omniscient and some questions not soluble, and that it is possible to find out and learn more about the matter himself, e.g. by searching in a book, or by some form of practical research or direct observation. If everything is too easily answered, he may lose the desire to explore.

Appropriate toys and games, as well as books, can, of course, be useful, but we have mentioned already the value of simple materials, which encourage ingenuity in converting them into some construction. A common practice in homes where there are one or more bright children is to keep a 'treasure chest' or cupboard for boxes, sheets of card or coloured paper, spools etc., which are potentially useful for such purposes. Scrap books for pictures relevant to a special interest (e.g. engines, architecture) are also valuable. From about the age of 8, the gifted child can be encouraged to keep a diary record of a holiday tour, including postcards, drawings, photographs, menus of memorable meals, entry tickets etc. Somewhat like the play of the 5 year old, this helps him to mull over and digest experience, and to build up organized and stable structures in his memory.

Even if the child has little graphic art talent, drawing and painting are worth encouraging as another means of organizing experience and expressing fantasy. The same holds for dramatic play or acting with small groups of friends, e.g. charades, or acting out stories from a book.

From very early years up to the time when they become really fluent readers, bright children enjoy being read to, or told stories — either of a fantastic or fairy-tale nature, or accounts of what happened to the parents when they were young, or stories of animals' or young people's adventures. They can be introduced, too, to considerably more advanced literature than they would be able to appreciate for themselves till many years later. In addition to the emotional content of stories (e.g. expressing and resolving fears and anxieties) they add to his knowledge of words and sentence structures, and hasten the desire to read for himself.

There are many word games, similar to 'I Spy', or 'What's My Line?', which bright children and adults can play together, for example, during long car journeys. Gifted children, like others, enjoy comics, and low-level TV, and should be allowed to do so within reasonable limits. Margaret Parker, like many cultured parents, regards TV as a waste of time that should be spent on doing something constructive, and as purveying violence and false values. She believes that viewing should be restricted to good programmes, in company with adults. On the whole we disagree: it would cut off the children from a source of interest which all their peers enjoy, and which probably does to some extent stimulate mental development. If the poorer programmes are not forbidden, or denigrated, the children are more likely to tire of them and move on to more advanced programmes and reading. However, they should also be encouraged to occupy part of their spare time by themselves, not in front of the TV screen, nor always in company with others. They can be helped, too, to organize their time more efficiently, e.g. to do homework at a specific time in a quiet room; and TV should be turned off for everybody during this study hour.

One of the most important aspects of the development of interests and skills is that both parents should share in the child's enthusiasms, and be ready to spend time giving any help that is needed. This is more useful than ample provision of material objects. Sometimes it may be difficult since the parents of such children are often very busy people with numerous commitments. If they show themselves willing to discuss the child's ideas and concerns, and ask about the day's happenings at school or at play, he is more likely to bring into the open any difficulties he has experienced with peers or teachers, or conflicts which might otherwise build up into serious problems. If there are open relationships in the preschool and elementary periods, less reticence and lack of communication are likely to accompany adolescent development. At the same time the parents should avoid being intrusive, and try rather — as the child grows older — to convey their confidence in his capacity to develop along his own lines.

Schooling

Parents of gifted children tend to expect them to learn to read by 3 or 4 years, but there is no need to try to teach them so early. On the other hand, if they do begin to recognize printed words for themselves, e.g. on TV, advertisements or road signs, or story books, and seem spontaneously interested, it would be foolish to delay, even though some teachers are opposed to it. There is no evidence for a common belief that early attention to print is bad for children's eyesight. Reading should be accompanied by writing, since both are extensions of oral communication. Here a blackboard and chalk have advantages over paper and pencil.

Another common belief is that gifted children should go to nursery school or kindergarten as early as possible. While this may indeed contribute to their social development, and broaden the range of experiences, it is not necessarily the best policy. Some gifted children are less mature than others in independence and confidence, and may not be ready to cope with the school situation till nearer 6 years. Obviously, too, there is less necessity if the child has brothers and sisters who are not much older or younger than he (or she) is.

One would naturally expect parents to take great care in choosing a school — when a choice is available — which seems most likely to foster their child's abilities and interests. It may be difficult to find out beforehand whether one school is over-formal, mechanical and impersonal, or another too lax, or (particularly at secondary level) whether there is a strongly anti-intellectualist climate of attitudes among the bulk of the pupils. But enquiries from acquaintances, or visits to the school, can help.

Some parents of gifted children are overambitious and unreasonable in their demands for special privileges for their offspring, and are therefore apt to be regarded as a nuisance. Thus as far as possible parents should content themselves with the usual channels of communication such as parent meetings and regular interviews. Where necessary, appeals can usually be made to area education officers. If no provision is available for the needs of exceptional children, groups of parents can often do a useful job in galvanizing the education authorities into action. Their joint efforts may influence school trustees and administrators, or induce more interest among the general public in special education (for the gifted as well as the handicapped). Again they may seek to provide funds for special equipment or books. Margaret Parker (1975) points out that parents of the gifted should study local school legislation to find out what provision it actually makes for such children, and how far this is put into practice; also how other community agencies might help. However, they should avoid battles with other groups of parents, such as those of handicapped children. Discussion groups among parents, perhaps with an occasional invited speaker, can also be valuable in showing how others have overcome their problems of education and upbringing.

Parents should realize that children's complaints about occurrences at school need to be taken with a grain of salt. The gifted would hardly be normal children if they did not find some things boring, some teachers unsympathetic, some pupils bullies or snobs. The parents may be able to help their child more by pointing out to him that the teacher cannot give him as much individual attention as his mother does, than by attacking the school in his hearing, or being overly sympathetic.

Requests for early entry, grade-skipping or other forms of acceleration (cf. chapter 9) should be made only if they are sure that their child is sufficiently mature socially, as well as advanced in achievement, to work along with older pupils. Some requests tend to be rejected by the school, not merely because of administrative inconvenience, but also because they are not always in the best interests of the particular child. Also the parents are apt to forget that many others besides themselves would like the same privileges.

To sum up: parents of gifted children must realize that no school can ever be ideal for all its pupils, though most principals and teachers will cooperate if approached in a reasonable manner. They should also regard it as their responsibility to make up some of the shortcomings by appropriate activities at home.

9 Methods of provision: acceleration

Some American writers comment that actually less is being done in the 1970s to cater for the needs of gifted children than in the early sixties when, as we have seen, there was a spate of interest in the selection and encouragement of scientific and creative talents (cf. US Commission of Education, 1971). Often quite useful schemes, which may have worked effectively for years, are phased out, partly because of criticism by the general public, teachers or administrators, partly because other needs, e.g. for the handicapped or for early childhood education, seem more urgent, and sometimes because School Boards come up with a new plan, such as 'continuous progress' which, if fully put into practice, should make any extra provision for the outstandingly gifted unnecessary.

In 1971, a special report was presented to the US Congress of *Education of the Gifted and Talented*, based on consultation with 239 educational and psychological experts, and on extensive surveys of selected regions. It was found that 21 of the States had specific legislation mentioning the gifted, though this did not mean that any practical steps had been taken by all of them. In 24 States there was someone responsible for administration of education for the gifted, though more often than not he or she was part-time and had no support staff. Although Federal aid was available for innovative programmes, little use had been made of it. Nevertheless, there were systematic and well-organized programmes in certain States, particularly in California, Connecticut, Georgia and Illinois; and other noteworthy schemes were operating in many cities, some of which will be mentioned later. Perhaps the most striking finding from surveying a representative group of principals across the country was that 57½ per cent of them stated that they had no gifted pupils in their schools. Apart from a few notable exceptions, there was little or no formal provision in elementary schools, though occasional teachers and principals were doing what they could to give some enrichment to individual children in the classroom. A greater degree of differentiation of courses, and more part-time special classes, occur in many secondary schools, though again it is rare for additional personnel or facilities to be made available. However, it was reckoned that about one fifth of the likely total of gifted and talented students in the country were receiving some form of special services, and that the proportion is rising. One of the main recommendations asked for greater emphasis on the training of specialists in the field; and as a result a Leadership Training Institute on the Gifted and Talented has been set up by the US Department of Health, Education and Welfare.

The situation is similar in Canada. Most of the provinces have permissive legislation, but the total number of gifted students for whom some active provision was claimed was less than 1 in a thousand of the school population in 1969 (cf. Ballance and Kendall). Probably this did not include students who were accelerated, nor those receiving informal enrichment in their classrooms. Ontario and Manitoba appeared to be the most active, though the latter province is now switching to 'continuous progress'. However, there are notable exceptions to the general apathy such as special classes for gifted children in Grades 5 to 8, which have been running in London, Ontario and in Saskatoon for over forty years.

In England, as explained in chapter 1, less need has been felt until recently because of the high degree of stratification of the educational system. Besides the private (preparatory) and traditional public schools, there were — by the 1950s — grammar schools for the 20 per cent or so most able from age 11, a few technical high schools, and 'modern' schools for the majority. Also there was streaming or homogeneous grouping of classes within the majority of primary and secondary schools which had fair-sized yearly intakes, say of fifty pupils or over.

However, with the recent growth of unstreamed and of comprehensive schools, the Schools Council of the Ministry of Education commissioned a report on *Gifted Children in Primary Schools* (Ogilvie, 1973). This was based mainly on a broad sampling of teacher opinions and panel discussions. It revealed that many Local Education Authorities do not consider that gifted children constitute a special problem, and claim that they are adequately catered for by present methods of school organization; also they dislike any measures designed for particular groups (other than the handicapped). Nevertheless, there was a wide range of attitudes among teachers; a majority did agree that gifted children are not usually recognized at present, and that they merit as much attention as do the handicapped. But they generally insisted that any scheme should not cut them off from the normal school environment, implying that they should not be segregated full-time. In practice, head teachers have considerable freedom to make their own arrangements, and several examples of schools with interesting programmes are described. Some common misconceptions were noted among the teachers, for example, that the gifted are going to make good regardless of what the school does, or fails to do; also that the only remedy required for greater individualization of instruction is smaller classes.

Summarizing his panel discussions, Ogilvie lists the following as the main requirements for an effective scheme for gifted children.

1 They should be able to work along with others of similar ability level.

2 They should maintain ample contacts with peers of average ability.

3 Though not set apart, they should have the opportunity to work by themselves on occasion.

4 They need to be stretched or challenged, even to the point of experiencing failure, and being humbled thereby.

5 They should pass rapidly through the elementary stages of a subject to more advanced work, for which appropriate resources should be available.

6 They should be guided rather than directed toward a greater depth of treatment in their studies.

7 They should be able to pursue their own lines of research.

8 They require contacts with teachers who are expert in their various fields.

9 They should have opportunity and encouragement in exercising special talents.

10 Both children and their parents should have access to counselling.

11 Last, but not least, they need to be treated like ordinary children.

Some additional points may be gleaned from various sources (e.g. De Haan and Havighurst, 1957; Martinson, 1973; Roth and Sussman, 1974 etc.)

12 Attention should be paid to fostering personal and social, as well as intellectual, development, including understanding of, or empathy with, the needs of others.

13 Efforts should be made to bring into the scheme as many children as possible from minority group or lower-class families, even though they may initially appear less qualified linguistically or less outstanding in achievement than gifted or talented middle-class children.

14 It is necessary to win wide support for any scheme among local teachers, administrators, school board members, and parents generally. Schemes which have broken down have usually been those which failed to convince one or more of these groups. Particularly vulnerable are schemes which provoke competitiveness among parents, or resentment among those whose children fail to receive privileges accorded to others.

15 Many schemes provide solely for the academically gifted. If possible, help should be given to those highly talented in some special area, not usually covered in the normal curriculum, who may not be greatly superior in all-round academic promise.

16 Any scheme to be applied throughout a Local Education Authority, or School Board, district must be accompanied by some plan for producing trained personnel, e.g. through workshops and in-service training, university courses etc.

17 Any proposal should be carefully costed. Although inevitably more expensive than the education of the general run of children, the costs are likely to be much lower than those required for special education of handicapped children.

18 Any scheme should incorporate procedures for systematic evaluation of its success or failure. It is not sufficient to show that gifted children do better academically, or in other respects, than average children of their own age. It must be demonstrated that they do better than could have been expected in the absence of special provision, or better than a control group of comparable ability who received no such provision.

The following classification of possible methods is a somewhat modified version of a list published by Roth and

Sussman (1974). Naturally there is a good deal of overlapping between the items, and many schools or districts may combine elements from two or more.

I *Acceleration*
   1 By early admission
   2 Grade-skipping
   3 Grade telescoping, or intermediate classes
   4 Continuous progress — non-grading
   5 Additional courses in High School, and early admission to universities
   6 Advanced placement

II *Segregation*
   1 In separate schools, full-time
   2 Grouping or streaming according to ability, also referred to as 'multi-track', or differentiated instruction
   3 Specialization by multiple curricula, options or electives
   4 Setting
   5 Special classes, part-time, serving one or more schools
   6 Summer or Saturday schools; and extracurricular interest groups

III *Enrichment*
   1 Individual study, or small-group work within classes
   2 Library or resource room projects
   3 Use of community resources etc.

Acceleration

Conventionally this implies that a child with superior ability is promoted to higher classes or grades more rapidly than usual, and thus is able to work along with others who more nearly approximate to his level. It should not mean pushing him, so much as allowing him to progress at his own rate. Incidentally, this policy should reduce the range of ability present in classes promoted strictly on an age basis, and thus make the teacher's task easier. Usually, though, it involves skipping one or more grades, and thereby creates problems for the student in making up what has been missed, and for the teacher of the higher grade who may have to provide some individual (or at least small-group) tuition for a few weeks until he has caught up. This criticism tends to be exaggerated since, in fact, there is always a lot of overlapping between the work of successive grades. By giving a diagnostic test (even an informal, unstandardized one) it is quite simple to discover topics which the promoted child has not covered, and to restrict coaching to these.

Anyhow, teachers tend to disapprove of acceleration (particularly those who are convinced of the inviolacy of the conventional curriculum), and often rationalize by objecting that the bright student is not sufficiently mature, physically or socially, to work along with others older than himself. Though fairly common in Canada, the great majority of American schools nowadays disallow it, probably largely for administrative convenience, and because a rigid rule protects them against pressure by vocal middle-class parents who want their child to be advanced. However, the schools are much less hesitant about retaining the opposite device of requiring very backward students to repeat one or more grades.

The policy is far the most economical to apply, since it does not require any additional staff (except perhaps the services of a school psychologist for testing likely candidates). In so far as bright children might be able to complete 12 grades in 10 years, there would be a very substantial saving of costs for the School Board, and increased financial rewards to the ex-student who becomes qualified for a job that much earlier.

Although ambitious parents do often try to break the rule, possibly without sufficient evidence of their child's competence, a greater number tend to accept it, partly because they do not want the child to appear 'different', or they are not sure of his ability to cope with more advanced work, and largely because they fear disruption of his friendships with other children. Worcester (1956) mentions that some parents discourage acceleration since they hope that their bright boy who is kept back will be physically more mature, and thus stand a better chance of being chosen for school athletics teams.

Another danger sometimes occurs in rather rigid educational systems where there is insufficient continuity between successive stages; namely that children who have gained a year through acceleration in the elementary school are not accepted by junior high schools, but forced to mark time, or put back to working with their age-peers. Also, if parents move to another area, the principal of the new school may not accept the child's advancement, and return him to the usual grade for his age.

Canadian and British secondary schools tend to be somewhat more flexible, though it is seldom that more than 5 to 10 per cent are accelerated by 1 year, and the maximum is generally 2 years.

Most educators and psychologists indeed agree that it would be quite impracticable to organize classes completely on a mental age rather than a chronological age basis (cf. chapter 1). Two years of acceleration would mean covering the 12 years of schooling in 10: but a child of IQ 150 could, presumably, cover the 12 years in 8 years or less — other things being equal. However, Laycock (1957) makes the pertinent point that the accepted convention of organization on the basis of C.A. implies that such age groups are in some sense homogeneous. In fact, a class of children of the same C.A. vary enormously in physical ability and personality characteristics, especially at the junior high school level, when pubertal changes are occuring quite haphazardly.

Terman, in Vol. IV of his studies of gifted children (1947), carefully examined the evidence regarding the dangers of acceleration, and concluded that students who had been accelerated (in the 1910s and twenties when it was more commonly allowed) not only fully maintained their academic position and achieved better than their older classmates, but also showed no more social or emotional maladjustment than occurs among non-accelerated bright students. Other follow-up studies have given unanimous results. Individual cases may be cited by teachers or parents where acceleration appears to have been harmful but, at least with the present limitation to 1 to 2 years, it is far more often beneficial. There can be little doubt, also, that greater harm is done to the development of many children's personalities and abilities by refusal to accelerate than by acceleration. Worcester (1956) claims to have found that high IQ children kept back with their age-peers are less well adjusted than those accelerated.

We would strongly urge, then, that schools be more willing to consider this measure, in individual cases. Probably the decision should be based on a school psychologist's recommendation, reached after individual testing and interview with

the child, and consultations with principal and parents, as well
as the prospective teacher. However, this is only a partial
palliative in the case of the highly gifted (e.g. IQs well above
130), and is obviously inappropriate for those who are talented
in one or two areas, but not much above average in most
academic subjects. Let us turn, then, to other ways of
effectively bringing about acceleration, which help to
circumvent some of the disadvantages.

1 *Early admission* Although many school systems continue
to impose a rigid minimum age for entry to Grade 1, and
admit only in September, others allow greater latitude. For
example, some younger children may be admitted if the
principal decides, after seeing the parents and the child, that
he is sufficiently mature and independent. Sometimes
informal tests may be given, or the Binet IQ taken into
account. Also it is easier to assess the child's readiness if he is
already attending a nursery school or kindergarten since,
although his experiences there do not necessarily make for
better adjustment or progress in the primary school, the staff
can report on his developmental maturity. When bright
children are admitted a year under age, they can usually
maintain this advancement throughout their school careers,
and even be eligible for further acceleration later. More often,
however, the schools limit the concession to 6 months; and in
Canada (in some areas at least) and the UK, there is a regular
double entry per year system. This of course does nothing to
accelerate children who are well above the minimum age; but
it can provide up to 6 months' acceleration for brighter
children who are lucky in their birthdates. In addition, later
entry is often useful for retarding some very immature or dull
children, and perhaps save them the stigma and boredom of
having to repeat a year's work.

M.C. Reynolds (1962) has surveyed the pros and cons of
early admission, and concluded that it works well when
applied to limited numbers of bright children, who are also
superior in physical and social qualities; and it does not
produce difficulties of emotional or social adjustment. One of
the best known examples has been running at Brookline,
Massachusetts, since 1932. About one-sixth of all entries to
kindergarten (perhaps one-half of those who apply) are
entered 3 to 9 months earlier than the regular age of 4:9, on

the basis of an individual intelligence test and physical examination. They are found to maintain their superiority throughout their school careers, to take more part in extracurricular activities, and eventually to enter college more frequently than average (Hobson, 1963). Note that the early entry does not enhance their superiority as students; it simply picks out rather effectively those with superior qualities. Similar results have been obtained in Nebraska by Worcester (1956) In Saskatoon, Canada, some use was made of reading readiness tests and of the Vineland Social Maturity scale for early admission of about 10 per cent of Grade 1 pupils. However, with the wider availability of kindergartens it is being discontinued.

We should be aware of the unreliability of predictions of the future progress of 4 to 5 year old children, even when evidence from Binet or other tests is available. However, the follow-up studies indicate that they do possess substantial validity. In particular it is unlikely that any of the published group intelligence tests would be of diagnostic value at this age. If possible, any early entrance scheme should be supplemented by later identification and promotion of those not detected at entry.

Naturally early admissions cause some inconvenience to Grade 1 teachers, especially if newcomers can enter at almost any time, not merely once or twice a year. However, in so far as numbers are usually small, and as grading in the early elementary years is tending to become more flexible, there is no good reason why this device should not be more widely used.

2 *Grade telescoping* In many school systems in North America the total 12 year period is divided into 4 blocks of 3 years, e.g. Elementary Division I and II, Junior High and Senior High. In large schools with, say, 5, 6 or more classes to each grade, it is comparatively easy to arrange for one of these classes to cover in 2 years the instruction which the remaining classes do in 3. Thus there is no lack of continuity as with grade-skipping. Obviously the fast-route students have to be chosen carefully, e.g. on the basis of previous achievement and a recent intelligence test (a minimum IQ of 115 would seem desirable). But it should not be too difficult to select on entry either to Grades 4-6, or to Grades 7-9; and occasional errors of allocation can be recognized fairly early and rectified.

This plan seems to be applied most often in Junior High

Schools in the USA, that is at the period which is often the most bleak for the very bright young adolescent. He may have experienced some help and encouragement in individual work in elementary school, but is now thrown into a much larger, more impersonal, institution, where different subjects are taken by different teachers in a somewhat sausage-machine manner, and there is little regard for individual differences. The problem is less acute in English secondary modern or comprehensive schools because, as we have seen, ability grouping is generally, though not universally, accepted.

We have not met any reports to suggest that the 2 year Junior High for bright children is socially divisive, either because it creams off the upper 15-20 per cent or so and reduces their mixing with the remainder, or because parents resent some getting privileges which are not accorded to all. 'Special Progress' classes of this type have operated successfully in New York for many years.

At a younger age level a scheme for telescoping the first 3 grades into 2 years operated in the writers' own area, Calgary, for several years. All Grade 1 pupils took the Detroit Beginners test and were assessed by their teachers for achievement and emotional, social and health status. Some 10 per cent were admitted to the accelerated programs after consultation with their parents. A follow-up to Grade 12 indicated overall superiority to an average group, though the accelerated group were usually no better than, or somewhat below, a matched group of the same initial IQ who had spent 3 years in Division 1. However, the scheme lost popularity and was eventually discontinued, mainly because the pictorial group test given in Grade 1 had quite poor predictive validity. Thus many children were picked out by it as being exceptionally bright, but turned out later to be of only average ability, and some suffered adverse effects from their mistaken acceleration. As a result of what was essentially a faulty identification procedure, the policy of acceleration fell into disrepute, and is now replaced by the continuous progress scheme.

An interesting variant of acceleration through condensation is suggested by Syphers (1972). Bright children from several schools who have done well in the first two Grades are brought together for a 6-week summer programme, which equips them to move straight on into Grade 4. In this way they make up the necessary essential of Grade 3 work.

3 *Nongraded classes or continuous progress schemes* These, by contrast, are most frequently tried in Division 1, or occasionally extended to Division II. Another common label is the 'Levels' or 'Units' system. The whole of the work normally covered in 3 years is divided into a sequence of blocks or units, through which children move at their own pace. Thus they can accomplish it all in 2 years (or 2½ if there is Double Entry), and relatively slow learners can take 4 years. The system is being widely adopted in Canadian elementary schools. The details of organizing and administering such schemes appear to be formidable, though they have been successfully overcome in some schools, particularly those based on Open Plan buildings. In other instances, however, Open Plan schools seem to produce more chaos than organized instruction. Sometimes, also, continuous progress exists in theory, but there is considerable reversion to grade organization, with all children of a given year-group receiving the same instruction.

There is a marked trend in the USA to hand over much of the organization of continuous progress plans to the computer. Cowley and Glaser (cf. Weisgerber, 1971) describe the IPI system (Individually Prescribed Instruction) developed at the Learning Research and Development Center of the University of Pittsburgh. The elementary curriculum, particularly in mathematics and English, is divided into a large number of short steps or 'behavioral objectives', and instructional materials are provided for each of these. Tests of present ability and past achievement allow each child to be allocated to a suitable topic, and he studies this until he achieves 85 per cent success on a criterion-referenced test. The computer keeps a cumulative record of accomplishments and shows whether more practice is needed or what topic he should proceed to next. This is CMI (computer managed instruction), not instruction by computer or computer-assisted (CAI), though the two can be combined, as when parts of the instruction are supplied by computer programmes. The children can do their work at their own pace in heterogeneous classrooms or in open plan centres; and different students follow alternative paths, depending on the rate and extent of their progress. The teachers do little class teaching, though they provide a lot of individual tutoring, and small group work with a few students who are in difficulties. They also play a large part in writing prescriptions for the courses, and in diagnosing student needs, and evaluation. It is recognized that they require considerable retraining in order to undertake this type of education.

While agreeing that such technology can be of considerable help to teachers in keeping track of the progress of each individual child, it seems dangerous to suppose that the whole of education could be reduced to a series of predetermined objectives, particularly in the early years when children cannot read the instructions for their work units. Another point to bear in mind is that this kind of system is far too costly to be adopted widely outside urban schools in the United States, though progress is being made in the UK and Canada. Other ways of promoting individualized instruction are discussed in chapter 11.

4 *Additional courses in high school, and early admission to college* In many high schools in North America there is a fair amount of flexibility in choice of courses. Sometimes, therefore, the brighter students can take additional courses in advance of the normal age, which allows them to graduate from school a year earlier. Alternatively, since schools may lack the equipment and the staff for college-level work, arrangements may be made with local universities or Junior Colleges for outstanding 11th and 12th grade students to be released from school and take certain first-year college courses, and thus shorten the period needed to achieve a degree. In an experiment on early admission where high school students took such courses 1 or even 2 years younger than average, they outdid the performance of their normal-age classmates (cf. Fund for Advancement of Education, 1957). Nevertheless, early admission has not caught on to the same extent as our next category.

5 *Advanced placement* This likewise means giving high school students college level work, and offering them credit if they successfully past entrance examinations. Thus, while they do not enter college till the normal age, they obtain exemption from certain elementary first-year courses, and can gain their degrees earlier. This scheme started in a small number of American schools and cooperating colleges in the early fifties, and has spread rapidly. It is now operated by the College Entrance Examinations Board. Such students not only get

their degrees in a shorter time, but also tend to obtain above average grades (cf. School and College Study of Admission with Advanced Standing, 1956). Correspondence courses are provided by some Canadian universities with a similar object, though usually only for students in rural high schools, or for mature (post high school students).

Some educationists nevertheless argue that it is preferable for very bright students to spend the full period in secondary school and to undertake more enriched activities at their normal grade level, instead of making accelerated progress.

In Britain there is some flexibility over age of entry to university, but, so far as we are aware, no arrangements comparable to the American Advanced Placement. One obvious reason would be that English university work is not organized in the same way around set courses and credits.

Yet another approach which has attracted considerable attention is the 'positive intervention' carried out by Julian Stanley (1973) at Johns Hopkins University. He searches out highly talented mathematicians and scientists at the age of 14 or under, using specially designed tests of high-level abilities. He then plans special programmes in the school or at university to bring them on at their own pace. These are often quite unconventional, and involve cutting much of the red tape which normally restricts educational advancement. He has also been able to show that this rapid acceleration and early entry is not accompanied by severe social or emotional problems. Unfortunately, of course, it is only a few who are lucky enough to gain this privilege; but the fact that it does work on a small scale should encourage secondary schools and universities generally to experiment with more adventurous policies.

10 Segregation — full or part-time

1 *Separate Schools* The British system of selecting for secondary grammar schools by the eleven-plus tests was briefly described in chapter 1, together with its erosion and gradual replacement by comprehensive (non-selective) schools. While there are some justifiable criticisms, it did and still does yield undoubted benefits for the more able pupils.

Thus it is commonly noted that students entering British universities from the grammar and independent (or 'public') schools are approximately two years ahead of their American and Canadian counterparts. Part of this difference would be due merely to the much smaller proportion who receive tertiary education in the UK. Naturally the average ability of the top 10 per cent of the population is higher than the average of the top 20 to 50 per cent. But, in addition, higher standards are expected, and obtained, when almost all students in selective schools are likely to have IQs over 115; when they are more strongly motivated and receive more encouragement from their homes, and when they are usually taught by more highly qualified teachers, in smaller classes, and have access to better facilities (e.g. science and language laboratories). Morale, or pride in the school and its traditions, tends to be stronger, and the teachers are generally backed up by the parents in maintaining firmer discipline than is commonly found in non-selective schools.

At the same time there are certainly disadvantages, and though these tend to be exaggerated by the critics, it is worth looking at them in some detail (cf. Vernon, 1957a), since many of the same difficulties are apt to recur when any form of grouping by ability is tried out in North America.

The major complaint is that selective schooling promotes snobbery and élitism, and that it exacerbates and perpetuates socioeconomic class differences. It removes the bright student from everyday contacts with the general run of his age-peers.

Moreover, students who fail to gain entry to such schools are largely (though not entirely) barred from entry to university, and likewise from most professional or executive type employment, or even from clerical jobs, regardless of their personal qualifications. Thus selection at eleven-plus was not merely selection for a superior education, but selection for a life career.

There is considerable substance in this criticism as applied to the English public school or to the private schools which exist in the USA and Canada. Nevertheless, if parents prefer to pay large fees to give their children what they regard as a superior education and type of upbringing, it would seem undemocratic to deny them the right. In the UK, moreover, selection to grammar schools is based on ability, not on parental wealth, hence the argument is weakened in so far as the most able and intelligent children from the working classes receive the same privileges as children of middle- and upper-class families. Indeed, intelligence tests were introduced into the eleven-plus mainly on the grounds that they would help to negate, rather than perpetuate, social class influence. This answer is, however, unsatisfactory in so far as we admit that intelligence and achievement depend considerably on advantaged *v.* disadvantaged background. Left-wing critics are also suspicious that the system simply removes the bright working-class child from his natural setting and tends to imbue him with middle-class values.

The question of social mixing or separation is also a complex one. According to Passow and Goldberg (1962), bright students in segregated schools or classes in the USA do *not* develop feelings of superiority, nor is there a change in their attitudes to children in other, less favoured, schools. Indeed, they tend to become more humble when working along with others of similar ability than when they were obviously more able than the great majority of children in a regular (unselected) classroom. Nevertheless, a study by M. Smith *et al.* (1971) of students in London, Ontario, who had spent four years in a selective school showed clearly that they did tend to lose neighbourhood friends, and instead to form more friendships with fellow-students.

Another point that has been raised is that, in the selective school, able children get less opportunity for leadership than when they are spread out among regular schools. We would doubt this because the club and other activities tend to be much more developed in selective schools, and thus provide more opportunity for various kinds of initiative.

Probably more serious than the boosting of self-concepts among the selected students is a possible lowering of morale among those not accepted. There is little direct evidence for this, but presumably it would occur mainly among the borderline students whose parents had strongly pushed them to pass the entry examination or tests. Much has been written too, on the inferiority feelings and consequent lowered motivation of children who know that they are regarded as stupid; and this point will come up again when discussing homogeneous grouping. Thus tests like the eleven-plus are apt to become self-fulfilling prophecies. On the other hand, the critics often fail to realize the remarkable resilience of childhood, and to ignore the obvious likelihood that the moderately bright, average and dull children may be happier working with others like themselves, than they are when the very bright members of the class always get the top marks and most of the teacher's approval. Goldberg (1965) did find improved self-concepts and more contributions to class discussions when slow-learning pupils were in a class by themselves. A further aspect of this issue is whether average and duller children benefit from contact with the more advanced thinking of the bright child. Possibly this is so, though De Haan and Havighurst cast doubts on it, and evidence is hard to come by. It is equally arguable that the less bright are depressed by realizing that they can never emulate the bright. Even if there is some loss to the less able, the challenge to the bright child of working and discussing with intellectual equals or superiors surely more than compensates. A point which we admit below is that bright children who remain in the regular classroom can sometimes help duller ones in understanding their mathematical or other work better than the teacher can. But this involves deliberate organization of small-group work which is rather uncommon in the majority of schools.

An entirely different, yet at least as important, criticism is that no predictions of ability to profit from selective secondary education can be completely accurate, since children's intellectual growth is irregular. Some blossom in their abilities and interests during the secondary years, others fail to fulfil the promise of their elementary school achievement of IQ. The English eleven-plus tests (usually English, arithmetic and verbal intelligence), when compared with later performance in the secondary school, yielded validity coefficients which were probably higher than those quoted for any other large-scale examination or other type of selection procedures. After correcting for restriction of range, these often exceeded 0.80. And yet even this figure permits of a considerable number of erroneous predictions. The situation can be illustrated by the following table:

		subsequent	
		success	*failure*
		20	80
selected by eleven-plus tests	20	13	7
rejected	80	7	73
	100		

Assume that we use the tests to pick out the top 20 per cent, and that it is possible, later, to find out who actually were the most successful 20 per cent. The table, representing a correlation of 0.80, shows how many were wrongly accepted or wrongly rejected. It can be seen that approximately one third of those selected (7 out of 20) fail to do well, and that 7 of the rejectees (nearly one tenth) would have done better, if given the chance.

Some follow-up studies have been carried on to university level, and here the correlation between eleven-plus results and getting a good university degree are much lower, especially among scientists (Nisbet and Buchan, 1959). It is only to be expected that students should change and develop during their secondary schooling, and yet the separation of the more from the less able at 11 years is supposed to pick out all those who will be likely entrants to university 6 or 7 years later. It follows, then, that the eleven-plus system of selection is wasteful in that it prevents some proportion of potentially able students from receiving the education they deserve. However, this has to be balanced against the wastefulness of trying to provide advanced secondary education for the great majority of students who could never reach university standards.

Even more obnoxious was the common tendency, at least in larger English primary schools, to grade their children into upper, middle, and lower streams at about the age of 7 years. This would be done largely on the progress made in reading from 5 to 7, and would naturally give an advantage to children from middle-class backgrounds who had received better linguistic training, and were generally more adaptable to school learning. Once in these A, B and C classes, they would mostly tend to stay in them, with rather little regrading (cf. Barker Lunn, 1970), since the As would progress at a faster rate, and it would be difficult for a B, virtually impossible for a C, to catch up. So that although all children took the eleven-plus examination, almost all the As and perhaps a few Bs would be certain to pass, and none of the Cs. In effect, the, a child's life career was being largely determined by a teacher's grading of achievement at age 7. Thus the major weakness of the eleven-plus system was that it made almost irreversible educational decisions at too early an age. We say 'almost' since a few transfers were possible after age 11, and more advanced courses were made available to the 80 per cent in the secondary modern (non-selective) schools whereby an alternative route to higher education and university was provided for a small minority.*

Under these circumstances, it is not surprising that selection had a tremendous 'backwash' effect on primary schools, parents and pupils. Teachers tended to concentrate most of their efforts, at least in the two final years, on training those skills which were required for success in the tests; and although new tests were made available every year, their format and content were pretty standard. Many schools even spent considerable time on coaching children to do group intelligence tests; or if they did not do this, parents frequently sent their children to outside tutors for coaching, e.g. on Saturdays. Careful investigations revealed that coaching and practice were to some extent effective in raising scores, though less so than the schools and parents believed (cf. chapter 3). And once a certain degree of sophistication in taking tests had been reached, very little further improvement in scores was possible (cf. Vernon, 1960). Many activities, probably of

*Universities of the Air, or the Open University in Britain, nowadays provide further opportunities for people whose education was inadequate. But obviously they cannot make up for talent that was wasted during schooldays.

greater educational value, were dropped from the curriculum as a result. Also — except in areas where a written composition was set — children could succeed in passing the multiple-choice English test and enter secondary school without ever having had to write complete sentences, or to formulate their thoughts on paper.

The critics further claimed that great stress and strain were imposed on 10-11 year olds, partly by the schools, but mainly by naturally ambitious parents. However, an attempt was made to obtain evidence from schools psychologists of mental disturbance attributable to the eleven-plus, and it appeared that serious anxieties were apt to occur only among children who were already emotionally maladjusted (Vernon, 1957a). Again then, we must insist that children of this age are highly resilient; they have already had to cope with many stressful situations and will face worse ones in the future. When both the school and the parents take a reasonable stand, and avoid conveying the notion that failure to 'pass the eleven-plus' will be catastrophic, children can readily take it in their stride. However, this does not condone the obvious fact that the system of once-and-for-all selection can have undesirable emotional and instructional effects on children with less sensible parents and teachers. And it is very necessary to avoid the recurrence of similar circumstances in planning for special (segregated) schooling of gifted children at the present time.

It is sometimes claimed, too, that students in selective schools are overworked, and that the competitive atmosphere is unhealthy. With this we have little sympathy since, if the students are selected for high ability, they are more likely to fulfil their promise if they are fully extended. A demanding climate is by no means inconsistent with encouragement of individual study and initiative.

Another line of argument draws attention to the current trend towards reduction of segregated education for any type of exceptional child. Instead of special schools or classes for the mentally subnormal, the maladjusted or the physically handicapped, the tendency is towards 'normalization', or integrating the deviates as far as possible into schools for the ordinary range of students; and many advantages are claimed (cf. Dunn, 1973). Surely then this is hardly the time to press for greater segregation for children who are exceptionally bright, rather than exceptionally backward. Actually, of course, integration of the handicapped into normal schools is almost always partial, not complete. Though there is intermingling for many school activities, the severely handicapped receive the major part of their instruction in separate classes, where specially qualified teachers employ specialized methods and equipment. Were this not so, there would be considerable danger that the education of the majority would deteriorate through the teachers having to spend so much time helping the handicapped minority. Many of the alternatives for gifted children, described later in this chapter, likewise aim at part-time segregation only.

A very different approach to the advantages and disadvantages of selective education is provided by the large-scale international comparative studies of achievement by Husén (1967) and his collaborators. Representative samples of students in a dozen or more countries, aged around 13, or in the last pre-university year around 18, were given tests — first in mathematics, later in a number of other subjects — which were designed as far as possible to cover the consensus of educators as to the objectives of their teaching. Obviously no one achievement test (even when suitably translated) can be equally suited to the aims of teachers in every country sampled, particularly when, for purposes of objective scoring and analysis, the tests all had to be multiple-choice. Nevertheless, extremely interesting data were forthcoming on the relation of mean achievement scores to national differences in educational organization and policy, to school differences within the countries (e.g. the qualifications and attitudes of the teachers), and to individual differences (e.g. the students' home backgrounds). One of the major themes of the authors is that educating larger proportions of the population to higher levels does not lower achievement; in other words, achievement is not raised by restricting such education to a selected few. For example, only some 8-12 per cent of children in Northwest European countries stay on at school for 12 years, compared with 70 per cent in the USA. Naturally the mean scores of the USA sample at this age were lower than the mean scores in a highly selected sample, such as Belgium. Nevertheless, the percentage of the total population aged 18 who reach a certain high standard in mathematics is greater in the USA than in Belgium. Clearly the Belgian (and English) systems have excluded large numbers of students from attempting higher mathematics, and the nonselective US system has given them the chance. However, the determining factors are extremely complex; e.g. the overall costs of producing good mathematicians in the US must vastly exceed those in Belgium where only the most promising are selected, and it may well be that European countries (still more so the less developed nations) are unable to afford the luxury of providing advanced education for a great many unfit students in order to equip a larger proportion of fit ones. Moreover, the obtained comparative results are much affected by student motivation, and probably by teaching aims and methods, as well as by the selective *v.* nonselective policy. Nevertheless, these results tend to confirm the point already made that selection is liable to be unfair to many students who might have turned out as well as, or better than, some of those selected but for the imposition of an arbitrary bar to higher- or better-quality schooling; and that our preference should be for a more flexible policy which avoids irreversible decisions, particularly at an early age.

One other point should be mentioned; the various selective systems cream off 10 to 20 per cent of the population, and it might be thought that this would not be of great advantage to the 2 per cent or less whom we regard as highly gifted. However, the common practice even within selective schools is to group, or stream the entrants into classes of different ability levels. Hence, the top class, at each age, in an English grammar or public school, would usually consist almost entirely of students of such high ability that the most gifted 2 per cent do get plenty of challenging instruction at their own level.

Let us turn to a few examples of well-known and apparently successful selective schools. Hunter College school in New York arose from the work of Leta Hollingworth in the 1920s (cf. Brumbaugh and Roshco, 1959). It takes children from Grade 3 to 6 level all of whom have IQs of 130 up, averaging about 150.* Originally it went down to nursery school, but now seems to postpone the identification of suitable pupils until the age of about 7; and it uses a specially constructed battery of verbal and reasoning tests, as well as interviews with parents and children before admission. The children are drawn from any

*This estimate was based on classical IQs (cf. p.60) and would need to be scaled down to be comparable with present-day Deviation IQs.

part of New York, and many are of quite low economic class. The curriculum is highly varied and stimulating, and considerable responsibility and freedom are given since, even at entry, the pupils are as intellectually developed as average 11 year olds.

The Bronx High School of Science also recruits widely, admitting its students mainly on examinations in mathematics and science, and good achievement record in the elementary school. Their median IQ is approximately 140. While it teaches all school subjects, it concentrates particularly on science, and has excellent laboratories, and numerous clubs to foster individual interests. There are comparable schools in New York for musical and for artistic children. Note that all of these are situated in a large urban area, so that they can draw the best from a wide population. Moreover, although entry is to some extent competitive, the overall numbers are so small that they are unlikely to provoke social jealousies or ill-feeling in the community. Havighurst *et al.* (1955) describe a number of other outstanding examples, and suggest that such schools work best in large communities because the clientéle are largely anonymous; they are less successful in smaller ones where parents are jealous of anyone getting special privileges. Also they tend to be regarded as unnecessary in upper- and middle-class areas where school provision is already superior, and almost all students are of good ability. And they are least popular in smaller centres, where the population is heterogeneous.

Branch and Cash (1966) describe some examples in England, for instance Millfield, an independent boarding school. Here the fees are very high, but by means of scholarships a number of students from non-wealthy backgrounds are admitted, on the basis of intellectual promise or talent. Classes average some 10 to 12 per teacher, and each student has a personal programme which allows for individual study and pursuit of interests, in addition to general academic excellence.

As in New York, there are specialized schools in England for, e.g. ballet dancers, or musicians, one of the most famous being that run by Yehudi Menuhin. These require good all-round ability in addition to special talent, and provide a thorough general education along with vocational training. Frequently the Local Education Authorities will pay the fees for a talented child, whose parents cannot afford them. In North America it is sometimes possible to gain the interest of some community group in subsidizing the education and training of such children. Probably the USSR carries further than any other country the training of the specially talented in separate schools. It is ironic indeed that the Soviet system, so often applauded by socialist writers who inveigh against élitist education in the West, actually practises more intensive selection for special schools and colleges than any western country. Russian educators regard the absence of selection of the most talented as a waste of the nation's most valuable resources.

Other examples of small private schools which offer unique curricula are the bilingual schools in parts of Canada for children of 3 to 4 years up. Children from English-speaking homes are given 'total immersion' in French for half or more of each school day. They are not 'taught' French, but are taught other subjects in French. Play activities are also conducted in French, so that they become fluent speakers of the language at an age when they are most capable of acquiring it.

A less divisive, yet clearly successful, plan for separate schooling of the gifted has been running in Cleveland, Ohio, since 1922, and, for over 40 years in Saskatoon, and London, Ontario. The Cleveland 'Major Work Classes' catered for elementary and secondary students with IQs of 125 upwards, drawn from numerous city schools. When followed up by Barbe and Norris (1954), it was found that the great majority of students went on to college, and that two-thirds of their grades fell in the top quarter of the distribution. S.R. Laycock (1957) was influenced by the Cleveland scheme and was largely responsible for initiating Canadian programmes, one of which we will describe in more detail.

In Saskatoon, the most intelligent 3 to 4 per cent of children are picked out in 4th grade on the basis of preliminary group tests and teachers' assessments, followed by an individual Binet or WISC. Previous achievement is not used as a criterion. The total number selected depends on the number of places available. If the parents approve, the selected children then spend the next four years in special classes which are located in one or more ordinary schools. They have specially chosen teachers working under the same principal, and they can and do mix with the nonselected or regular children in the same school for many activities. In other words they are not completely segregated. They have, of course, to be bussed or privately transported to the particular school, and this partly explains the fact that up to about one half of the parents offered admission for their bright child refuse it. Other reasons are that children tend to lose neighbourhood friends, though picking up new friends nearer to them in ability at the new school; that many parents are reluctant for their children to appear 'different', or to be accelerated; and that some feel that their local school already provides comparable, though less formally organized, instruction and facilities. Moreover, the total numbers involved are quite small, say 60 to 90 per year in a medium-sized city, rather than 20 per cent of the entire secondary school population, as in England. Hence other schools in the area suffer very little because the top cream has been skimmed off. Generally then this plan has not led to the kind of competitiveness that marred the English eleven-plus; and rather little criticism is heard from parents or administrators on the grounds that it involves costly provision for an élite group. Nevertheless, Laycock (1957) admits certain difficulties, particularly in the early days when public opinion was hardly ready for such a break with tradition. He suggests that there should have been more systematic consultation and cooperation with parents, and that remedial measures should have been made available for the appreciable proportion of selected children who failed to achieve as well as expected.

It should be noted that the numbers of boys and girls included in the scheme are roughly equal. Particular attention is paid to locating likely students from schools in the poorer areas of the city, not just good middle class areas. Martinson (1973) likewise records special efforts in the USA to bring black students into schemes for the gifted.

In the Saskatoon classes for the academically talented, instruction is not aimed at acceleration, but rather at enrichment, or study in depth, and at challenging intelligent minds. It includes a wide range of supplementary activities, such as field work and museum visits. Though each grade is usually taken as a group, there is more opportunity for projects and small-group research, and individual assignments. Considerable recourse is made to parent helpers for fostering special interests. After 8th grade the students return to normal secondary or Collegiate schools, often at their own age level (Grade 9), though sometimes promoted a year. Some

secondary schools make little allowance for their advancement, though others do place them in more advanced 'tracks',
or otherwise provide special programmes. There is much
evidence of the later success at school and college of these
students, though so far little proof that they do better than
control groups of comparable initial ability who do not attend
the selective classes.

A major point of attractiveness in such schemes is their low
cost. No extra school buildings or teachers are required,
beyond what would be needed for the same students in regular
schools. The individual testing of about twice as many children
as actually enter the scheme is costly in psychologists' time; for
example, it may mean diverting all the school psychologists for
several weeks from their normal work of diagnosis and
remediation of the handicapped. The special classes make use
of the libraries and audiovisual equipment of the regular
schools in which they are housed, but do, of course, require
rather more advanced materials, books, money for field trips
etc., than the regular students. In London, Ontario, an
Advancement Classes Consultant coordinates the scheme for
identifying gifted students, and plans appropriate instruction
(M. Smith, 1971).

2 *Homogeneous grouping, or streaming* This plan was at
one time almost universal in all large British schools, primary
and secondary, and according to Esposito (1973) it is spreading
rapidly in the USA, especially in large urban centres.
Essentially it aims to reduce the range of individual differences
in ability within any one class, so that the teacher can adapt his
or her instruction to suit the average level. At once this raises
the problem that when pupils are selected as relatively
homogeneous on any one criterion (e.g. intelligence, or
English achievement), they will inevitably be more heterogeneous in other respects (e.g. mathematics), though less so
than when they are grouped merely by age. Moreover, the
range may still be quite large; thus if there are three streams
classified by IQ, the top third will generally include IQs of 107
upwards. However, even under these circumstances, the gifted
(say IQ 130 +) are enabled to work rather more at their own
level than when their classmates range all the way from IQ 80
or 70. As Ogilvie (1973) points out, streaming does not solve all
the problems of catering for the highly gifted, though one
might expect it to help.

The dangers are much the same as in segregated schooling, e.g. over-pressuring by parents, and social divisiveness, in so far as the top streams will be mainly middle and upper class, the bottom mainly lower class and ethnic minority children. However, this should be less serious in so far as there is free mixing in nonacademic activities. Children in the lower streams generally realize that they are regarded as inferior, and their self-esteem may be impaired, while motivation is more likely to improve in the upper groups. Much depends on the particular circumstances such as the morale or climate in the school, and the quality and attitudes of the staff, so that generalizations are dangerous. It has been claimed that children themselves, on the whole, prefer the system. Another criticism, already noted above, is the tendency of the classification to rigidify, so that it becomes increasingly difficult to switch streams. And no doubt many teachers are apt to develop stereotypes of the bright and the dull, which become self-fulfilling prophecies.

There have been many researches which attempted to compare grouped or streamed with mixed-ability classes, but the results have been highly contradictory. Some studies were too brief, other lacked proper comparison or control groups; most often there was inadequate control of methods of instruction, and of teachers' attitudes. Thus Ekstrom (1959), Goldberg *et al.* (1966), and Esposito (1973) suggest that improvement in achievement with grouping occurs only when the content and methods of instruction are modified to suit each level of ability. However, the most extensive study, carried out by Barker Lunn (1970) again found no consistent differences in achievement or progress in English primary schools, 36 of which were streamed, and 36 unstreamed. She notes that about half the teachers in the nominally unstreamed schools in fact resorted to a lot of grouping within their classes, and laid more stress on formal subjects and competition than did the other half who were genuinely more child-centred and permissive. The latter group, where the school *and* the teacher favoured nonstreaming, scored significantly higher on a short battery of divergent thinking tests, though the differences were not large. More important, the average and below average pupils in streamed schools, and those in unstreamed who were taken by stream-oriented teachers, showed poorer attitudes, self concepts and relations with their teachers. Thus the findings were definitely unfavourable to streaming as affecting social and emotional adjustment, and gave no support to the claim that it enhances achievement among the superior group in the elementary school (cf. also Jackson, 1964).

The results might, of course, differ in the secondary school, where the range of achievement tends to be wider. However, a study in Sweden at junior secondary level lent no support. Two types of school organization were operating in different parts of the country, one streamed, the other unstreamed. No overall differences in achievement were found between these. But there was some tendency for bright working-class children to benefit from grouping. Presumably bright middle-class generally get more stimulation at home, and are therefore less dependent on receiving advanced instruction at school.

Note that these predominantly negative findings refer to students who are assigned to groups or streams within a school for *all* subjects. Thus they should not be taken to apply to the separation of small groups of gifted children part-time for certain topics; nor to the segregated schools such as the English grammar and modern schools described above.

A minor difficulty which sometimes occurs in schools with streamed classes relates to teachers' gradings. Some teachers tend to expect much the same distribution of marks in classes at all levels, rather than allowing that the top stream should almost all achieve high grades or marks, almost all the bottom stream poorer grades. This seems likely to have harmful effects only when an undue emphasis is put on achievement grades; and currently school report cards are trying to reduce such emphasis. If it is necessary for certain purposes to bring out the real differences between streamed classes in the same grade, standardized tests, or examinations common to all classes, can readily be set.

It may be of interest to record the introduction, and eventual abolition, of one such grouping scheme which operated in the junior high schools of a large Canadian city from 1963-1970. This was called an Honours Programme. Approximately the most able 3 per cent of students were identified at the end of elementary school by means of group and individual intelligence tests and school records. Only high achievers were referred for testing. If parental assent was received they were transferred in Grades 7 onwards to separate classes in a number of the larger junior high schools, where they worked at their own level independently of the rest of the school. There was a very definite aim *not* to accelerate, but 'to challenge students to think, to create, and to understand, and in so doing to maintain a high standard of scholarship, and to accept the challenge of responsibility and leadership in our complex society.' However, very frequently the work departed rather little from the standard curriculum; there was more increase in quantity than change in type of work. Though the teachers were specially chosen, some were over-rigid and had little experience in individualized education. Actually all but about 6 per cent of students admitted did obtain A or higher grades in their examinations, and when transferred to senior high schools at Grade 10, they subsequently achieved better than average, despite having spent a good deal of time on topics outside the ordinary curriculum. (It could hardly have been otherwise, considering how carefully they had been selected in the first place.)

It is difficult to pin down the main reasons for terminating the scheme, considering that the great majority of students involved and their parents were highly favourable. Some of the latter considered their children overworked, or cited transport difficulties. Some senior high school teachers criticized the students' grounding in formal skills, and some junior high teachers objected to the removal of the cream from their classes. Many people disliked the competitive aspects involved both in the initial selection and in the programme itself. Probably the main opposition came from the general public (especially parents whose children failed to get places). Many children, also, were subjected to intense pressure to 'pass' the necessary tests; and sometimes the relations between the Honours class students and the rest of the school were not too happy, the former being accused of snobbishness. Because of the pronounced emotionality permeating both criticism and defence of the programme, it is hardly surprising that, after a few years' duration, the decision was made by the Board of Education to drop this uncomfortably hot potato, and to divert the funds which had been allocated to it into less controversial areas. What is more unfortunate is that the scheme has left a significant residue of negative feelings in the city towards any fresh attempts to provide special education for the gifted. Many similar schemes have been tried out elsewhere, again with varying, though seldom lasting success.

3 *Multiple curricula, elective programmes and options*
There seems to be far less objection to grouping within secondary schools, for example, into college-oriented, general, and vocational programmes. This kind of differentiation is based less on arbitrary selection than on student achievement and parent choice, or the advice of school counsellors. Those who are not interested in, or capable of, tertiary academic education are usually aware of this by the age of 15, at the beginning of senior high school. In English secondary schools, it is also generally accepted that there should be specialization by subject, e.g. classical or modern languages, physical or biological sciences, social studies etc., after the 'O' level examinations have been taken at about age 15. When there are many alternative courses, less kudos or social stigma is apt to be attached to any one of them.

In many North American high schools, students can elect to take honours classes in 1, 2 or more subjects. A simpler variant, often introduced at junior high school level, is to set aside so many periods a week for optional subjects, which offer a choice of, e.g. foreign language, orchestra or band, drama etc. Often the choice may be severely restricted by the capabilities and interests of the teachers, especially in smaller schools or by the numbers of places available for any one option. Though three-quarters or more of the school week may still be spent on core subjects in heterogeneous (unstreamed) classes, such a scheme does provide some leaven for the development of talent, in company with other students who are similarly motivated.

Obviously there is considerable overlapping with voluntary school clubs, which meet after school, or at lunch hour etc. These can be extremely various, e.g. school magazine, photography, chess, radio, drama etc. The more specialized ones may be dependent on staff guidance, and therefore limited by available talent; but many can be self-supporting. Again the mere fact of putting individual effort into something one is interested in tends to promote better adjustment and study habits in the more conventional and less stimulating class work.

4 *Setting* An extension of streaming which is very common in British schools is regrouping students for different school subjects. Thus one boy can be in a high stream for

mathematics, low for French, another the reverse. While this creates time-tabling difficulties, it obviously provides more adequately for variations in abilities along different lines; and it is less discriminative than allocating students to high or low streams for everything.

5 *Part-time special classes* Here we turn again to schemes which are of special benefit to the highly gifted few — usually those with all-round superior ability, rather than those with specialized talents. Some 2 to 5 per cent are selected by the usual criteria of teacher nominations and intelligence tests, often at the end of 4th grade, for entry to special classes during 5th and 6th grades. However, similar plans can well be operated at other age levels. In an average school with say 90 entries per year, this may yield about 5 pupils in each of Grades 5 and 6. They spend most of their time in the ordinary class of their own age, but go to a special teacher for anything from one to five half-days a week for enriched instruction and activities. If there are insufficient numbers or inadequate space in one school, pupils from several neighbouring schools can combine in a central location. But the size of such special groups should seldom exceed 10, if they are to get adequate help with individual studies.

Syphers (1972) indicates that a full half-day or day per week is preferable to short daily periods. Such schemes are inevitably rather costly, since they require an additional teacher full-time if, say, five gifted groups are taken for a day each week.

There is great diversity among schemes of special classes for the gifted — with respect to their aims, composition, facilities, methods of operation, and acceptance by the community. Sometimes the emphasis lies on covering the major subjects, English and mathematics, at a more advanced or deeper level during the special periods. But more often these are dealt with in the regular classes, and the meetings are devoted to special interests, especially in social studies or science or arts. The work need not be wholly individualized: the children benefit from being introduced as a group (or subgroup) to a new topic, discussing it with intellectual peers and planning further exploration; also from cooperating in research activities, or in carrying out a science project, writing a story etc.

One experimental scheme may be described which covered

about a dozen Grade 5 and 6 children in a Canadian elementary school. Being self-contained, and receiving a special grant for personnel and for materials (books, equipment, kits etc.), it showed great flexibility and vitality. The children usually came together for half of each school day and, apart from covering the core curriculum adequately, they had freedom to develop their interests in almost any direction, with the help of a specially appointed teacher. For example, two boys wrote an extended adventure story, complete with maps and illustrations. Rapid progress was made in mathematics, since an individual hand calculator was available for each child, and a very large range of resource materials was collected and filed.

Some of the staff of the classes from which the children were chosen, or teachers of other classes, had initial misgivings, but became progressively more positive in their support. There seemed to be no particular social difficulties. Children not chosen came to realize that the activities of the gifted group were beyond their ken — not just doing what they wanted, but having harder work than that demanded by the regular instruction. Those who were selected seemed to find the regular periods more tolerable in so far as they had to spend less time on them, and could do what really interested them, at their own pace, in the special periods.

This particular experiment might have been even more successful had psychological help been enlisted in choosing the children. There were a few who were experiencing difficulties, either because they were not sufficiently intelligent, or because they lacked the motivation necessary for sustained independent effort. Another possible improvement would be to involve the other teachers more fully in the provision of enrichment materials to use in their own classes, e.g. when the gifted children were being taught science or social studies along with the rest.

Ogilvie (1973) found that his panels of teachers, who were opposed to full-time segregated classes or schools, approved this type of programme, at least for children aged 9 and over, though usually not for those of 8 years or under.

Even this form of provision is liable to be greeted by objections on the ground of promoting snobbishness, élitism, and so forth. Curiously, the critics never seem to object to partial segregation or special instruction for outstanding members of athletic teams, though this is closely parallel to what we are asking for the gifted. Provisions for students talented in music or drama are also not regarded as undemocratic. Nor are objections raised to the almost universal practice of grouping children within the class for the early stages of teaching reading, or to special classes for backward pupils, whether within the school or in a special remedial centre. It is only grouping on the basis of high intelligence which is attacked, presumably because it is so value-laden. Thus we frequently hear of promising experiments in helping the gifted which initially attracted funds, but then petered out for lack of continuing financial support in the face of some public criticism. The acceptability of any scheme depends on many complex social factors, in addition to the size and heterogeneity of the area from which pupils are drawn (referred to on p.159). Local politics, cultural traditions, and the kind of publicity which the press decides to give to educational innovations often seem to override strictly educational considerations.

A few additional examples will be referred to briefly. In England, the Brentwood experiment has been written up by Bridges (1969). Here, one or two children from each of several primary schools in an area were brought together for an afternoon a week at a Training Centre for teachers, where the students supervised a varied assortment of small-group activities. One of the major benefits is said to be the realization by the previously isolated gifted children that there were others with similar interests, curiosity, and abstract level of conceptualization. A drawback, however, was that there was little connection between the special class activities and the work done in the feeder schools.

In the USA, the Colfax Plan, operated at a school in Pittsburgh, is often cited. Over 10 per cent of the most able children were separated for part of each day in special 'workshops'. Los Angeles had a scheme for the brightest children from 24 schools; and Edmonton, Alberta, is similar in drawing several small groups from different schools for one or two half-days a week. At present these classes cater for roughly 1 per cent of children in Grades 5 to 6, and a smaller number of junior high school students, all with IQs of 130 or more, who are also selected for superior school achievement and apparent maturity to undertake independent work. The main emphasis is on art or music, outdoor studies, or social and community studies; while the older students undertake their own research projects. The aims of the programme appear rather ambitious in view of the relatively small amount of time allocated to it. Such general skills are emphasized as proficiency in oral presentation, research abilities, divergent thinking, role playing, imaginative artistic expression, decision making, and receptivity to the 'cultural heritage'.

6 *Summer, or Saturday, schools, and extracurricular interest groups* Particularly popular in the United States are summer workshops which run for a few weeks during the holidays, and may cover a great variety of specialized scientific or other topics, or artistic training. It may seem surprising that bright students are willing to give up time for these, but presumably they make possible the pursuit of interests, along with equally able peers, and self-initiated study, which are not usually gratified during the regular school year. In some instances they may be run in conjunction with in-service training for groups of teachers who wish to gain more experience of identifying and handling the gifted. Examples are the Cullowhee experiment in North Carolina, and the Kootenay Centre for the Gifted in British Columbia. More usually they are held in local secondary schools, or even attached to universities, where there are superior facilities and equipment. Where the credit system operates, students can gain extra credits and thus complete high school at an earlier age.

Privately organized Saturday morning or after-school classes for special tuition are likewise common in N. America, for example those run by ethnic subgroups (Chinese, Jews etc.) for fostering and passing on their own cultural traditions and language. Public libraries also often arrange reading and instructional circles, under qualified tutors, e.g. in environmental studies. In England, as Ogilvie points out, many education authorities provide Saturday classes, mainly in music, or other arts. In Toronto, special Saturday courses constitute one of the main services provided for gifted children. Many different topics are offered for pupils in Grades 6-8, e.g. computer science, journalism, archaeology, philosophy, drama, ceramics (cf. Furr *et al.*, 1972). About 100 students are selected each year on the basis of tests given in

Grade 5, and teacher nomination. An interesting feature is that both an omnibus verbal group test and the Raven Matrices nonverbal test are used, and high scores on either (not both combined) qualify. This should give a better chance to 'new Canadians', i.e. recent immigrants, who might be handicapped in the verbal test.

Obviously such provision does little or nothing to help gifted children cover the normal curriculum at their own pace, though presumably it often compensates for boredom during the school week. Such short-term programmes, without any follow-up, seem unlikely to be of lasting benefit. For example they can do little to train good study habits and scholastic motivation generally. The Toronto scheme is devised mainly 'to stimulate new courses of study and extend existing fields of interest', also to stimulate schools to develop their own enrichment activities. A particular point in their favour is that, because of their voluntary nature, they do not arouse any public criticism.

A final point to emphasize in this chapter is that an education system which provides a variety of alternative routes for children with different abilities, interests and needs is likely to be healthier and more effective than one which aims to provide the best available single system for everybody, or one which arbitrarily allocates children to a particular form of instruction whether it be on the basis of age, sex, ethnic background, or intelligence. Many of the plans here described do allow for parental and pupil choice, which is surely highly desirable. For schools were invented to supplement, rather than to replace, home upbringing. A number of educational writers in the UK and USA are currently advocating some sort of voucher system, each family being allowed to expend their vouchers for their children's education as they think best. Instead of just one unified authority, independent bodies would be allowed to establish schools of various types to suit varied needs, and appropriately subsidized. Obviously some kind of coordination and overall control would be required, and this is not the place to discuss the merits and difficulties of the plan. So far attempts to put it into practice have failed largely because of the opposition of the majority of teachers. But clearly it would make for much greater flexibility than the present state-maintained, or provincial systems, which bear so hardly on the children most worth educating.

11 Enrichment

The provision of enriched education for individual gifted children (or small groups) within the ordinary school is the most popular approach in North America, since it does not appear to require any formal organization such as we have described in chapters 9 and 10. It is a teaching procedure rather than an administrative device, and it avoids most of the controversial aspects of either acceleration or special grouping. This point of view is disputable, as we shall see later. But for the moment let us define enrichment simply as the provision of some form of additional educational experience which supplements the regular classroom activities, and is available for gifted students who are able to complete these activities more rapidly and competently than the majority of their classmates. Or to quote Worcester (1956), enrichment is 'providing experiences for which the average or below-average child lacks the time, the interest, or the ability to understand'.

Unfortunately, though, the term is so vague that it is commonly applied to almost anything. In its simplest and least structured form it may be just a shelf or table of books on a variety of topics to which the bright child has access when he or she has finished the regular classroom work. At a slightly more organized level, the teacher may require of that student a well-researched and well-prepared presentation to be completed within a certain time. Sometimes, rather than select a particular topic, the teacher may encourage the more able student to initiate his or her own learning project with virtually no structure imposed. If there are two or three gifted students in the same class, the teacher may suggest that they work together on a project, and then possibly present this to the class on completion. Sometimes two or more teachers may collaborate to the extent that they share the gifted students in their classes and pool their own talents in order to devise more varied and challenging activities for them. These activities need not necessarily be confined to the classroom, but may involve visits to places of interest outside the school, and instruction by members of the community other than teachers. However, a series of snippets such as the occasional trip to the zoo or museum should not be regarded as an enrichment programme.

In view of the many and varied forms which enrichment in the classroom can take, it is hardly surprising that, as a method or organization, it is viewed rather warily by those who are concerned with the education of gifted children. Even when written into the policy of the school system, with a goodly number of laudable, but very general, objectives, all too often the mechanics of the process are not spelt out. Admittedly, a too highly structured statement of policy could, by its inflexibility, restrict the efforts of the able and creative teacher, and thus defeat the purpose of providing the most appropriate educational experiences for gifted students. But unfortunately all teachers are not equally able and creative, and many of them experience great difficulty in interpreting and implementing a general exhortation to 'enrich' their regular classroom programme. Furthermore, they are often not at all sure who the recipients of that enrichment should be, before they even begin to consider the form that it should take. Thus a school system may have on paper a policy for the provision of enriched activities for gifted children, but what occurs in fact may be very far from what was envisaged. However good the intentions, the amount of impact they have is decidedly chancy when so much is left to the particular teacher, principal and school. It becomes a lottery in which the winners are those gifted children who, fortuitously, find themselves in the classrooms of teachers with the time and talent for devising stimulating and challenging additional activities for them; while other equally gifted children in other classrooms can be almost total losers.

Organization

If a policy of enrichment is to be effectively implemented, even more careful definition and organization are required than they are for regular instruction. In the first place the selection of students who are to be included raises as many problems as does selection for any other type of programme. Obviously a classroom teacher should not be expected to be a diagnostician and a curriculum developer in addition to performing his or her ordinary duties, though many can make valuable contributions in either direction. We have already seen, in chapter 7, that it is insufficient merely to tell the school to require certain scores on particular intelligence and achievement tests. They can carry out fairly effective identification procedures, but it is preferable to have input from a psychologist who can collate the needed information on the child's range of abilities, skills and interests, and relate these to his family and previous educational background.

A second aspect of the work is the compilation of an extensive repertoire of materials, equipment, 'modules' or programmed units, learning kits, and audio-visual aids. This should be the responsibility of one or more specialists in the school system, who are versed in a much wider range of subjects than are covered by the resources centre which services the general run of students. As well as helping the schools to choose materials suitable for their gifted pupils, such specialists might be able to stimulate local groups of teachers to devise learning packages of their own.

Thirdly, the key persons should be consultant teachers, who would initiate and conduct part of the work with individual children or small groups, advise the regular staff on how to carry on, and keep in touch so as to evaluate each child's progress, and recommend needed changes. They could also indicate cases where acceleration was desirable, and suggest part-time segregation of groups of pupils within a school, or among neighbouring schools.

In Ogilvie's survey (1973) English teachers frequently favoured peripatetic help of this kind, especially for 9 to 13 year olds, also indicating that parent assistants could be useful in looking after gifted children. But he noted that very few Education Authorities possess advisory staff for this purpose. However many American and some Canadian cities do appoint consultants for enrichment activities.

Another possibility might be to delegate in each school some interested member of staff, whole or part-time, who would look after the identification of, and activities for, the gifted in that school. But it would obviously be difficult to find sufficient people with suitable qualifications in all aspects of enrichment described above.

Naturally the question of expense arises, and it is unfortunately true that the implementation of an effective and comprehensive scheme of enrichment must be more expensive than one based mainly on either acceleration or segregation. However, attempts have been made to cost programmes which are running successfully in different parts of the United States (cf. Gallagher, 1964); and although they certainly do involve increased expenses per child who is included, current programmes for handicapped children are considerably more costly. De Haan and Havighurst (1957) make the point that, although acceleration is both more economical and more effective in enabling children to progress at their own rate, yet one has to balance this against the desirability of allowing such children to experience a richer, more spread-out, childhood, rather than speeding them up. They themselves prefer the latter alternative, but admit that any decision depends on a value judgment. There is no scientific answer to the question whether enrichment is superior to acceleration, or vice versa; but this does not provide an excuse for sitting back and doing nothing for the gifted minority.

As an indication that an effective scheme need not be excessively expensive, we will outline the organization of one which is running successfully in a small Californian city, where the total school student population is about 12,500. The area is largely, though not wholly, professional or upper-middle class, hence the proportion of children covered, with IQs exceeding 130, is over 10 per cent, rather than 2 per cent. The budget in 1975-6 amounted to some $250,000, about three-quarters for salaries, and one quarter for books, materials, supplies etc. The staff consist of an overall coordinator, three resource teachers in the elementary schools, one part-time coordinator on the staff of each secondary school, one psychometrist, several part-time counsellors or guidance consultants, and the equivalent of two clerical staff. The parents in the neighbourhood are extremely keen; they are consulted over the planning and do a lot of voluntary work, including: evaluations of what is going on in each school and in other parts of the country, acting as teacher assistants, giving 'mini-courses', designing and preparing enrichment materials, transporting groups of children, e.g. to the local university, and clerical chores. A 'mini-course' would typically deal with some branch of science, which would be studied by a small class from one or more schools for one hour per week for about six weeks.

Each resource teacher looks after enrichment activities in seven schools, which she visits for half a day each week. She observes gifted children in their classrooms, works with teachers on their programmes, demonstrates enrichment activities with groups in the classroom or elsewhere, sets up mini-courses, field trips etc., introduces teachers to new materials, carries out in-service workshops for teachers and evening courses for parents.

Early admission is possible from the age of 5:0 (instead of the usual 6:0) to bright children who have had a year in kindergarten. Acceleration can be arranged at any stage, and there is some ability grouping such as Honours classes from Grades 7 to 11. Through a kind of Advanced Placement, selected 6th graders can attend some junior high school courses, and 8-9th graders attend senior high courses. Though tests and teacher nominations are used for identifying the children requiring enrichment, everyone concerned is strongly against labelling particular children as gifted; and they regard their efforts as part of the general aim to provide opportunities for any children with special needs. Children in enrichment groups also take an important part in ordinary classroom activities, and techniques or materials developed for them are often adapted so as to be useful to average and duller children too. Particular attention is paid to the educational careers of the exceptionally bright (i.e. Terman-Merrill IQs of 154 + or WISC IQs of 145 +), and attempts are made to promote their social adjustment. Likewise care is given to gifted children who are under-achieving.

Individualization

There is one further preliminary question to discuss — the relation between enrichment programmes for gifted children and individualization of instruction for all children. Syphers (1972) urges, and others support her, that provision for the gifted should be: 'one phase of providing for individual differences in children, and not an arrangement for giving special privileges or rewards to a select few'. While all would agree in principle that every child is entitled to the best education available, this ideal seems rather unrealistic in view of the enormous variations between teachers. A very good, dedicated teacher, who is prepared to spend many hours in the preparation and organization of materials and approaches, and who has the insight to assess her students relatively accurately, may be able, unaided, to provide a considerable degree of individualization of instruction for all the students in her class, including appropriate remediation for the slower ones and enrichment for the brighter ones. Her task will be made easier if the school in which she works has optimal conditions such as open plan building, extensive library and audio-visual equipment, low student-teacher ratio, good inter-staff relations etc. But we are just as likely to come across the exact opposite — the non-innovative teacher in an overcrowded classroom in a school with few facilities.

Even in the case of an average teacher in traditional conditions, the most that we can reasonably expect is that she should be able to cope with the general run of pupils, i.e. usually those in the IQ range 80-120. But she should receive assistance in the more extreme cases both of backwardness and of giftedness. If he or she can adequately challenge the 125s, 130s and over, so much the better; and this chapter tries to outline the sort of things that can be done. But just because the task is almost superhuman, we advocate the special measures already described, or ask that enrichment be largely entrusted to a special teacher, consultant, or aides. Gold (1965) likewise takes the view that provision for the gifted should be combined with greater individualization for all, but that it cannot wait for the millenium. There is certainly no conflict between overall progress in educational methods and improved programmes for the gifted.

Normally, indeed, a great many children other than the gifted do receive individually prescribed programmes at some time in their school careers, notably the intellectually and physically handicapped. The average child tends to come lower in the scale of priorities simply because, much less frequently, does he display any special need. Nevertheless, side benefits do accrue to him too, since when enrichment activities are provided primarily for gifted students, other class members are not excluded and often participate in them, although the projects or other work that they produce are not expected to be as high in quality as those of their intellectually more able classmates.

Virtually complete individualization is sometimes possible, given the right principal and outstanding staff, together with local support. A good example is described by D. Glines (cf. Weisgerber, 1971) — namely the Wilson Campus School at Mankato, Minnesota. This caters for children from nursery school to Grade 12, though in fact there are no grades and no examinations. No courses are taught as such, and there are no required classes. Even attendance is optional, though students are expected to attend for a minimum of 170 days per year, and often greatly exceed this. In other words, maximum student freedom is encouraged, and is not — as in more conventional schools — seen as a threat; in general, also, it is not abused. Very good relations are built up between students and staff, and there are seldom any problems of student discipline.

Very varied activities, at all levels, are laid on every day, in a kind of smorgasbord, and students can choose which they will attend, and choose which teachers they prefer to work with. However, there are consultations between a member of staff and the parent(s) and child for planning suitable programmes; and particularly in the case of the younger children there is some pressure to follow programmes likely to be of most use to them. Occasionally there are large lecture-type meetings, but more often a small group meets a teacher to discuss the topic, and then carry on, largely on their own. The work is entirely self-paced. Well developed programmes are available in the arts and music, as well as in more conventional subject areas. Older students can often carry on parts of their studies outside the school, e.g. Spanish language in Mexico, psychology in a mental hospital etc.

Frankly we do not believe that such radical schemes would often work effectively, though we would be glad to see many more schools of this type to serve as experimental models. The more successfully individualization is implemented in any class or school, the less need for any provision for the gifted. What one does find more frequently in North America are senior high schools where every student has his individual programme worked out with teachers as consultants or directors of studies. While some of the instruction is given in classes or small groups, a good deal of use is made of 'modules' such as the LAP (Learning Activity Packages) and UNIPACS, of which a considerable range are now published (cf. Weisgerber, 1971). Obviously a good deal of the work consists of reading, and library or laboratory activities. In many English secondary schools also, part of the work is done by individual study, especially in the upper sixth forms; though because of the demands of the 'O' and 'A' level examinations, to a greater extent the work has to be tied to a regular syllabus taught in classroom groups.

Reference was made earlier (p.148) to computer organized instruction in elementary schools, which likewise involves largely individualized learning. At a much less elaborate level, help can be given effectively to gifted children by means of programmed learning units, which cover many topics that could be studied by such children on their own, with a minimum of teacher supervision, and which are geared to a level of difficulty well beyond what the majority of the class, or the teacher herself, would wish to tackle.

Even though individualization is a laudable idea, one might point out that the conventional class instruction for at least part of the time is not only less costly, but also helps in conveying to all children a common core of fundamental skills which they require in our culture. As Gold (1965) suggests, education should try to strike a balance between passing on the cultural heritage, and giving children the freedom necessary for spontaneous intellectual growth. With a little more resourcefulness among teachers, every class should be able to spend part of each day in unstructured educational activities. Not only gifted, but average and dull children have some capacity for, and enjoy self-initiated learning; they are not merely knowledge-absorbing machines. Likewise an appropriate balance must be struck for the exceptionally gifted; they too require the same fundamentals, but in so far as they need less explanation and drill to acquire these than most of the class, a different blend of structured and unstructured activity should be attained. That is, they should follow the same basic curriculum as the rest of the class, but be given more demanding work for part of the day. It is indeed sometimes found that children who have been provided with many enriched activities in the elementary school do come on to secondary school with insufficient grounding in, e.g. spelling or accurate arithmetical computation.

Though the permissive and progressive *v.* the formal and traditional classroom climate is not the same thing as unstructured *v.* structured education, they are obviously linked. Many writers seem to assume that the progress of gifted children, and indeed the productive creativity of all children, will flourish best under a permissive régime. Ogilvie (1974) gives reasons for doubting this view, and reports an investigation of divergent-thinking test performance of children in five primary schools which ranged from highly informal to highly formal. As he anticipated, the moderately informal school did best, then the more highly formal, and scores were worst in the highly unstructured and permissive school. He points out that creative children must have a good background of knowledge and skills to be creative with. In Haddon and Lytton's (1968) study of two relatively informal, and two more traditional schools, divergent thinking scores were significantly superior in the former. But the authors describe the informal not as a *laissez-faire* régime, but rather an enterprise where all children are busy, and where learning is more self-initiated than imposed by the teacher. Lytton (1971) points out too that criticisms of conventional schooling for thwarting creative children have sometimes been exaggerated. It may be the child who is maladapted to the institution, rather than the instituion to a large number of children.

General principles of enrichment

Havighurst *et al.* (1955) list 10 points which cover the essentials of a programme of enrichment, as follows:

1 There should be emphasis on creative and experimental activities
2 Emphasis on developing skills of investigating and learning
3 Independent work, involving initiative and originality
4 High standards of accomplishment
5 Opportunities for leadership and social adjustment
6 Individual attention from a teacher
7 Firsthand experiences
8 Flexibility of organization and procedure
9 Extensive reading
10 Concern with community responsibility

Advocates of the approach through enrichment usually insist that it consists in 'horizontal' rather than 'vertical' extension; that it does not aim to advance the gifted child to a higher level on the educational ladder, but to give him a broader and/or deeper knowledge and experience at the same level as that of average children of his age. We would question whether this aim is a realistic one, or whether extension in breadth and depth do not in fact mean advancing to more abstract and more comprehensive ideas very similar to those of students who are one, two, or more grades ahead. More often the difference between enrichment and advancement seems to consist in the gifted child being encouraged to study and explore things which are not usually included in the conventional curriculum, and in this way to provide more stimulating activities which compensate for the boredom and frustration of having to do most of his work at the same level as that of his average and below-average age peers.

In more detail: enrichment activities should not be thought of primarily as acquiring masses of factual information. Yet at the same time many gifted children around 9-14 years obviously enjoy acquiring an extraordinary range of knowledge on a variety of topics; and if they like to read avidly and absorb quantities of useful or apparently useless information, there is no need to discourage them. They should not do so, however, for the sake of showing off to peers or adults. But it is true that enrichment aims rather at the higher levels of Bloom's taxonomy of educational objectives: comprehension, application, analysis, synthesis and evaluation. Also, wherever possible, it should give opportunity for creative production and expression of ideas, rather than just accepting other peoples'.

Particularly important is the training of general strategies or techniques of study, which can be applied to intellectual work in general. These are more important than extension of content knowledge in any particular area. For example, they should gain experience in the use of tools such as dictionaries and encyclopaedias, atlases and large-scale maps, audio-visual aids such as filmstrips and programmed learning packages. The problem-solving approach should be emphasized, and the students learn the necessity of collecting all available evidence before jumping to conclusions, of attacking problems in a systematic, orderly, fashion, of evaluating the evidence and of distinguishing logical arguments and facts from emotional opinions. They can learn when to skim in reading, when to concentrate and how to take notes. Techniques of exploration, discovery and research can be developed in almost any scholastic area. They should learn, too, to plan their work, and to develop the skills of report writing, communicating their ideas to their peers and discussing them rationally. The sort of problem set to them should preferably override conventional subject boundaries, and require interdisciplinary reading: for example, some key social problem can be considered from the economic, scientific, historical and sociological viewpoints.

Teachers should realize that gifted children work best at self-initiated activities, and need much less supervision than usual. Such children can often devise their own outlets if they are given reasonable opportunities. But of course the teacher should be available for advice, and should keep an eye on continuity and relevance. Enrichment does *not* consist simply of letting a bright child who has time on his hands do anything he feels like.

Martinson (1973) lays particular stress on self-determination of learning activities; for if teachers supply most of the ideas and planning, and answer any question the student asks, much of the point of the enrichment will be lost. The student will once again merely be trying to produce the sort of work the teacher wants. Whereas if the teacher shows that she expects him to be an active learner who is able to produce positive results on his own, she will find that he does so. Syphers points out that any instruction given should not take the form of lecture-like statements, but should ask provocative questions; and that even apparently 'far-out' responses from, or discussions among, students should be welcomed. At the same time it should be made clear that high standards are expected, not shoddy or superficial work. Enriched activities are not justified unless they involve persistent, careful, effort, and thus lead to developing better habits of study than do the conventional activities of the classroom.

Laycock (1957) urges teachers to accept gifted children as persons, neither regarding them as threats, nor just as super-brains. Only by helping them to develop positive self-concepts, will they learn to recognize their own talents and take pleasure in improving them. At the same time they should not be encouraged always to seek the limelight. Their abilities should be used not merely for self-advancement, but as something they can use responsibly for the benefit of others (cf. Wall, 1960).

Underachievement

It is important for the visiting psychologist or teacher, or the school counsellor, to take a continuing interest in each gifted child since, even when what appear to be suitable programmes have been worked out for them, a considerable proportion may fail to progress as expected, or become underachievers. This term — underachievement — has to be treated cautiously. In the early days of testing it was commonly assumed that intelligence tests showed the child's potential educability, and that therefore his achievement should be at the same high level as his mental age. If, for example, a child aged 10 had a MA of 14, but his performance on achievement tests averaged only 12 year level, his Accomplishment or Achievement Quotient was: $\frac{12}{14} \times 100 = 86$, that is, he was considered inferior although his performance considerably exceeded that of children of the same age but of average intelligence. Such low quotients were generally ascribed to maladjustment or to defects of personality (e.g. laziness) which prevented him from working 'up to capacity'.

We realize now that the concept of the Achievement Quotient is statistically fallacious: intelligence and achievement never correlate perfectly, hence the high IQ child will almost always tend to 'regress towards the mean' (cf. p.24), i.e. to achieve at a lower level than his MA. Correspondingly, very dull children will more often than not achieve higher than their MAs, i.e. they will appear to be overachievers who are producing above their capacity, which is surely absurd. However, it *is* legitimate to calculate the expected achievement (whether in any one subject, or all-round) from the correlation with IQ.* Our 10 year old with 14 year MA will most probably be found to have a predicted achievement of 12 to 13 year level, though quite a wide range is possible around this mean; he might score all the way from 16 year to 9 year level. Thus it would seem reasonable to refer to those performing at 11 year level or lower as poor achievers. Very seldom should they achieve only at the average level of the class, or below it.

Views have changed also regarding the causes of underachievement. It is not simply the student's 'fault'. It may well

---

*The procedure, based on the regression coefficient, is somewhat technical and is therefore not described here. Naturally the example given in the text would not necessarily apply to other children with different IQs.

arise from weaknesses in his previous instruction, which may have taught him poor study habits; or from lack of support by his home. Innumerable investigations have been published into the attitudes and personalities of underachievers, often giving contradictory results. But De Haan and Havighurst, also Gallagher, summarize the general trend as follows: he (or she) tends to see himself as inadequate; he has low aspirations, is apathetic and does not enjoy studying; he is poorly adjusted or anxious, or sometimes rebellious against all that school stands for, often low in popularity. Such students tend to come more frequently, though not exclusively, from unstable or broken homes, of low socioeconomic background, where there is little tradition of or concern with higher education.

Gallagher, and other writers, therefore stress that a programme for the gifted should include the counselling of less successful students, and sometimes their parents, by the visiting psychologist or a school counsellor. But he has to admit that experiments designed to demonstrate the usefulness of such counselling have been notably unsuccessful. In one study by Goldberg, a group of underachieving secondary school boys were put together in a class with a flexible, warm and skilled homeroom teacher who combined social studies with a good deal of group counselling. He was able to bring about considerable improvement in all-round achievement over a year, but this was lost when, in the subsequent year, they were transferred to a more rigid and conventional teacher. In general, male teachers are more likely than females to stimulate underachieving boys in the later elementary years and in adolescence.

Gallagher further suggests that where deprived children are identified as potentially gifted, special efforts are needed on their behalf, such as putting them in smaller classes with much individual tutoring, opportunities for counselling and remediation of deficient skills, and attempting to involve their parents in the programme. This approach was successful when applied to Puerto Rican and negro children in New York; more of them stayed on at school longer than usual.

Training for creativity

Torrance (1965) believes that creativity is largely a learned skill, which can be improved when it is encouraged and rewarded, and inhibited when greeted with disinterest or criticism. He has studied the opinions of teachers in several different countries regarding the behaviour of gifted children, such as their independent thinking, asking unusual questions etc. He found these characteristics disapproved of by many (certainly not all) teachers, but to a much greater extent in more traditional cultures such as the Phillipines than in the USA. Also he gave a battery of divergent thinking tests to a wide range of age groups in different countries, and showed that while scores generally increased with age, there were often plateaus or regressions occurring at ages when pupils are subjected to more formal pressures in their curriculum (e.g. Grades 4 and 7 in the USA).

In another article (Torrance, 1972) he summarizes the results of 142 experimental studies, 72 per cent of which, he claims, yielded clearly positive results. However, in the great majority, the criterion of creative achievement consisted of scores on divergent thinking tests, usually his own batteries. As pointed out in chapter 6, it is fairly easy to increase the numbers of ideas produced, or their unusualness, by altering the instructions, or indicating to the students what sorts of answers are required. It is much more difficult to prove that any form of training enhances the productivity or quality of writing, painting, scientific or other problem solving, or the enjoyment of creative activities. However, as Lytton (1971) shows, there is some positive evidence, including his own studies, with Haddon.

Torrance subclassified the 142 studies according to the type of training. One of the most successful appeared to be the Osborn-Parnes technique of brain storming, i.e. producing as many ideas as possible, however 'wild', and deferring evaluation of these till later. Actual experience of graphic, writing, or dramatic activities was also highly effective (in relation to the criterion mentioned above). Special pro- grammes like Covington and Crutchfield's (1969) series of self-instructional exercises for developing productive thinking, were about average; whereas administrative or curricular devices for stimulating creativity, and studies focused on classroom climate, seemed less successful.

Much has been written, also, on techniques for developing effective thinking, though again one doubts how far any improvement results from practice in tackling a particular kind of problem (usually just on paper), or if it does spread to practical daily life or scholastic thinking (cf. Burton, Kimball and Wing, 1960; Getzels, 1964).

Quite apart from Torrance's attempts at validation, he has published a useful list of precepts for teachers to follow in handling creative children (1962); and since many of these are relevant to the academically gifted and talented in general, a somewhat condensed list is given below.

1 Teachers should show that they value unconventional ideas and creativity in the classroom, not discourage them. They should respect the ideas put forward, even if they seem 'wild', and encourage other children to be tolerant, not to ridicule them;

2 Provide opportunities for children to develop sensitivity to sensory stimuli in the world of colours, sounds, pictures, touches, smells, and to express their feelings about them;

3 Teach children to trust their own perceptions even when different from others' and to have confidence in their own creative thinking;

4 Encourage acquisition of knowledge and hobbies in varied fields, however unusual they may be;

5 Provide opportunities for, and give credit to, self-initiated learning;

6 Make available resources for working out ideas, e.g. library, laboratories, museums, visits, clubs;

7 Provide for quiet periods as well as active, so that the creative child can write, draw, read, on his own;

8 Beware of insisting on set patterns of work, e.g. in arithmetic. Many things can be done in a variety of ways;

9 Sometimes practise 'brain-storming' and deferred evaluation, showing how original ideas can emerge more fluently;

10 Train children in testing ideas systematically, and working out their full implications; also verifying solutions to problems. Show how to clarify the issues and carry out relevant experiments. Introduce situations that involve problems that call for creative and rational thinking, and stimulate children to see where there are problems;

11 When criticizing or evaluating ideas, make the criticism constructive. The child should not feel that he is rejected by being greeted with sarcasm;

12 Show the creative child ways of avoiding group

disapproval, not to be bossy, and to be helpful to the less talented. When he is the only one to grasp a topic quickly, not to seek the limelight;

13 Help parents and others in the community to understand him, to welcome and encourage his ideas;

14 Maintain his own curiosity and openness to experience; provide a model of independent thinking and adventuresomeness; to be keen to explore anything new;

15 Welcome research on creative thinking, and better facilities for training new teachers or retraining older ones in handling creative children.

What principals and teachers can do

Notwithstanding our plea for systematically planned, and centrally coordinated enrichment programmes, there is much that the reasonably resourceful and flexible teacher can do (in consultation with the principal) to keep gifted children profitably employed when they have completed their regular assignment. De Haan and Havighurst quote an instance from a 7th Grade class where the average pupil did 20 arithmetic problems in one period, and four bright boys averaged 139 problems each! Laycock (1957) provides a useful list of ten common forms of enrichment which could, indeed, apply to children of any level of ability, but which are particularly appropriate for the brighter ones:

1 Encourage general reading, and guide the child to suitable books, magazines pamphlets etc., at his own level of competence;

2 Stimulation of hobbies, collections, handwork etc. Encourage sharing of interests with other children;

3 Participating in extracurricular school activities — committees, athletics, clubs;

4 Producing, acting in, or otherwise contributing creatively to school plays;

5 Organizing excursions to museums, zoos, industries, community centres, nature trips;

6 Exploiting community resources — libraries, classes in art galleries, scouts or guides, church activities etc.;

7 Arranging contacts with gifted adults, having them speak in the school, or give individual interviews;

8 Arrange for children to work after class hours in laboratories or art rooms;

9 Organizing additional elective courses — metal work, typing, foreign language etc;

10 Encourage the undertaking of community service.

Quite a number of contemporary school textbooks already include suggestions for enrichment activities (for example branching out from the regular mathematics curriculum). The most obvious step for the teacher who has difficulties in coping with the needs of their brightest students is to allow them to bring in books from the library, or to go and work there. In some schools, each classroom has a small, but quite varied supplementary library (and this is something that Parent Teacher Associations could aim to supply). Likewise it does not take much extra effort to amass a small collection of resource materials, either those recommended by the district centre or specialist, or others obtained from miscellaneous sources or self-constructed. Even with quite large classes it should be possible to arrange for small groups to work on some project as supplementary to the regular work, since they can largely look after themselves. Desks can be moved around to put them in a secluded corner, or a large table can be provided if the classroom has sufficient space; or again they might work in a section of the library. Note that the constitution of the group would vary with the subject matter. Those capable of some special activity in maths or science would often differ from those engaged in an English or social studies project. While it is common to pin up specimens of children's paintings on the classroom wall, more interest and stimulus might be provided by letting such groups produce displays of scientific or environmental studies projects.

Some schools already employ brighter children from the same class, or children from older classes, to coach the backward ones. True the more advanced child may often be able to explain things to the backward more effectively than the teacher in the time at her disposal. But, of course, the child tutor is likely to know only one approach, e.g. in teaching reading, and this may be the approach whereby the backward have already failed to make progress. Also, except as a kind of social service, this is of very little benefit to the tutor, who should rather be developing his own abilities.

The principal might be able to draw on volunteer parent assistants to take gifted children weekly, or establish a connection with a local Training College (UK) or Education

Department (North America) whereby university students or teachers in training could work individually either with very backward, or very talented children. This will contribute to their own studies. The principal himself, or visitors, might take seminars with the gifted pupils, on some extracurricular topic.

The principal and staff of each school should periodically discuss which children show special gifts, and what can be done for them. Merely issuing edicts is less effective than cooperative planning.

We will not attempt here to provide detailed suggestions for topics, or relevant materials, in each subject area. Valuable advice can be found in the books by Laycock (1957), Gold (1965), Jones (1972), Gallagher (1964) and others. However the following notes may provide some starting points.

English Generally this is the easiest area to enrich, since it can so largely be assisted by reading, and oral discussions. Students need to learn to read efficiently, both for immediate comprehension and long-term retention; also to communicate both by speech and writing. Far more advanced reading can be recommended than what is normal for the child's age, both classical and modern writers.

Creative writing and utilitarian writing are quite different, and both are important. The former is something to be enjoyed, and done under relaxed conditions, without stress on mechanics, spelling and handwriting, which are necessary for the latter. Correctness in utilitarian writing is certainly desirable, and will lay a foundation for clear thinking among future university students. But many teachers insist on it in all kinds of composition to the extent of stifling the student's imagination. One should remember also the extreme unreliability of assessment of creative English; use should be made of outside judges where real talent is supected. Gifted children can usually supply their own themes, e.g. for poetry, but can also be stimulated by pictures or listening to music. Writing short stories can start quite early, though not much originality should be expected till adolescence. Written productions should sometimes be read to others.

Other useful activities include editing and publishing a school newspaper, and writing book reviews. The latter both helps critical evaluation, and provides models of style.

Attention should be paid to recognizing a variety of styles, and to aesthetic appreciation of creative prose and poetry. Without being pedantic, the teacher can build up an interest in etymology and the structure of language.

Gifted children are generally fluent speakers, but this can be stimulated, e.g. by debates. It is particularly important to try to get the less verbal students, e.g. scientists, to participate.

Foreign languages Most gifted children should readily learn to read and to communicate in a foreign language such as French (especially in Canada and Britain), Spanish (especially in the US), or German. For the talented whose needs cannot be met in school, there are often out-of-school classes and foreign language clubs, especially in cities with large non-Anglo populations.

Immersion programmes for younger children have already been mentioned (p.160). Special techniques with language laboratories are particularly needed for those who start in the later elementary or secondary years, since the available broadcast programmes and gramophone records are too limited unless the student is exceptionally motivated, and also has wider opportunities to practise his skills.

Supplementary materials can be obtained from foreign literature, journals and newspapers, even some foreign movies, and pen pals. The most effective way of bringing on oral competence is by living in a foreign-language community, e.g. through exchange.

Arts and crafts Gifted pupils who do not show exceptional talents in any of these should still be encouraged to spend some time on them, since they help to enhance cultured leisure pursuits. There is very little value in producing drawings etc. of what adults like, and it is more important to stimulate expression of personal feeling, with freedom to explore a wide range of materials and techniques, e.g. pottery, linocuts etc. Too much evaluation at an early stage is apt to destroy confidence, though obviously help should be available when the student feels frustrated by his technical limitations. Handwork activities can be linked to, or develop into, avocational hobbies. In music, appreciation and under-standing of many types of music — classical, modern, jazz and pop — may be of more value to larger numbers than the acquisition of formal techniques such as sight reading. However, for those who do show keenness and talent, many schools can arrange to lend instruments which may well be enjoyed even by those who have grown tired of conventional piano lessons and practice. Likewise for those who are talented in the graphic or other arts, but who happen to be in schools without an expert teacher, advice and materials might be sought from the administrative or supervisory staff of the school system.

Drama and/or the art of movement should again be thought of, not for showing off to adult audiences, but as using the voice and body as media of communication of ideas and feelings.

There are a great many aids in this area — films, filmstrips, plays, concerts, exhibitions and other displays. Also, of course, there is ample literature on the arts or crafts themselves, and in the form of biographies.

For those really talented, who show vocational promise, it is obvious that expert instruction is necessary, beyond what schools can usually provide. But it is still desirable for the psychologist and consultant to help plan the student's education and training, not letting them become too onesided.

Social and environmental studies In this and the remaining areas there is currently a strong trend in North American education to forsake the conventional approaches, and to base instruction more on concrete, practical topics which will interest the average and duller students. In social studies there may indeed have been too much emphasis in the past on learning geographic details, or historical chronology. But American elementary and comprehensive high schools have attempted to substitute a watered down and fragmented syllabus. This is just what the gifted student does not need; he should concentrate in depth on generative concepts and methodologies of collecting data and reaching generalizations. De Haan and Havighurst suggest such key topics as problems of civilization, conquering the environment, food supplies, transport, development of common objects and new ideas such as clothes, writing, newspapers etc. Besides acquiring knowledge the main aim should be to help the student to think critically on the issues that these raise.

A major difficulty is that bright students want to study, and think logically about such controversial topics as justice, religion, politics, sex, and crime; and any consideration of these is apt to shock the community, or be regarded as a threat to the status quo. However, questions of values can hardly be avoided, and the good teacher should be able to encourage research and discussion without laying himself open to charges of onesidedness or indoctrination. We might remember that gifted adolescents are likely to be able to talk much more sensibly about such topics than average adults.

Here too a wide range of materials is readily available — newspapers, broadcasts, free pamphlets, brochures from travel agencies, films and filmstrips, programmed packages, as well as biographies and other books. The project approach is particularly appropriate and can be applied even from 4th grade up. We have admitted earlier that evaluation of such productions is very subjective, but marking is less important than welcoming the initiative shown, and commenting constructively when there are weaknesses. Displays can again be useful, provided they do not always draw too much attention to the same few students. However, some projects are mere time-wasters: Laycock mentions making an Indian village as an example.

With younger children it is well to start from the familiar and concrete, and to extend their understanding of times and distances by stories and pictures. In leading on to more abstract ideas, outings to explore various aspects of the community are useful, and perhaps actual surveys, e.g. of ecology or transport. Some schools have found it worth the effort to apprentice individual students for a week or two in an industry, business, or social welfare agency.

Mathematics Again there is the clash between the New Math approach, or pure mathematics, which are more suitable and interesting to bright students than to the great majority, and the tendency to concretization and applied mathematics for the sake of the weaker brethren. A main difficulty in elementary schools is that the teachers need a thorough knowledge of mathematics in order to design enrichment for the mathematically talented. Many, however, are not themselves interested in the subject, and thus tend to inhibit keenness or creativity among their pupils.

Brighter children can be introduced to the joys of the

discovery approach right from Grade 1 with the help of such apparatus as Cuisenaire, Stern or Dienes. Ordinary computation should not, of course, be neglected, but such children require far less rote drill than the average pupil. If provided with hand calculators, unnecessarily tedious calculations can be avoided, at the same time stimulating a more advanced understanding of number relations.

Many enrichment materials are available, together with programmed courses on a variety of topics, which allow more individualized instruction. Unusual topics can be explored such as other number systems, probability — including dice-throwing, calculus in high school etc. Social applications should not be ignored because they have less abstract significance, for example budgeting, instalment buying, costs of community or governmental services and so on. Books of puzzles and problems can be stimulating, though it is unlikely that they have much transfer value. There are likely to be numerous mathematicians with varied specializations in any large community, and some of these might be persuaded to give talks to gifted mathematical students.

Natural scientists The superficially trained science teacher is very limited, so that much school science consists of learning strings of facts. Other handicaps to the scientifically gifted are the anti-intellectualist bias in contemporary society, and the common stereotype of the scientist as cold, inhumane, pedantic etc. However, on the positive side, Science Fairs are justly popular, and these give unexcelled opportunities for initiative and for small-scale research investigations by high school students. Also the modern curricula devised by outstanding scientists both in the United States and Britain are particularly suited to gifted students. By concentrating more on the method than the product, they help the student think like a scientist.

In the elementary school, work should initially be mainly content-based, moving on to process-based. Stimulation of curiosity lays a foundation for scientific exploration, and even the early grades can make a start in observing, naming, classifying, and playing e.g. with sand and water quantities. Biological or mechanical experiments are possible in later elementary grades. In secondary school, however, the emphasis should be more on abstract considerations of method and history than on practical or technological interest; though this should not deter those who prefer it from studying topics like the weather, pollution, engineering or agriculture, or making radio sets. While it is useful for groups of pupils, with or without the teacher, to follow the discovery method, it should be remembered that many children gifted in science may be lone wolves who like to get to the bottom of things by themselves.

A great deal of helpful literature is available like young people's encyclopaedias, magazines etc., together with films, filmstrips and programmed units which could be loaned from the resource centre. The number of science and constructional sets for children is legion. With greater cooperation among schools at different levels, elementary and junior high teachers with less advanced qualifications should be able to get invaluable help from secondary teachers in handling their scientifically gifted pupils.

Training of teachers of the gifted

We have asked both for specialist consultants and for teachers who can take part-time segregated classes of gifted children, and even for teachers who would be responsible for all activities for gifted children in their own schools. The more progress that is made in provision for the gifted, the more serious will become the bottleneck in finding suitable staff. There are few courses of specialized training for such teachers even in North American universities, let alone in British universities or training colleges — courses which focus on the identification, needs of, and methods and materials for the gifted. Where they do exist they may amount only to a few weeks of a course on special education, mainly concerned with the handicapped.

True the situation is improving, but very slowly, as more university education departments become interested. Such departments should also undertake in-service training of already experienced teachers, whether by full-year diploma courses or by occasional workshops. They should become centres of research, and of community leadership, for work with the gifted. Many such departments have attached to them demonstration schools where, since the majority of the pupils tend to be of superior ability, it should be all the easier to provide models of procedures for the gifted.

Gallagher argues that it would be impossibly expensive to train the needed numbers of teachers to cover all the gifted, and envisages as more feasible a Technical Assistance Centre, which would supply experts for diagnosing and planning the needs of a particular city or education authority, showing how to lay on teacher training and workshops, and circulating information on methods and materials. Our experience would suggest that such special institutes are seldom very effective, and that growth is more likely to occur through the gradual spread of programmes which have proved themselves in particular areas, leading to greater awareness among administrators and the general public; and this can be greatly aided by such bodies as The Association for the Gifted, and by university participation.

The training would need to differ considerably from that given to regular teachers or teachers of the handicapped; indeed, it should aim to break down the conventionalizing effects of the students' own formal education and teaching experience. People are needed whose personalities and attitudes are more adventurous and flexible than usual, and whose cultural background and abilities are varied and wide-ranging. If possible they should themselves be talented in at least one of the arts, yet also educated in the natural and social sciences and mathematics. Besides requiring knowledge of the psychological and psychometric characteristics of bright children, and their development, they should be skilful in stimulating group activities and discussions, in instructional procedures, and in devising materials. A useful source of information on teacher qualities is provided by the opinions of actual gifted students. These were surveyed in a study by W.F. Bishop (1968), and it was found that the children chiefly asked for mature and experienced teachers, who are themselves intellectually superior, who are systematic and business-like, yet stimulating and imaginative. Probably all this sounds like demanding that teachers of the gifted should be paragons. But until systematic training becomes more widespread it is hardly possible to lay down the desired qualifications in more specific terms.

Conclusion

In conclusion we would suggest that a programme for the

gifted based entirely on individual enrichment is likely to be too costly and difficult to organize to work effectively in a large school system. Usually, therefore, it should be combined with a variety of part-time segregated small group or special class activities, and with more frequent resort to acceleration than is customary at present, as in the scheme outlined on p.175.

Having surveyed the many ways of educating gifted children, and of supplying suitable materials and personnel, we certainly do not underestimate the difficulties to be overcome. Yet we believe that more and more School Boards are beginning to realize the need for better facilities than are currently available for the gifted minority. Finally, we would reiterate that such measures are not — as so many critics state — 'creating an élite'. This minority already exists, whether we decide to ignore or repress it, or to educate it as it deserves.

Bibliography

Anastasi, A. and Schaefer, C.E. (1969) Biographical correlates of artistic and literary creativity in adolescent girls. *J. Appl. Psychol.* 53, 267-73.

Arnold, M.B. (1962) *Story Sequence Analysis*. New York: Columbia University Press.

Ausubel, D.P. (1968) *Educational Psychology: A Cognitive View*. New York: Holt, Rinehart and Winston.

Baldwin, A.L., Kalhorn, J. and Breese, F.H. (1945) Patterns of parental behavior. *Psychol. Monogr.* 58, no.268.

Ballance, K.E. and Kendall, D.C. (1969) *Report on Legislation and Services for Exceptional Children in Canada*. Council of Exceptional Children in Canada.

Barbe, W.B. and Norris, D. (1954) Special classes for gifted children in Cleveland. *Except. Children* 21, 55-8.

Barker Lunn, J.C. (1970) *Streaming in the Primary School*. Slough: National Foundation for Educational Research.

Barron, F. (1969) *Creative Person and Creative Process*. New York: Holt, Rinehart and Winston.

Barron, F. and Young, H.B. (1970) Rome and Boston: a tale of two cities and their differing impact on the creativity and personal philosophy of Southern Italian immigrants. *J. Cross-Cult. Psychol.* 1, 91-114.

Bayley, N. (1955) On the growth of intelligence. *Amer. Psychologist* 10, 805-18.

Bereiter, C. and Engelmann, S. (1966) *Teaching Disadvantaged Children in the Preschool*. Englewood Cliffs, N.J.: Prentice-Hall.

Bishop, W.E. (1968) Successful teachers of the gifted. *Except. Children*, 34, 317-25.

Bloom, B.S. (1964) *Stability and Change in Human Characteristics*. New York: John Wiley.

Branch, M. and Cash, A. (1966) *Gifted Children: Recognizing and Developing Exceptional Ability*. London: Souvenir Press.

Bridges, S.A. (1969) *Gifted Children and the Brentwood Experiment*. London: Pitman.

Bronfenbrenner, U. (1974) Is early intervention effective? *Teachers Coll. Rec.* 76, 274-303.

Brumbaugh, F.N. and Roshco, B. (1959) *Your Gifted Child: A Guide for Parents.* New York: Holt, Rinehart and Winston.

Bühler, C. (1935) *From Birth to Maturity.* London: Kegan Paul.

Burks, B.S. (1928) The relative influence of nature and nurture upon mental development. *27th Yrbk. Nat. Soc. Stud. Educ.* pt. I, 219-316.

Burt, C.L. *et al.* (1926) A study in vocational guidance. *Industr. Hlth Res. Board Rep.*, no.33.

Burt, C.L. (1943) Ability and income. *Brit. J. Educ. Psychol.* 13, 126-40.

Burt, C.L. (1958) The inheritance of mental ability. *Amer. Psychologist* 13, 1-15.

Burt, C.L. (1962) The gifted child. *Yearbook of Education.* London: Evans, 1-59.

Burt, C.L. (1963) Is intelligence normally distributed? *Brit. J. Statist. Psychol.* 16, 175-90.

Burt, C.L. (1966) The genetic determination of differences in intelligence: A study of monozygotic twins. *Brit. J. Psychol.* 57, 137-53.

Burt, C.L. (1975) *The Gifted Child.* London: Hodder and Stoughton.

Burton, W.H., Kimball, R.B. and Wing, R.L. (1960) *Education for Effective Thinking.* New York: Appleton, Century, Crofts.

Cattell, J. McK. (1906) A statistical study of American men of science. III. The distribution of American men of science. *Science* 24, 732-42.

Cattell, R.B. and Butcher, H.J. (1968) *The Prediction of Achievement and Creativity.* New York: Bobbs-Merrill.

Claiborn, W. (1969) Expectancy effects in the classroom: a failure to replicate. *J. Educ. Psychol.* 60, 377-83.

Coopersmith, S. (1967) *The Antecedents of Self-Esteem.* San Francisco: W.H. Freeman.

Cornwell, J. (1952) *An Orally Presented Group Test of Intelligence for Juniors.* London: Methuen.

Covington, M.V., Crutchfield, R.S. and Davies, L.B. (1969) *The Productive Thinking Program.* Columbus, Ohio: Charles Merrill.

Cox, C.M. (1926) *The Early Mental Traits of Three Hundred Geniuses*. Stanford, Calif.: Stanford University Press.

Cronbach, L.J. (1968) Intelligence? Creativity? A parsimonious reinterpretation of the Wallach-Kogan data. *Amer. Educ. Res. J.* 5, 491-511.

Cropley, A.J. (1966) Creativity and intelligence. *Brit. J. Educ. Psychol.* 36, 259-66.

Cropley, A.J. (1967a) *Creativity*. London: Longmans.

Cropley, A.J. (1967b) Divergent thinking and science specialists. *Nature* 215, 671-2.

Dearborn, W.F. and Rothney, J.W.M. (1941) *Predicting the Child's Development*. Cambridge, Mass.: Sci-Art.

De Haan, R. and Havighurst, R.J. (1957) *Educating Gifted Children*. Chicago: University of Chicago Press.

Dennis, W. and Narjarian, P. (1957) Infant development under environmental handicap. *Psychol. Monogr.* 71, no.436.

Dewing, K. (1970) The reliability and validity of selected tests of creative thinking in a sample of seventh grade West Australian children. *Brit. J. Educ. Psychol.* 40, 35-42.

Drevdahl, J.E. (1956) Factors of importance for creativity. *J. Clin. Psychol.* 12, 21-6.

Dudek, S.Z. (1968) Regression and creativity. *J. Nerv. Ment. Dis.* 147, 535-46.

Dunn, L.M. (1973) *Exceptional Children in the Schools*, 2nd ed. New York: Holt, Rinehart and Winston.

Ebel, R.L. (1966) The social consequences of educational testing, in A. Anastasi (ed.), *Testing Problems in Perspective*. Washington, D.C.: American Council on Education, 18-28.

Eiduson, B.T. (1958) Artist and nonartist: A comparative study. *J. Pers.* 26, 13-28.

Ekstrom, R.B. (1959) *Experimental Studies of Homogeneous Grouping: A Review of the Literature*. Princeton, N.J.: Educational Testing Service.

Elliott, J.M. (1964) Measuring creative ability in public relations and advertizing work, in C.W. Taylor (ed.), *Widening Horizons in Creativity*. New York: John Wiley, 396-400.

Ellis, H. (1904) *A Study of British Genius*. London: Hunt and Blackett.

Esposito, D. (1973) Homogenous and heterogeneous grouping:

principal findings and implications for evaluating and diagnosing more effective environments. *Rev. Educ. Res.* 43, 163-79.

Flesch, R.F. (1955) *Why Johnny Can't Read.* New York: Harper.

Fraser, E. (1959) *Home Environment and the School.* London: University of London Press.

Freeman, F.N., Holzinger, K.J. and Mitchell, B.C. (1928) The influence of the environment on the intelligence and school achievement and conduct of foster children. *27th Yrbk. Nat. Soc. Stud. Educ.*, 103-217.

Freud, S. (1908) Creative writers and day-dreaming. *Standard Edition of the Complete Psychological Works of Sigmund Freud,* 9 (1959) 143-53.

Fund for Advancement of Education (1957) *They Went to College Early.* The Fund.

Furr, K.D., Landrus, G. and Goldie, H. (1972) Canadian programming for the gifted. *Gifted Child Quart.* 16, 32-40.

Gallagher, J.J. (1964) *Teaching the Gifted Child.* Boston, Mass.: Allyn and Bacon.

Gallagher, J.J. (ed.) (1965) *Teaching Gifted Students: A Book of Readings.* Boston, Mass.: Allyn and Bacon.

Gallagher, J.J., Aschner, M.J. and Jenné, W. (1967) Productive thinking of gifted children in classroom interaction. *Council for Exceptional Children, Res. Monogr. Serv. B.,* no.5.

Getzels, J.W. (1964) Creative thinking, problem-solving, and instruction. *63rd Nrbk. Nat. Soc. Stud. Educ.*, pt.I, 240-67.

Getzels, J.W. and Jackson, P.W. (1962) *Creativity and Intelligence: Explorations with Gifted Students.* New York: John Wiley.

Ghiselin, B. (ed.) (1952) *The Creative Process: A Symposium.* Berkeley, Calif.: University of California Press.

Ghiselin, B. (1963) The creative process and its relation to the identification of creative talent, in C.W. Taylor and F. Barron (eds), *Scientific Creativity: Its Recognition and Development.* New York: John Wiley, 355-64.

Götz, K.O. and Götz, K. (1973) Introversion-extraversion and neuroticism in gifted and ungifted art students. *Perc. and Motor Skills* 36, 675-8.

Gold, M.J. (1965) *Education of the Intellectually Gifted.* Columbus, Ohio: Charles Merrill.

Goldberg, M.L. (1965) *Research on the Talented*. New York: Teachers College, Columbia University.

Goldberg, M.L., Passow, A.H. and Justman, J. (1966) *The Effects of Ability Grouping*. New York: Teachers College, Columbia University.

Goldfarb, W. (1947) Variations in adolescent adjustment of institutionally reared children. *Amer. J. Orthopsychiat.* 17, 449-57.

Gough, H. (1961) Techniques for identifying the creative research scientist. *Conference on the Creative Person*. Berkeley, Calif: University of California, Institute for Personality Assessment and Research.

Guilford, J.P. (1950) Creativity. *Amer. Psychologist* 5, 444-54.

Guilford, J.P. (1967) *The Nature of Human Intelligence*. New York: McGraw-Hill.

Haddon, E.A. and Lytton, H. (1968) Teaching approach and the development of divergent thinking abilities in primary schools. *Brit. J. Educ. Psychol.* 38, 171-80.

Haddon, E.A. and Lytton, H. (1971) Primary education and divergent thinking abilities — four years on. *Brit. J. Educ. Psychol.* 41, 136-47.

Harding, R. (1940) *An Anatomy of Inspiration*. London: Cass.

Hasan, P. and Butcher, H.K. (1966) A partial replication with Scottish children of Getzels and Jackson's study. *Brit. J. Psychol.* 57, 129-35.

Havighurst, R.J., Stivers, E. and De Haan, R.F. (1955) *A Survey of the Education of Gifted Children*. University of Chicago: *Suppl. Educ. Monogr.*, no.83.

Hebb, D.O. (1949) *The Organization of Behavior*. New York: John Wiley.

Heber, R. and Garber, H. (1971) An experiment in prevention of cultural-familial mental retardation, in D.A. Primrose (ed.), *Proc. 2nd. Congr. Intern. Assoc. Scient. Stud. Ment. Defic.* Amsterdam: Swets and Zeitlinger, 31-5.

Hebes, R.D. (1974) Hemisphere specialization in commissuratomized man. *Psychol. Bull.* 81, 1-14.

Heist, P. (ed.) (1968) *The Creative College Student: An Unmet Challenge*. San Francisco: Jossey-Bass.

Helson, R. (1966) Personality of women with imagination and artistic interests: the role of masculinity, originality, and other characteristics in their creativity. *J. Pers.* 34, 1-25.

Hildreth, G.H. (1952) *Educating Gifted Children*. New York: Harper and Row.

Hills, J.R. (1955) The relationship between certain factor-analyzed abilities and success in college mathematics. *Reports from the Psychol. Lab.*, no.15, Univ. of Southern Calif.

Hobson, J.R. (1963) High school performance of underage pupils initially admitted to kindergarten on the basis of physical and psychological examination. *Educ. Psychol. Measmt.* 23, 159-70.

Hoffman, M.L. and Hoffman, L.W. (1964-6) *Review of Child Development*. New York: Russell Sage Foundation.

Hollingworth, L. (1942) *Children Above 180 IQ*. New York: Harcourt, Brace.

Hopkins, K.D. and Bracht, G.H. (1973) Ten-year stability of verbal and nonverbal IQ scores. *Amer. Educ. Res. J.*, 12, 469-77.

Hudson, L. (1966) *Contrary Imaginations*. London: Methuen.

Hudson, L. (1968) *Frames of Mind*. London: Methuen.

Husén, T. (1951) The influence of schooling upon IQ. *Theoria* 17, 61-88.

Husén, T. (ed.) (1967) *International Study of Achievement in Mathematics*. Stockholm: Almquist and Wiksell.

Jackson, B. (1964) *Streaming: An Educational System in Miniature*. London: Routledge and Kegan Paul.

Jensen, A.R. (1969) How much can we boost IQ and scholastic achievement? *Harvard Educ. Rev.* 39, 1-123.

Jensen, A.R. (1973) *Educability and Group Differences*. London: Methuen.

Jensen, A.R. (1974) Kinship correlations reported by Sir Cyril Burt. *Behavior Genetics* 4, 1-28.

Jones, M.C., Bayley, N., Macfarlane, J.W. and Honzik, M.P. (1971) *The Course of Human Development*. Waltham, Mass.: Xerox Publications.

Jones, T.P. (1972) *Creative Learning in Perspective*. London: University of London Press.

Kent, N. and Davis, D.R. (1957) Discipline in the home and intellectual development. *Brit. J. Med. Psychol.* 30, 27-33.

Klineberg, O. (1935) *Negro Intelligence and Selective Migration*. New York: Columbia University Press.

Koestler, A. (1964) *The Act of Creation*. London: Hutchinson.

Koluchova, J. (1972) Severe deprivation in twins: A case study. *J. Child Psychol. and Psychiat.* 13, 107-14.

Kretschmer, E. (1931) *The Psychology of Men of Genius*. New York: Harcourt, Brace.

Kris, E. (1952) *Psychoanalytic Explorations in Art*. New York: International Universities Press.

Laycock, S.R. (1957) *Gifted Children*. Toronto: Copp Clark.

Lee, E.S. (1951) Negro intelligence and selective migration: A Philadelphia test of the Klineberg hypothesis. *Amer. Sociol. Rev.* 16, 227-33.

Levine, S. (1960) Stimulation in infancy. *Scient. American* 202, 80-6.

Lieblich, A., Ninio, A. and Kugelmass, S. (1972) Effects of ethnic origin and parental SES on WPSSI performance of preschool children in Israel. *J. Cross-Cult. Psychol.* 3, 159-68.

Lombroso, C. (1891) *The Man of Genius*. London: Walter Scott.

Lorge, I. (1945) Schooling makes a difference. *Teachers Coll. Rec.* 46, 483-92.

Lytton, H. (1971) *Creativity and Education*. London: Routledge and Kegan Paul.

Lytton, H. and Cotton, A.C. (1969) Divergent thinking abilities in secondary schools. *Brit. J. Educ. Psychol.* 39, 183-90.

MacKinnon, D.W. (1962) The personality correlates of creativity: A study of American architects. *Proc. XIV Congr. Appl. Psychol.* vol.2. Copenhagen: Munksgaard, 11-39.

Maier, N.R.F. (1930) Reasoning in humans. *J. Compar. Psychol.* 10, 115-43.

Martinson, R.A. (1973) Children with superior cognitive abilities, in L.M. Dunn, *Exceptional Children in the Schools*, 2nd ed. New York: Holt, Rinehart and Winston, 191-241.

Martinson, R.A. and Lessinger, C.M. (1960) Problems in the identification of intellectually gifted pupils. *Except. Children* 26, 227-31.

Maslany, G.W. (1973) *The Long Term Predictive Validity of Intellectual Tests with Respect to Non-Academic and Academic Criteria*. University of Calgary, Ph.D. Thesis.

McClelland, D. (1962) On the dynamics of creative physical scientists, in H.E. Gruber, *Contemporary Approaches to Creative Thinking*. New York: Atherton, 141-74.

McKellar, P. (1957) *Imagination and Thinking*. London: Cohen and West.

Mednick, S.A. (1962) The associative basis of the creative process. *Psychol. Rev.* 69, 220-32.

Miller, G.W. (1970) Factors in school achievement and social class. *J. Educ. Psychol.* 61, 260-9.

Moss, H.A. and Kagan, J. (1961) Stability of achievement and recognition seeking behavior from early childhood through adulthood. *J. Abn. and Soc. Psychol.* 68, 504-13.

Munsinger, H. (1975) The adopted child's IQ: A critical review. *Psychol. Bull.* 82, 623-59.

Newman, H.H., Freeman, F.N. and Holzinger, K.J. (1937) *Twins: A Study of Heredity and Environment*. Chicago: University of Chicago Press.

Nichols, R.C. and Holland, J.L. (1963) The prediction of the first year college performance of high aptitude students. *Psychol. Monogr.* 77, no.570.

Nisbet, J. and Buchan, J. (1959) The long-term follow-up of assessments at age eleven. *Brit. J. Educ. Psychol.* 29, 1-8.

Ogilvie, E. (1973) *Gifted Children in Primary Schools*. London: Macmillan.

Ogilvie, E. (1974) Creativity and curriculum structure. *Educ. Res.* 16, 126-32.

Parker, M. (1975) *The Joy of Excellence*. Kootenay, B.C.: Kootenay Centre for the Gifted.

Parkyn, G.W. (1948) *Children of High Intelligence*. Wellington: New Zealand Council for Educational Research.

Parloff, M.B., Datta, L., Kleman, M. and Handlon, J.H. (1968) Personality characteristics which differentiate creative male adolescents and adults. *J. Pers.* 36, 528-52.

Passow, A.H. and Goldberg, M.L. (1962) The effects of ability grouping. *Education* 82, 1-6.

Paterson, D.G. and Elliot, R.M. *et al.* (1930) *Minnesota Mechanical Ability Tests*. Minneapolis: Minnesota University Press.

Pegnato, C.W. and Birch, J.W. (1959) Locating gifted children in Junior High Schools: A comparison of methods. *Except. Children* 25, 300-4.

Pilliner, A.E.G., Sutherland, J. and Taylor, E.G. (1960) Zero error in Moray House 11 + verbal reasoning tests. *Brit. J. Educ. Psychol.* 30, 53-62.

Quay, L.C. (1971) Language dialect, reinforcement, and the intelligence test performance of negro children. *Child Devlmt* 42, 5-15.

Renzulli, J.S. and Hartman, R.K. (1971) Scale for rating behavioral characteristics of superior students. *Except. Children* 38, 243-8.

Reynolds, M.C. (1962) *Early School Admission for Advanced Children*. Council for Exceptional Children. Special Publication.

Rickover, H.G. (1963) *American Education —, A National Failure*. New York: Dutton.

Roe, A. (1946) Artists and their work. *J. Pers.* 15, 1-40.

Roe, A. (1952) *The Making of a Scientist*. New York: Dodd Mead.

Rogers, C.R. (1954) Toward a theory of creativity. *ETC: A Review of General Semantics* 11, 249-60.

Rosenthal, R. and Jacobson, L. (1968) *Pygmalion in the Classroom*. New York: Holt, Rinehart and Winston.

Roth, J. and Sussman, S. (1974) *Educating Gifted Children*. York, Ont.: Board of Education.

Samuel, W. (1976) Motivation, race, social class and IQ. *J. Educ. Psychol.*, 67, 273-85.

Schaefer, C.E. and Anastasi, A (1968) A biographical inventory for identifying creativity in adolescent boys. *J. Appl. Psychol.* 52, 42-8.

Schaefer, E.S. and Bayley, N. (1963) Maternal behavior, child behavior, and their intercorrelations from infancy through adolescence. *Monogr. Soc. Res. Child Develpmt* 22, no.87.

School and College Study of Admission with Advanced Standing (1956). Philadelphia: Central High School.

Shapiro, R.J. (1968) Creative research scientists. *Psychologia Africana, Monogr. Suppl.* no.4.

Skeels, H.M. (1966) Adult status of children with contrasting early life experiences: A follow-up study. *Monogr. Soc. Res. Child Develpmt* 31, no.105.

Smith, M. *et al.* (1971) *Attitudes and Opinions of Advancement Class Students and their Parents*. London, Ont.: Board of Education.

Spearman, C. (1927) *The Abilities of Man*. London: Macmillan.

Spitz, R.A. (1946) Anaclitic depression: An enquiry into the genesis of psychiatric conditions in early childhood, in

A. Freud (ed.), *The Psychoanalytic Study of the Child*. New York: International Universities Press.

Stanley, J. (1973) Accelerating the educational progress of intellectually gifted youth. *Educational Psychologist*, 10, 133-46.

Strang, R. (1960) *Helping Your Gifted Child*. New York: Dutton.

Syphers, D.F. (1972) *Gifted and Talented Children: Practical Programing for Teachers and Principals*. Arlington, Virg.: Council for Exceptional Children.

Tannenbaum, A.J. (1962) *Adolescent Attitudes Toward Academic Brilliance*. New York: Teachers College, Columbia University.

Taylor, C.W. (1962) Who are the exceptionally creative? *Except. Children* 28, 421-31.

Taylor, C.W. and Ellison, R.L. (1964) Predicting creative performance from multiple measures, in C.W. Taylor (ed.), *Widening Horizons in Creativity*. New York: John Wiley, 227-60.

Taylor, I.A. (1959) The nature of the creative process, in P. Smith (ed.), *Creativity: An Examination of the Creative Process*. New York: Hastings House, 51-82.

Terman, L.M. (1925) *Genetic Studies of Genius*, Vol.I. *Mental and Physical Traits of a Thousand Gifted Children*. Stanford, Calif.: Stanford University Press.

Terman, L.M. (1930) Vol. III. *The Promise of Youth*. Stanford, Calif.: Stanford University Press.

Terman, L.M. (1947) Vol. IV. *The Gifted Child Grows Up*. Stanford, Calif.: Stanford University Press.

Terman, L.M. and Oden, M.H. (1959) Vol. V. *The Gifted Group at Mid-Life*. Stanford, Calif.: Stanford University Press.

Thorndike, R.L. (1973) *Stanford-Binet Intelligence Scale: 1972 Norms Table*. Boston: Houghton Mifflin.

Thurstone, L.L. (1938) *Primary Mental Abilities*. Chicago: University of Chicago Press, Psychometric Monographs No.1.

Torrance, E.P. (1962) Developing creative thinking through school experiences, in S.F. Parnes and H.F. Harding (eds.), *A Source Book for Creative Thinking*. New York: Scribner, 31-47.

Torrance, E.P. (1965) *Rewarding Creative Behavior*. Englewood Cliffs, N.J.: Prentice-Hall.

Torrance, E.P. (1969a) Curiosity of gifted children: Performance on timed and untimed tests of creativity. *Gifted Child Quart.* 13, 155-8.

Torrance, E.P. (1969b) Prediction of adult creative achievement among High School seniors. *Gifted Child Quart.* 13, 223-9.

Torrance, E.P. (1971) Long range prediction studies and international applications of the Torrance Tests of Creative Thinking. *Proc. XVII Congr., Intern. Assoc. Appl. Psychol.* Liege.

Torrance, E.P. (1972) Can we teach children to think creatively? *J. Creative Behav.* 6, 114-43.

U.S. Commission of Education (1971) *Education of the Gifted and Talented.* Washington, D.C.: Report to the Congress of the United States.

Vernon, P.E. (1955) The assessment of children, in University of London, Institute of Education, *Studies in Education* no.7, 189-215.

Vernon, P.E. (ed.) (1957a) *Secondary School Selection.* London: Methuen.

Vernon, P.E. (1957b) Intelligence and intellectual stimulation during adolescence. *Indian Psychol. Bull.* 2, 1-6.

Vernon, P.E. (1960) *Intelligence and Attainment Testing.* London: University of London Press.

Vernon, P.E. (1961) *The Structure of Human Abilities*, 2nd ed. London: Methuen.

Vernon, P.E. (1966) A cross-cultural study of 'creativity tests' with 11-year-old boys. *New Res. in Educ.* 1, 135-46.

Vernon, P.E. (1969) *Intelligence and Cultural Environment.* London: Methuen.

Vernon, P.E. (1971) Effects of administration and scoring on divergent thinking tests. *Brit. J. Educ. Psychol.* 241-57.

Vernon, P.E. (1972) The validity of divergent thinking tests. *Alberta J. Educ. Res.* 18, 249-58.

Wall, W.D. (1960) Highly intelligent children. *Educ. Res.* 2, 101-11, 207-17.

Wallach, M.A. and Kogan, N. (1965) *Modes of Thinking in Young Children.* New York: Holt, Rinehart and Winston.

Wallach, M.A. and Wing, C.W. (1969) *The Talented Student: A Validation of the Creativity-Intelligence Distinction.* New York: Holt, Rinehart and Winston.

Wallas, G. (1926) *The Art of Thought.* London: Jonathan Cape.

Weisgerber, R.A. (ed.) (1971) *Developmental Efforts in Individualized Learning.* Itasca, Ill.: Peacock.

Weissberg, P.S. and Springer, K.J. (1961) Environmental factors in creative function. *Arch. Gen. Psychiat.* 5, 64-74.

Wertheimer, M. (1959) *Productive Thinking.* London: Tavistock.

Wiener, N. (1953) *Ex-Prodigy: My Childhood and Youth.* New York: Simon and Schuster.

Witty, P.A. (ed.) (1951) *The Gifted Child.* Boston, Mass.: D.C. Heath.

Worcester, D.A. (1956) *The Education of Children of Above-Average Mentality.* Lincoln, Neb.: Nebraska University Press.

Yamamoto, K. (1963) Relationships between creative thinking abilities of teachers and achievement and adjustment of pupils. *J. Exper. Educ.* 32, 3-25.

Index of names

Subject index